NEW CONCEPTS IN LATINO AMERICAN CULTURES
A Series Edited by Licia Fiol-Matta & José Quiroga

Ciphers of History: Latin American Readings for a Cultural Age
by Enrico Mario Santí

Cosmopolitanisms and Latin America: Against the Destiny of Place
by Jacqueline Loss

Remembering Maternal Bodies: Melancholy in Latina and Latin American Women's Writing
by Benigno Trigo

The Ethics of Latin American Literary Criticism: Reading Otherwise
edited by Erin Graff Zivin

Forthcoming Titles

Modernity and the Nation in Mexican Representations of Masculinity: From Sensuality to Bloodshed
by Héctor Domínguez-Ruvalcaba

White Negritude: Race, Writing, and Brazilian Cultural Identity
by Alexandra Isfahani-Hammond

NEW DIRECTIONS IN LATINO AMERICAN CULTURES
Also Edited by Licia Fiol-Matta & José Quiroga

New York Ricans from the Hip Hop Zone
by Raquel Rivera

The Famous 41: Sexuality and Social Control in Mexico, 1901
edited by Robert McKee Irwin, Edward J. McCaughan, and Michele Rocío Nasser

Velvet Barrios: Popular Culture & Chicana/o Sexualities
edited by Alicia Gaspar de Alba, with a foreword by Tomás Ybarra Frausto

Tongue Ties: Logo-Eroticism in Anglo-Hispanic Literature
by Gustavo Perez-Firmat

Bilingual Games: Some Literary Investigations
edited by Doris Sommer

Jose Martí: An Introduction
by Oscar Montero

New Tendencies in Mexican Art
by Rubén Gallo

The Masters and the Slaves: Plantation Relations and Mestizaje in American Imaginaries
edited by Alexandra Isfahani-Hammond

The Letter of Violence: Essays on Narrative and Theory
by Idelber Avelar

Intellectual History of the Caribbean
by Silvio Torres-Saillant

None of the Above: Contemporary Puerto Rican Cultures and Politics
edited by Frances Negrón-Muntaner

Forthcoming Titles

New York Ricans from the Hip Hop Zone, 2nd Edition
by Raquel Z. Rivera

Juanito Xtravaganza, Keith Haring, and Queer Latino Testimonio: *Hard Tails*
by Arnaldo Cruz-Malavé

Puerto Ricans in America: 30 Years of Activism and Change
edited by Xavier F. Totti and Félix Matos Rodríguez

THE ETHICS OF LATIN AMERICAN LITERARY CRITICISM

READING OTHERWISE

Edited by
Erin Graff Zivin

THE ETHICS OF LATIN AMERICAN LITERARY CRITICISM
Copyright © Erin Graff Zivin, 2007.

All rights reserved. No part of this book may be used or reproduced in any manner whatsoever without written permission except in the case of brief quotations embodied in critical articles or reviews.

First published in 2007 by
PALGRAVE MACMILLAN™
175 Fifth Avenue, New York, N.Y. 10010 and
Houndmills, Basingstoke, Hampshire, England RG21 6XS
Companies and representatives throughout the world.

PALGRAVE MACMILLAN is the global academic imprint of the Palgrave Macmillan division of St. Martin's Press, LLC and of Palgrave Macmillan Ltd. Macmillan® is a registered trademark in the United States, United Kingdom and other countries. Palgrave is a registered trademark in the European Union and other countries.

ISBN-13: 978–1–4039–8496–8
ISBN-10: 1–4039–8496–4

Library of Congress Cataloging-in-Publication Data

    The ethics of Latin American literary criticism : reading otherwise / edited by Erin Graff Zivin.
      p. cm.—(New concepts in Latino American cultures)
    Includes bibliographical references and index.
    ISBN 1–4039–8496–4 (alk. paper)
      1. Criticism—Latin America. 2. Criticism—Moral and ethical aspects—Latin America. I. Zivin, Erin Graff.

PN99.L29E85 2007
809.898—dc22
                                        2007003059

A catalogue record for this book is available from the British Library.

Design by Newgen Imaging Systems (P) Ltd., Chennai, India.

First edition: September 2007

10 9 8 7 6 5 4 3 2 1

Printed in the United States of America.

For Josh and Simon

Contents

List of Figures   ix

Acknowledgments   xi

Introduction: Reading Otherwise   1
Erin Graff Zivin

Part I   Ethics, Politics, Representation

1. The Ethical Superstition   11
   Bruno Bosteels

2. Ethics, Perhaps   25
   Gabriela Basterra

Part II   Ethics and Cultural Studies

3. Ethics and Citizenship in the Blogosphere: Academics Meet New Technologies of Online Publication   45
   Idelber Avelar

4. Modernist Ethics: Really Engaging Popular Culture in Mexico and Brazil   63
   Esther Gabara

Part III   The Limits of Literature

5. A Few Notes on Constructed Worlds: The Contradictory Legacy of Past Decades   105
   Sergio Chejfec

6. Saying the Unsayable: Saer, or for an Ethics of Writing   115
   Gabriel Riera

7. Infrapolitics and the Thriller: A Prolegomenon to Every Possible Form of Antimoralist Literary Criticism. On Héctor Aguilar Camín's *La guerra de Galio* and *Morir en el golfo*   147
Alberto Moreiras

Part IV THE EXPERIENCE OF READING

8. Ethical Asymmetries: Learning to Love a Loss   183
Doris Sommer

9. Reading for the People and Getting There First   201
Francine Masiello

List of Contributors   217

Index   221

List of Figures

4.1 "Toada," *S. Paulo*, August 1936. Biblioteca, Instituto de Estudos Brasileiros, Universidade de São Paulo.   76
4.2 "The Paulista Sense of Brazilian Life Means:" *S. Paulo*, January 1936. Biblioteca, Instituto de Estudos Brasileiros, Universidade de São Paulo.   78
4.3 *S. Paulo*, September–October 1936. Biblioteca, Instituto de Estudos Brasileiros, Universidade de São Paulo.   81
4.4 El Caballero Puck, "Masks," *El Universal Ilustrado*, March 4, 1926. Hemeroteca Nacional, Universidad Autónoma de México.   92
4.5 "Our Artists in Masks," *El Universal Ilustrado*, March 4, 1926. Hemeroteca Nacional, Universidad Autónoma de México.   93
4.6 Xavier Villaurrutia, "The Mask," *El Universal Ilustrado*, March 4, 1926. Hemeroteca Nacional, Universidad Autónoma de México.   95

ACKNOWLEDGMENTS

The publication of this book would not have been possible without the collaboration of a great number of people. The nine chapters that form this volume are based upon presentations made at a colloquium hosted by the Department of Hispanic Languages and Literatures at the University of Pittsburgh on October 21–22, 2005, cosponsored by the Arts and Sciences Office of the Dean, the University Center for International Studies (UCIS), the Center for Latin American Studies (CLAS), the Office of the Provost, and the School of Arts and Sciences. The faculty, staff, and students of the Department of Hispanic Languages and Literatures generously gave of their time to make the colloquium a great success, among them John Beverley, Connie Tomko, Suzanna Publicker, and Citlali Martínez.

I would like to express my appreciation to Heather Cleary, whose flawless translation of Sergio Chejfec's essay is included here; Gabriella Georgiades and Joanna Mericle at Palgrave Macmillan for their astute advice throughout the editorial process; and Licia Fiol-Matta and José Quiroga, the editors of the New Concepts in Latino American Cultures series. Several institutions and publishers have generously cooperated with the publication of the current volume. In chapter 4, three images from the periodical *São Paulo* have been reproduced with permission of the library of the Instituto de Estudos Brasileiros at the Universidade de São Paulo. A segment of Mário de Andrade's *Paulicea desvairada. Hallucinated City. A Bilingual Edition* (1968) has been reprinted with permission of Vanderbilt University Press. Manuel Horta's "Masks" and "Our artists in masks," as well as Xavier Villarrutia's "The Mask"—which appears in chapter 4 as well as the cover of the present volume—have been reproduced with permission of *El Universal Ilustrado*. The second section of chapter 7 subsumes a previously published article by Alberto Moreiras entitled "Ethics and Politics in Hector Aguilar Camín's *Morir en el golfo* and *La guerra de Galio,*" *South Central Review* 21:3 (2004) and has been reprinted with permission of the Johns Hopkins University Press. I would like to thank Adriana Hidalgo Editora for granting permission to include in chapter 9 an excerpt of Diana Bellessi's "Notas del presente" from *La rebelión del instante* (2005).

Finally, I would like to extend a warm *abrazo/abraço* to all the contributors to this book: it has been a pleasure and an honor to get to know you during the past two years, and I look forward to continuing the fruitful and provocative dialogue that has been cultivated here.

INTRODUCTION: READING OTHERWISE

Erin Graff Zivin

Reading Otherwise

The last several decades have witnessed a reorientation of the political and a globalization of the cultural in Latin America, shifting literature's function as a homogenizing, citizen-forming institution to a more dispersed, fragmented, and (potentially) democratic and liberating practice. At the same time, and perhaps in response to this cultural shift, the field of Latin American literary studies has expanded to include cultural studies, postcolonial theory, performance studies, gender studies, Africana studies, and subaltern studies, at once expanding and disrupting the boundaries of literature, criticism, and of Latin America itself. In light of these dramatic transformations within a globalized Latin American culture, as well as within the field of Latin American literary studies itself, what value can we attribute to aesthetics today? Is a reconsideration of artistic creation a mere return to the hegemonic lettered city described by Angel Rama? Or can we begin to think about an "ethical potential" inscribed within the act of reading, that is, an encounter with otherness that irreversibly alters the reading subject?

I posed these questions to the contributors to this volume with the intention of initiating a discussion about the shifting role of Latin American literature and literary studies. More precisely, I asked the contributors to consider the place of what we might call "ethics," "ethical subjectivity," or "ethical responsibility" within these practices. Ethics, here, could be understood in a number of ways: as a response to the demand of the Other within the same (as Levinas would have it); as fidelity to an event, following Badiou; or as an adherence to the Lacanian dictum to not give way on one's desire [*ne pas céder sur son desir*], to name only a few models taken from recent Continental philosophy and psychoanalytic theory. Regardless of the model, if we believe that the ethical subject could be constituted through encounters with otherness that represent an interruption of the status quo, what does this mean for the practice of literary criticism?

If literature seeks to represent the other—whether we understand the other to be the subaltern, the popular, the other within the same, the event, the real, or everything outside the order of representation—it is vital that we consider the ethical implications of literary production, as well as of our own practice of literary criticism, which, in turn, aims to interpret and therefore represent the text as other. Does literature necessarily involve the violent thematization of difference, the reproduction of the status quo, the replication of preexistent power relations, or the production of these very systems of hierarchy and inequality? Or can we locate within literary discourse an "other side" of representation, some element within the confines of the text (or within our encounter with the text) that resists representation, a signifying process that bears within it the sign of its own impossibility? What happens when we shift the focus of our discussion to the scene of reading, to the moment of encounter with the alterity of the text? Is there something about aesthetic language—visual, poetic, or otherwise—that interrupts or undoes us as reading subjects? Can the act of reading be understood as an event? What are the political implications of such an ethics? Finally, what does it mean to be posing these questions from the perspective of Latin American literary and cultural studies?

To my delight, several thematic clusters emerged from the responses I received. The chapters in this volume not only represent divergent perspectives on the issues at hand, they also take the proposed topics in new and unexpected directions. The current volume collectively explores the potential intersection of ethics and literary criticism by pursuing four distinct but interrelated avenues of inquiry: ethics, politics and representation; ethics and cultural studies; the limits of literature; and the experience of reading. Because these methodological or thematic clusters are ultimately inseparable, we see a number of overlapping questions and problems treated in each section: the turn to ethics in literary studies, art's relationship with the popular, the rapport between ethics and politics, the role of the critic, visuality and aurality, affect and the unsayable. At the same time, the chapters in this volume do not (nor should they) form a cohesive whole. Rather, in their provocative inquiries into the subject(s) at hand, they present diverse and even competing theses, questioning the assumptions we too often leave unexamined in our work as literary critics. This volume is divided into four parts, each of which I discuss hereunder.

Ethics, Politics, Representation

The following section ("Ethics, Politics, Representation") includes two contentious essays that engage with and question philosophies of ethical subjectivity and that serve, albeit from differing perspectives, as a warning against an ethics that would depend upon an essentialized notion of the other as an identitary category. In "The Ethical Superstition," Bruno Bosteels questions the recent turn to ethics in literary criticism in general, and in Latin American literary criticism in particular. The pitfalls of such epistemological or critical approaches to the study of literature, he argues, are related to what he sees as a set of misguided or superstitious assumptions, above all the reliance upon the idea of the "other" as a basis for ethics (inside or outside of the realm of the literary). He warns against an ethics that would turn each subject into a victim, following Rancière, ethics as "a state of indistinction in which we are all ultimately victims of some originary trauma, witnesses to some radical evil, or subjects to an overwhelming catastrophe." Turning to Enrique Dussel's *Etica de la liberación* [Ethics of liberation], Bosteels challenges us to imagine a politics that might, in the end, "liberate us from ethics."

Gabriela Basterra's chapter ("Ethics, Perhaps") also tackles the problematic turn to an "ethics of the other" by developing a conceptual distinction between what she has perceived as two different Western traditions: "tragic subjectivity" and "ethics of the break." Far from being confined to the realm of antiquity, tragic subjectivity pervades modernity, constituting itself around identity and difference, enabling the illusion of autonomy, and making politics and representation possible. Perhaps counterintuitively, she locates an ethics of the other within the structure of tragic subjectivity, arguing that "[i]nsofar as this subject promotes 'respect for the other,' 'ethics of difference,' or 'identity politics,' it ultimately represents itself as victim (and agency as powerless), thus evading responsibility, inflicting suffering and creating real victims." An ethical break is related, in turn, to the experience of noncoincidence that constitutes the subject as other than itself. In the later work of Emmanuel Levinas, Basterra claims, we see an example of the "break" through the idea of the trace, which de-essentializes exteriority as such. In detailing these parallel modes of subjectivity, Basterra asks whether it is possible to conceive a link between the tragic and the ethical, the experience of the "break" and the possibility of representation. It is here—in the act of representation—that we can begin to interrogate the relationship between ethics and politics, as well as the relationship between ethics and literature.

Ethics and Cultural Studies

The second section of this volume ("Ethics and Cultural Studies") travels beyond the narrow confines of both literature and literary criticism to consider, in an explicitly material way, the ethical implications of more democratizing modes of cultural production and cultural analysis. Idelber Avelar explores the shifting ethical imperative of intellectual work in light of the recent explosion of intellectual blogs (Web logs) in "Cultural Studies in the Blogosphere: Academics Meet New Technologies of Online Publication." If traditional academic debates take place within a well-defined discursive space in which one is able to anticipate (more or less) his or her public, on the Internet one writes to "a wholly other," posits Avelar. It is therefore necessary to think about what kind of ethics would govern such a space. How does the role of the intellectual in the public sphere shift, he asks, when the sphere itself has been changed so radically by the Internet? As academic writing enters the blogosphere, forging new links between those inside academia and those outside, how is the practice of criticism altered?

Of course, shifts in the field of criticism are ultimately inseparable from the modes of cultural production it attempts to engage. Esther Gabara's chapter is one such example. In "Modernist Ethics: Really Engaging Popular Culture in Mexico and Brazil," Gabara turns to the modernist avant-gardes of the first decades of the twentieth century in order to investigate the relationship between the artist and the masses. Underscoring the overlap between *cultura popular* [popular culture] and *cultura de masas* [mass culture] within the modernist imaginary, Gabara distinguishes Latin American avant-garde artists from their European counterparts who attempted to bridge ethics and aesthetics through an encounter with the "people." Turning to the potentially democratizing genre of photography and, in particular, the illustrated magazine, she demonstrates that "Mexican and Brazilian modernists did not simply mine the popular for exotic and scandalous images but rather actively located themselves within it," realizing in this way an ethics of visual representation.

The Limits of Literature

Avelar's and Gabara's analyses of the Internet and photography serve as clear examples of uses of modern media that exceed the narrow limits of traditional publishing and writing to forge links with the "public" or the "popular." But is it possible to find ethical elements in literary discourse, that is, nodes of resistance at work within writing itself? Section III, "The Limits of Literature," addresses this question by situating the question of ethics within the context of twentieth-century Latin American narrative. In his chapter "A Few Notes on Constructed Worlds: The Contradictory Legacy of Past Decades," Sergio Chejfec analyzes novels from the 1960s and 1970s by Osvaldo Lamborghini, José Revueltas, Renato Rodríguez, and Sebastián Salazar Bondy, who resisted the aesthetic mandates of the time. At the same time that the "Boom" was homogenizing an already uniform literary landscape, these works represented "acts of disobedience to the literary precepts issued by politicians," according to Chejfec. But while these works subverted the literary conventions of their generation by exhibiting enigmatic or illegible qualities, they anticipated practices and characteristics that have since become common or at the very least validated in critical circles. Chejfec therefore warns against the reification of these previously avant-garde practices, suggesting that by standardizing aesthetic norms we run the risk of creating another homogeneous "Boom," precluding the possibility of ethical or political work.

This notion of the "illegible" or the "enigmatic" as characteristics of literary language finds a parallel in the writing of Juan José Saer, whose work is discussed by Gabriel Riera in "Saying the Unsayable: Saer, or for an Ethics of Writing." Like the novels analyzed by Chejfec, Saer's resist the dominant modes of cultural expression of his generation, creating what Saer himself has called a "literature without attributes," that is, a body of work that defies facile categorization (as Baroque, as Argentine, as Latin American, or as subordinate to any preexisting agenda). Confronting literature's tendency to represent the real, Saer's narratives inscribe an inassimilable margin that Riera has termed the "writing of the affects." Rather than seeking to recover the representational void at the heart of the literary work, these novels aim to preserve "the unsayable"—that element of the text which announces its "impossible condition of possibility." This aporetic relationship between language and the real exposes the contradiction or betrayal inherent in ethical signifying, the attempt to recognize within the order of representation that which exceeds its limits.

Alberto Moreiras also considers the "secret" at the heart of the narrative in his discussion of the thriller as a literary genre that is, by definition, ethical in "Infrapolitics and the Thriller." By seeking to investigate the enigma of murder—the relationship with the other in which ethics are suspended—the thriller establishes an ethicopolitical relation to crime. This perhaps unexpected association between murder, literature, ethics, and politics occurs because if the crime always conceals a secret (the extraliterary within the literary), in seeking to unconceal this secret, the crime novel realizes an "ethical aesthetization of politics." The deconstruction of the political by the ethical is always accompanied by the deconstruction of the ethical by the political in these novels, a phenomenon Moreiras terms *infrapolitics*. An ethics that can be characterized as infrapolitical is radically opposed to what he calls moralism, which aims to protect autonomy rather than privileging heteronomy—a distinction that must be taken into account when attempting to define a relationship between ethics and politics.

The Experience of Reading

If the textual practices discussed by Chejfec, Riera, and Moreiras are primarily concerned with the act of writing, or representation, how does a consideration of ethics change when we direct our attention to the experience of reading? What happens when the reading subject confronts the enigmatic, the unsayable, or the secret, that is, textual "others" that refuse our interpretation? How do we respond to that which escapes or alters an imperialistic reading tendency? The volume's final section analyzes such encounters with alterity within the scene of reading. In "Ethical Asymmetries: Learning to Love a Loss," Doris Sommer discusses the unequal and uncomfortable relationship between self and other, reader and text, within difficult scenes of bilingual aesthetics. By focusing on the privileged position of the readerly subject, her essay explores the ways in which it might be possible for this subject to be displaced, in particular by what she terms "minority" literature and bilingualism, combating the monological and the monolinguistic, mastery and "egolatry" in one fell swoop. Turning to the Levinasian notion of asymmetry, in which the "lowly" self exists in a relationship of inequality or nonreciprocity with the "exalted" other, Sommer points to the possibility of an ethics of reading, maintaining that it might be possible to conceive of a mode of politics grounded in the discomfort of the subject.

In the volume's final chapter, Francine Masiello ("Reading for the People and Getting There First") investigates the relationship between ethics and reading by reflecting upon Argentina's 2001 economic crisis and the subsequent obsession of Argentine intellectuals with emergent popular subjects (*cartoneros, piqueteros*) as a promised alternative for the future. After a critical reappraisal of such appropriations of "the popular," Masiello turns to the experience of reading, examining "the *effects* of a corporeal reading that may lead to the question of ethics." If the representation of *cartoneros* and *piqueteros* is problematic in its reification of the dominant critical subject who reads/interprets the popular, Masiello's chapter considers the effect of poetic discourse as an example of an aural aesthetic experience that just might irreversibly alter the reading—or listening—subject.

* * *

As is evident from the brief descriptions above, the contributions to this volume offer a variety of insights into the problem of ethics and representation, questioning many of the arguments that can be found not only in current debates on Latin American literature and culture, but also in the very chapters that make up this collection. The theses put forth here invite us not only to ponder the place of the "other" within the practices of writing and reading, but also to examine our reliance on the very notion of "otherness" as critics. They encourage us, moreover, to redirect our attention from the question of the other to the problem of the same by offering diverse interpretations of the subject: the reading subject, the critical subject, the ethical subject. Finally, they challenge us to be provoked, indeed, to be altered by the experience of reading, to open ourselves up to what it might mean to read otherwise.

Works Cited

Badiou, Alain. *Ethics. An Essay on the Understanding of Evil*, trans. Peter Hallward. London: Verso, 2001.
Lacan, Jacques. *The Seminar of Jacques Lacan, Book VII. The Ethics of Psychoanalysis, 1959–1960*, trans. Denis Porter. New York: Norton, 1992.
Levinas, Emmanuel. *Otherwise than Being or Beyond Essence*, trans. Alphonso Lingis. Pittsburgh: Duquesne UP, 1998.
Rama, Angel. *La ciudad letrada*. Hanover, NH: Ediciones del Norte, 1984.

Part I

ETHICS, POLITICS, REPRESENTATION

1

THE ETHICAL SUPERSTITION

Bruno Bosteels

Ethics Superstitious and Otherwise

In "The Superstitious Ethics of the Reader" from *Discusión*, Jorge Luis Borges attacks what he considers to be a disastrous habit among modern-day readers, referring to the habit of mistaking acoustic, metric, and other purely external technicalities for sufficient proof of literary greatness. However sarcastic and seemingly unforgiving, though, this attack against "a superstition of style" clearly implies that its author, like many critics today, believes in the possibility of an "ethics of the reader" that would *not* be superstitious—one that by contrast would be, let us say, truthful, or enlightened, or genuine.[1]

Does this mean that from this example among others, we are justified in seeking out an "ethics of Latin American literary criticism" by way of "reading otherwise," as the title of the present volume invites us to think? Based on Borges's own work, at least two critics—one of whom is included here as well—seem positively in favor of such an investigation. Let me briefly mention these examples, if for no other reason than that they illustrate what I consider to be two common models of answering the question about ethics, literature, and literary or cultural criticism in Latin America.

Sylvia Molloy, for one, ends the introduction to her book *Signs of Borges* with the following suggestion: "Any reading of Borges should take into account the ethics that sustains it," to which she adds: "By ethics I mean the honest conduct and conveyance of a text, seemingly deceitful yet aware of its deceptions, admitting to its inevitable traps, confessing to the creation of simulacra it does nothing to conceal. If a return to Borges, to his entire text, is worthwhile, it is because that text upholds a constant and honest disquisition on writing, his own writing, the writing of others."[2] Aside from the brief reference to the practice of confession as well as the mention of notions such as honesty and self-awareness, two notions that we certainly have come to expect, in postromantic times at least, from any ethical and moral discussion, the most striking feature of this description without a doubt involves the role of textuality, as a peculiar form of simulacrum, now made part of a careful disquisition about self and others. The question of worth, if not exactly literary worth in the older sense of evaluative criticism, thus comes to depend on a new kind of textual honesty, intrinsic to writing as such: perhaps not to all writing, though this is not excluded either, but at least those few writers to whom a return is worth our while.

No doubt closer to Maurice Blanchot than to Jacques Derrida or Paul de Man, who in any case are never mentioned by name in the book, Molloy's *Signs of Borges* (originally published in 1979) nonetheless in many regards stands as a high point of a certain deconstructive and more generally poststructuralist tendency in Latin American literary criticism. This tendency thus proves that the textual turn, despite frequent objections to the contrary, by no means ought to exclude a turn, or a return, to ethics—whether to an ethics of writing or, in a subtle slippage that seems to be openly embraced in the lines quoted above, to an ethics of reading as well.

From a slightly different angle, but writing within a tradition that is perhaps not as far removed from the ethics of textual self-reflexivity promoted by Sylvia Molloy, Idelber Avelar too turns to Borges in a quest for what he prefers to call an "ethics of interpretation" in his article "The Ethics of Interpretation and the International Division of Intellectual Labor." Thus, before taking inspiration from Borges's short story "The Ethnographer," he proposes to inquire into and ultimately takes issue with the common notion that critical theory, particularly of the textual and deconstructive kind, in the tradition of what he also calls "post-phenomenological thought," would have entailed a "bracketing," a "demise," or even a total "eclipse" of all moral and/or ethical concerns. Avelar at the same time goes against the unexamined ethnocentrism of some of our time's most erudite and well-intended liberal critics and moral philosophers such as Wayne Booth or Martha Nussbaum, authors whose benevolent humanism cannot conceal the profoundly unequal and asymmetrical global situation in which their pleas for pluralism and cosmopolitanism risk sounding like a shrill provincialism.

Rejecting the false alternative between the antitheoretical denial of an ethics of the text and its liberal-humanist reaffirmation, Avelar chooses to rely in detail on "The Ethnographer" as a pedagogical strategy because it would be "one of the most daring literary texts in its portrayal of the undecidable nature of the ethical encounter."[3] Rather than deceit, the issue now is undecidability, and instead of honest awareness, the ethical demands a daring portrayal that risks unveiling the dark motivations hidden behind even the brightest facade of honesty and tolerance. Borges's story, precisely because of the undecidability of its main character's success or failure in becoming one with the Other in the Indian reservation, in fact, places in crisis the allegedly universal and value-neutral access to the nature of "the human" that continues to undergird the approach even of as subtle and self-critical a thinker as Nussbaum.

Language, or textuality, and alterity: these are still, I would say, the dominant modes in which over the last decade or two the ethical turn has become part of literary and cultural studies at large. We could no doubt argue over minor points that might require clarification in the treatment of these modalities. Among such quibbles, I could briefly mention, first, the question of the prior selection of authors, texts, or genres worthy of ethical interrogations to begin with; second, the unclear differentiation between an ethics of writing and an ethics of reading or of interpretation; and, third, the question of knowing whether the ethical experience is wholly intrinsic to literature and/or to literary criticism, or whether this relation between the ethical and the literary is actually to some degree external to the two terms themselves.

Even in the case of Molloy's ethics of language, there seems to be a set of presuppositions about what constitutes the dimension of the ethical per se. These presuppositions, while not necessarily extraliterary, are not strictly immanent to the literature in question either. In Idelber Avelar's case, on the other hand, a comparable separation is present in the distance between Borges's short story and the theoretical references to Levinas, Derrida, and Simon Critchley, all of whom are pushed away in the footnotes, not to forget the overarching but silent figure of Alberto Moreiras, to whom the article is dedicated. Ironically, this "division of international labor" between a literary object from Latin America and theory or philosophy from Europe—a division that is one of the main targets of Avelar's article—is barely compensated for by the mention, in two other footnotes, of Patricio Marchant and Pablo Oyarzún, Chilean philosophers who thematize precisely the difficulty of redressing this situation of imbalance and uneven development.

Most importantly, both of these approaches remain inscribed in a certain use of literature (I am reluctant to call it "allegorical") as a model, or as an exemplary instantiation, of ethical notions that seem to be available outside of these models or exemplifications themselves, though perhaps not with the same vividness of portrayal. Aside from the qualities of honesty and self-awareness, both modalities rely above all on a certain notion of finitude as the principal key to the ethical experience today—finitude as enacted in and through language, writing, reading. Literature, then, is only one privileged site among others where this experience of finitude is exposed to the ethical light as such. Perhaps such exposure is even the very task of literary criticism.

Finitude Exposed

Regardless of these minor points, it is clear that we are certainly not lacking in ethical models for criticism in or on Latin America. Our question, therefore, cannot be an a priori one about the general conditions of possibility of an ethics of Latin American literary criticism; instead, this question must be addressed within the current historical and theoretical conjuncture. What, then, is the state of ethics today?

In the context of what Avelar calls "post-phenomenological" thought, I would argue that the dominant modes of ethics today are more specifically post-Heideggerian and post-Levinasian—in sum, finitude as exposed in language and in the face of the other. Even Lacan's ethics of desire, drive, or the real seems most often to fit this framework insofar as it too can be summed up in the notion of finitude. In more recent years, however, another tradition has emerged against the current consensus, producing quite a polemical stir in the process, in the guise of an ethics of truths as elaborated by Alain Badiou. Among these thinkers, Levinas and Badiou not only stand out but, what is more, they are now also frequently combined—despite the harsh polemic against, and ultimate dismissal of, Levinas's thought in Badiou's *Ethics: An Essay on the Understanding of Evil*.

Let me add a few comments about this surprising amalgamation of Levinas and Badiou, which was almost single-handedly spearheaded some years ago by Simon Critchley, author not only of the well-known books *Ethics of Deconstruction* and *Ethics-Politics-Subjectivity* but also of a number of articles in which he brings together Levinas, Derrida, Lacan, and Badiou into an all-encompassing notion of ethics that remains by and large Kantian in nature, and in which the polemics of Badiou against Levinasian and Kantian ethics apparently can be ignored without qualms.

In the context of the "formal structure of ethical experience"—as Critchley describes it, and which he also calls, following Dieter Henrich, "the grammar of the concept of moral insight"—ethics fundamentally consists in an individual's giving approval to a formal demand or call.[4] How this demand is filled out, ironically, turns out to be quite open, not to say indifferent, so that everyone from Plato to Lacan and from Paul to Kant to Adorno somehow fits this scheme. This is ironic because for this proponent of the ethics of the other, in the end it all looks pretty much the same. At this level of generality, of course, there is no real quarrel if one wishes to include Levinas, Derrida, Lacan, and Badiou as well. In the case of Levinas and Badiou, for example, the demand of the Other then becomes formally homologous to the call to fidelity to the event.

Without wanting to play the role of policing Badiou's thought, or anyone else's for that matter, some readers at least might have concluded that most of this confusion had been cleared up by Peter Hallward, both in his response to Simon Critchley titled "Ethics Without Others" and in his introduction to Badiou's *Ethics* itself. "Badiou's book does nothing less than *evacuate* the foundation upon which every deconstructive, 'multicultural' or 'postcolonial' ethics is built: the (ethical) category of alterity," Hallward writes in the translator's introduction. He adds, "The whole tangled body of doctrine variously associated with the *Other*—and developed by Levinas, Derrida, Irigaray and Spivak, among so many 'others'—is here simply swept away."[5] Since apparently this reply has not been enough, insofar as it could not deter a number of Critchley's followers to become reluctant or half-baked Badiouians overnight, perhaps we ought to revisit some of the reasons why Badiou and Levinas are in fact strictly incompatible.

Even aside from specific disagreements over concepts or contents, including the role of religion or the place of heroic figures of the subject, which Hallward addresses in his reply to Critchley, I want to raise the more formal prior question about the very place of ethics in the respective philosophies of Badiou and Levinas. I do not know how else to formulate this than by saying that almost nothing major is lost in Badiou's overall philosophy if we take away his tiny book *Ethics*, which in any case was written over the time span of barely a few weeks for an audience of mostly high school students, whereas the reader cannot claim to have even a minimal understanding of Levinas's thought without giving an absolutely central role to ethics.

A second discrepancy revolves around the question of temporality, perhaps better described in terms of sequencing, not just of alterity and sameness but also of ethics and politics as such. If one wants, there certainly is a place for a kind of otherness—even for victims and suffering—in Badiou's thought. But it is only the site for a possible event; it should not be confused with the event itself, which may or may not take place where there are victims.

Badiou's dismissal of the logic of victimization is often misunderstood by readers who are completely taken aback by his notion that the ethics of the other is nihilistic in that it reduces us to the role of mere victims, suffering beasts, mortal or really dying bodies: "In his role as executioner, man is an animal abjection, but we must have the courage to add that in his role as victim, he is generally worth little more."[6] This is often read as a brutal indifference, not to say a dogmatic exclusion, of those very real victims that populate the dark pages and television screens of history. Badiou's rejection of ethics as a nihilistic framework that reduces humans to the role of suffering animals always portrayed as victims, however, should not lead us to forget that for him, too, an event starts out from the site of the least protected, the most unsheltered, and usually the most harshly victimized part of a given situation, which his fellow post-Althusserian Jacques Rancière calls *la part des sans-part*, "the part of those who have no part."[7] The point is that oppression and victimization, which usually do characterize the site of an event, should not be turned into irrefutable reference points of an ethical responsibility that can then be invoked against any and all political efforts to right the original wrong. This invocation would keep the site from ever becoming the site of an actual event. But this is precisely the operation that, for Badiou, risks hiding behind the self-described radicalism of the ethical turn, which is why we should be wary of all speculative zeal to homologize his thinking to that of Levinas.

Fragments of a Critical Genealogy of the Ethical Turn in Latin America

To underscore this point, let me turn to two Latin American thinkers, the first of whom would have to be considered almost the radical opposite of Badiou. I am referring to Enrique Dussel, who in his lifelong philosophical project, leading up to the recent synthesis in *Ética de la liberación* [Ethics of Liberation], has attempted to combine an ethics of the Other with the inscription of Latin American specificity as a concrete Other: the Other of European modernity.

Let me go against the grain once more. Dussel himself, in fact, explicitly quotes Badiou in his *Etica de la liberación*: not as an opponent, as one might have expected, but in order to support his own argument. More specifically, he wholeheartedly embraces Badiou's definition of the subject as the bearer of a truth that results from fidelity to an event. "I call 'subject' the bearer of a fidelity, the one who bears a process of truth," as Badiou writes in his *Ethics*: "The subject, therefore, in no way preexists the process. He is absolutely nonexistent in the situation 'before' the event. We might say that the process of truth *induces* a subject."[8] Thus, what interests Dussel is *el devenir-sujeto de la víctima* [the becoming-subject of the victim], which is why, rather than staring himself blind on the polemic between Other and Same, victim and subject, he can actually find an ally in Badiou. From victims and injustice, in other words, we need to move toward a type of subjectivation, that is, toward a really transformative act that Dussel still describes in strictly Marxist or Marxian terms as the equivalent of revolution: "The 'question of the subject' (in its inter-subjective, socio-historical sense, as the emergence of the diverse subjects of *new* social movements in the diagrams of Power), then, is exactly the problematic of the becoming ethicocritical of the community of victims."[9]

The problem I see with this ethical turn is twofold. On one hand, I believe that the specificity of the ethical experience in this context is frequently lost, as the line of demarcation between ethics and politics seems to have become indiscernible. I see no reason, for example, why Dussel's book could not have been called *Política de la liberación* [Politics of Liberation]—no reason, that is, other than to go with the spirit of our time and its authoritarian consensus regarding the dignity of the ethical over and above all potentially illusory, if not purely voluntaristic political commitments and partisanships. An alternative effect of this preeminence given to the ethical dimension, in fact, relies on the irrefutable radicalism of one's openness to alterity in order to strike preemptively at the dogmatic nature of all processes of political subjectivation. Proof of this irrefutability lies in the fact that there exists no such thing as "ethically incorrect" behavior, whereas the reigning consensus can at least be broken in an act of "political incorrectness." Indeed, who in the world would want *not* to be ethical?

On the other hand, both the growing conflation between ethics and politics and the complete subordination or obliteration of the latter by the former are themselves the result of a historical process that still needs to be mapped out. This is, finally, what I would like to propose as an open-ended task: the history not just of the ethical turn (say, sometime in the early eighties, particularly thanks to the renewed interest in the ethical and the political overtones of deconstruction) nor only of various ethical theories (Kant, Levinas, Lacan, Badiou, Dussel, etc.) but rather the historical inscription of various ethical-theoretical frameworks within a specific political situation.

The history of this development, which would amount to a critical genealogy of the ethical turn, still needs to be written. Obviously I do not pretend to do so here. In the remaining pages, I would like merely to give a few pointers, or post a few signs, by reflecting on a single moment, captured in the movie *Memorias del subdesarrollo* [Memories of Underdevelopment] and the book on which it is partially based: I am referring not to Edmundo Desnoes's novel but to the still fairly unknown book *Moral burguesa y revolución* [Bourgeois Morality and Revolution], written by the Argentine philosopher and long-time Freudo-Marxist León Rozitchner. Indeed, long parts of this book are read by the main character's voice during the movie, in conjunction with both documentary and fictional footage.

Rozitchner's book is a close textual analysis of, and philosophical commentary on, the trials of the counterrevolutionaries taken prisoners after their failed attempt to overthrow Fidel Castro's regime in 1962 during the so-called Bay of Pigs crisis. Based on the written testimonies of the *contras* themselves, as voiced and recorded during their trial by the Cuban judicial system, this analysis tries to come to grips with what Rozitchner, in a later work, would call "the limits of bourgeois individualism." In fact, the books starts out with the following line: "The goal of the present work is to confront the moral conceptions of the bourgeoisie and the ethics of Revolution."[10] Bourgeois morality, at this point, can still be countered with a revolutionary ethics.

In the movie-version of *Memorias del subdesarrollo* directed by Tomás Gutiérrez Alea, however, we barely get a glimpse of the ethics of revolution. Instead, through the overpowering perspective of Sergio, the otherwise disoriented bourgeois individual who decides to stay on the Cuban island rather than join his wife and family when they flee to Miami, what we witness is an impressive montage of the sarcasms, witticisms, and neurotic broodings, both accusatory and self-deprecating, of a supreme example of bourgeois morality.

I would argue that this movie—including its uncanny mockery not only of writers and intellectuals such as David Viñas and the cigar-smoking Edmundo Desnoes himself, but, perhaps more importantly, even of Fidel Castro—marks an important stepping stone toward the complete obliteration of the *alternate* side in Rozitchner's dichotomy, that is, the ethics of revolution as opposed to bourgeois morality. By this I mean that with the gradual waning and subsequent collapse of the revolutionary idea, we have entered a period—"special" in a different sense—in which the ethical experience no longer leads *from* the injustice and victimization *to* a new sense of justice but instead remains entirely within a realm—henceforth the ethical realm as such—where everyone is a victim, or an other to someone else's sameness.

For Rozitchner, bourgeois ethics or morality can be perceived in the tactics by which the counterrevolutionaries systematically seek to evade all collective responsibility, either by blaming the group when they are at fault as individuals, or else by setting oneself apart from the group, when they feel worthy of praise as individuals:

> In bourgeois ethics, there is nobody, as we will see, responsible concretely for the whole. Nobody takes hold of the totality of meaning of action; all appear as dislocated elements of a global meaning that nobody assumes completely: everyone refers to his own individuality when wanting to distance himself from the misery of others which (he believes) undeservedly contaminates him, or else submerges himself in the indifferentiated group when having to hide one's own responsibility, and thus contaminating the others without qualms. Among them, there is no ethical sense, only a personal morality; there is not a single one who can take charge of his action and extend its meaning so as to reencounter in it the signification of the acts taken on collectively, by including the full materiality in which they are grounded. (Rozitchner, *Moral burguesa y revolución*, 17)

But precisely this inability to sustain any collective project, this disconnect between actions and their meaning, is seen by Sergio in the movie as a symptom—or better yet, as the very definition—of what he calls underdevelopment. The problem then lies in the fact that already in this movie from 1968 there seems to be no path, no program, not even as much as a critical perspective available to overcome the condition of underdevelopment.

For Rozitchner, in his theoretical case study on the trials from the Bay of Pigs, on the other hand, the solution can consist only of an ethics of collective revolutionary commitment. However, at this point in the early 1960s, the Argentine philosopher is already acutely aware of the dilemmas that will soon thereafter come to haunt with ever-growing intensity the consciousness of politically engaged left-wing intellectuals, all the way up to the unanswerability of Gayatri Spivak's pivotal question "Can the Subaltern Speak?":

> This also means that our commitment, in actualizing and validating the total connection that we maintain with the world, prepares us, as thinking human beings, to receive the object in its total interhuman signification. If we were not to do so, our act of knowing would not provide us with true knowledge. Why? Because it would mean assuming that there can be someone, the I who analyzes, or I as privileged subject, who manages at some point to evade the responsibility that in all orders of action I maintain with other human beings. Precisely, that is, at the point where I dedicate myself to think *for* them.[11]

Once the suspicion sets in that one is speaking *for* the other, ethical responsibility frequently displaces all notions of political commitment. Or rather, we should say that, both through the *critique* of the logic of commitment and through the *crisis* of the revolutionary ideal now turned state regime, the meaning of ethics undergoes a profound displacement.

Toward the Liberation from Ethics

Following Rancière's conclusion in the last chapter of his recent book *Malaise dans l'esthétique* [Aesthetics and Its Discontents], we could describe this development as the ethical turn in aesthetics and politics, provided we redefine our understanding of this turn itself: "The essential aspect of this process is certainly not the virtuous return to norms of morality. It is, rather, the suppression of the division that this same word of morals implied."[12] Using the contrasting examples of Bertold Brecht's plays and Lars von Trier's *Dogville*, as well as a similar contrast between Alfred Hitchcock's movies and Clint Eastwood's *Mystic River*, Rancière describes how morality today, instead of dividing our sense of justice and injustice as was the case before, due to a generalized turn to ethics, has led to a state of indistinction in which we are all ultimately victims of some originary trauma, witnesses to some radical evil, or subjects to an overwhelming catastrophe.

Unlike what happens in Rozitchner's *Moral burguesa y revolución*, ethics then no longer opens up a promise of emancipation; instead, as can be seen in the movie-version of *Memorias del subdesarrollo*, alienation and underdevelopment—also in the structural sense of the film's stark disjunctions between individual and group, image and sound, action and thought, documentary and fiction—come to define the human condition from which only a criminal lie can promise to liberate us. Art, after the ethical turn, bears witness to this impossibility, the noble philosophical and quasi-ontological name for which is finitude.

In the context of Dussel's work, this shift can be understood further if we reflect upon the structural tension, if not exactly an unacknowledged discrepancy, between, on one hand, the framework of dependency theory, which continues to determine his *Etica* in terms of center and periphery, Europe and its other, the exclusion of which is subsequently covered up, and, on the other hand, the strictly ethical theory, which, as I suggested, could be called political as well insofar as its aim is a transformative act that collectively would overcome the initial injustice by way of a new and hitherto impossible sense of justice. Once the newly developed ethics submerges the politics, however, one framework risks undermining the other. This ambiguity can be seen in the very title of the book with its two-pronged orientation: *Etica de la liberación en la edad de la globalización y de la exclusión* [Ethics of Liberation in the Era of Globalization and Exclusion]. A similar tension, in fact, appears in the title of Avelar's article, with "ethics of interpretation" pointing toward Levinas and the witnessing of the Other, whereas "international division of intellectual labor" begs the question of knowing whether the ideal of a revolution, though unspoken, still promises to be a way out as in the case of older dependency theory.

In Dussel's case, the origin of this tension may well lie in the qualification of the site of the transformative act as the space of victimhood. In the movement *from* (injustice, victimization, exclusion) *to* (justice, emancipation, the becoming-subject of the excluded), what happens then is that the latter half drops out of the picture altogether because any such attempt at subjectivation is now seen as entailing the inevitable creation of more sacrificial victims. In the name of these new victims, any subjectivation of the process thus is truncated from the start. Dussel's project, which in a sense has to be much closer to Badiou than to the general Levinasian trend behind the current ethical turn, nevertheless facilitates this trend by which its ultimate goal, which I believe can be said to be political rather than ethical, ends up being sacrificed at the altar of the general victimization of humanity.

To conclude, let me illustrate this point one last time with a passage from *Liberación latinoamericana y Emmanuel Levinas* [Latin American

Liberation and Emmanuel Levinas], in my eyes still one of Dussel's most compact anticipations of his *Etica de la liberación*. In the epigraph to this little book, the author quotes the following words from Levinas: "The least drunk and most lucid humanity of our time, in the most liberated instants of the preoccupation of existence with this existence itself, has no greater shadow in its clarity than that which stems from the misery of others."[13] Precisely by recalling the fact that the most liberated moments of our existence are also the clarity whose shadow is misery, the last two decades or so, in the name of ethics, have come to cancel any attempt to overcome this misery through a political act of liberation.

In this context, finally, it may seem entirely appropriate and understandable to seek a return to the ethics of textual honesty alone, without the impossible pretense of an ethics of liberation. The question with which I would like to end, though, asks whether we should not also consider the possibility that today, and for the time being, it might be more urgent to liberate us from ethics.

Notes

1. Borges, "The Superstitious Ethics of the Reader."
2. Molloy, *Signs of Borges*. 4.
3. Avelar, "The Ethics of Interpretation." 92.
4. Critchley, "Demanding Approval."
5. Hallward, *Ethics*. xxxv.
6. Badiou, *Ethics*. 11.
7. Rancière, *Disagreement*, passim.
8. Badiou, *Ethics*. 43. Quoted in Enrique Dussel, *Etica de la liberación en la edad de la globalización y de la exclusión*. 520.
9. Dussel, *Etica de la liberación*. 527.
10. Rozitchner, *Moral burguesa y revolución*. 9.
11. Ibid. 19.
12. Rancière, *Malaise dans l'esthétique*. 145.
13. Levinas, quoted in Dussel, *Liberación latinoamericana y Emmanuel Levinas*. 7.

Works Cited

Avelar, Idelber. "The Ethics of Interpretation and the International Division of Intellectual Labor." *SubStance* 91 (2000): 80–103.

Badiou, Alain. *Ethics. An Essay on the Understanding of Evil*, trans. Peter Hallward. London: Verso, 2001.

Borges, Jorge Luis. "The Superstitious Ethics of the Reader." *Selected Nonfictions*, ed. Eliot Weinberger. New York: Penguin Books, 1999. 52–55.
Critchley, Simon. "Demanding Approval: On the Ethics of Alain Badiou." *Radical Philosophy* 100 (2000): 16–27.
Dussel, Enrique. *Ética de la liberación en la era de la globalización y de la exclusión*. Mexico, D.F.: UAM-Iztapalapa/UNAM, 1998.
———. *Liberación latinoamericana y Emmanuel Levinas*. Buenos Aires: Bonum, 1975.
Gutiérrez Alea, Tomás, dir. *Memorias del subdesarrollo*. Cuba, 1968.
Hallward, Peter. "Ethics without Others: A Reply to Critchley on Badiou's Ethics." *Radical Philosophy* 100 (2000): 27–30.
———. "Translator's Introduction," in Alain Badiou, *Ethics. An Essay on the Understanding of Evil*, trans. Peter Hallward. London: Verso, 2001. vii–xlvii.
Molloy, Sylvia. *Signs of Borges*, trans. Oscar Montero. Durham: Duke UP, 1994.
Rancière, Jacques. *Disagreement: Politics and Philosophy*, trans. Julie Rose. Minneapolis: U of Minnesota P, 1999.
———. *Malaise dans l'esthétique*. Paris: Galilée, 2004.
Rozitchner, León. *Freud y los límites del individualismo burgués*. Mexico, D.F.: Siglo XXI, 1974.
———. *Moral burguesa y revolución*. Buenos Aires: Procyon, 1963.
Spivak, Gayatri Chakravorty. "Can the Subaltern Speak?" *Marxism and the Interpretation of Culture*, ed. Cary Nelson and Lawrence Grossberg. Urbana: U of Illinois P, 1988. 271–313.

2

ETHICS, PERHAPS

Gabriela Basterra

Immanuel Kant, Emmanuel Levinas, and Jacques Lacan describe ethical subjectivity as responding to a disruption of order caused by an event. Despite the important differences between them, all three evoke ethical experience as unrepresentable: existing outside of language, beyond the constellation of content, it is an experience outside of experience that interrupts the autonomous self. I will call it ethics of the break. Whether the break is provoked by the moral Law (Kant), by the other within the same (Levinas), or by fidelity to one's desire (Lacan), it has always already interrupted the self, compelling it to act in ways that lie beyond social legitimation and support. This ethical interruption constitutes ethical subjectivity as an otherwise than identity by exposing it to the difficult experience of lack of self-coincidence: it opens a gap within the self that compels it to act on an address that is unconditioned and unconditional, yet impossible to fulfill. Since this demand remains incommensurate with any particular act, the interval it opens within the self can never be reduced.

But why should the autonomous subject be interrupted, and what form does this disruption take? Isn't the notion of "autonomy" already an ethical one, at least in the sense initially intended by Kant? My claim is that the concept of autonomy that has prevailed in our Western societies is correlative to a mode of subjectivity based on victimization and guilt that I will call "tragic." To this paradigm of guilt belongs, perhaps surprisingly, the modern liberal subject that premises the rational political order. Insofar as this subject promotes "respect for the other," "ethics of difference," or "identity politics," it ultimately represents itself as victim (and agency as powerless), thus evading responsibility, inflicting suffering, and creating real victims. "Attention" to the other represents the other either as the victim that must be saved by projecting one's own idea of the good, or as the "diverse" other that must be carefully kept at a distance (through "tolerance" and "charity"), or as the enemy to be vanquished, or as the victim of a society that lacks democracy. Even when "well" intended, these depictions of the other deflect attention from the problem of the same, which is the problem that concerns Kant, Lacan, and Levinas. The "same" that Levinas describes in *Otherwise than Being* does not coincide with itself because it is not a "one" (neither a unicity, nor singular) but plural. In the plurality of the same lies the impossible possibility that is ethics.

To start exploring these ethics of the break, I will begin by proposing a conceptual distinction between two modes of subjective constitution that we could tentatively call "tragic" and "ethical"—or the subject of guilt and the subject of the break; the subject of the law and the subject of the event; or, in Lacan's terms, the subject desiring the desire of the other and the one not giving way on its desire. After a brief description of autonomous subjectivity as based on internalizing guilt, I will focus on ethical subjectivity as described by Levinas in *Otherwise than Being*. My account of Levinas's thought will include brief references to the structure of bearing witness and declaring the event as Alain Badiou depicts it in his book on *Saint Paul*. Any general comparison of Badiou's and Levinas's philosophical projects could easily amount to an act of violent reduction, so profound are the differences between them. However, since Badiou's evocation of witnessing resonates with that of Levinas (even if the event borne witness to in each differs in its immanence or transcendence), I will refer to it in the hope to bring inspiration to the difficult reading that I am about to propose.

As it may have already become evident in my initial distinction between "tragic" and "ethical" subjectivity, one of the problems in this account will be that concepts such as "subject," "the Law," "the good," "obligation," "obedience," or "truth," not to mention "the same," "self-division," or "subjectivation," can be used indistinctly to refer to ethical interruption (a heteronomous break) and to the situation being interrupted (the autonomous subject). Beyond any simple terminological challenge, at stake here is no less than the relation between heteronomy and autonomy. Since both modes of subjective constitution are linked to an experience of obligation, couldn't they come to coincide at some point? Though at first view it would seem that autonomy depends on representation, whereas ethical constitution does away with representation, we will see that the very ethical experience beyond experience that appeared to leave representation aside is also the very adventure of its birth.

Tragic Subjectivity

By "tragic" subject I refer, perhaps unexpectedly, to the modern subjectivity that premises the rational political order and the illusion of autonomy on which such order relies. Born with the Enlightenment, this subject achieves its position in society by internalizing guilt and desiring necessity. It is depicted in Hegel's "unhappy consciousness," and elaborated in Nietzsche's account of "conscience," Freud's distinction between ego and superego and his idea of melancholic self-beratement, Althusser's ideological interpellation as an originary assumption of guilt, or Foucault's distinction between body and soul, to name only a few instances.[1] In all these accounts, the subject emerges by internalizing external coercion as a critical agency that turns against the material and sensitive part of the self, splitting it (hence the so-called modern split).[2] The identity models that still define us today presuppose the existence of an essentialized force of otherness—call it power, law, the state—that has come to replace tragic fate in rational times. This mystified "other" produces through internalization a rent and bound identity that I denominate "tragic subjectivity." Though this subjectivation is premised on some kind of death of the sensible self (which in tragedy is brought about by an inevitable destiny), tragic heteronomy is extremely fruitful. It produces subjective identity, the illusion of autonomy, the fiction of the autonomous subject, social recognition, duties determined and legitimized by the law, symmetrical and reciprocal intersubjective relations, the social equalities enabled by universal principles, and subject-based liberal politics. This fruitfulness often requires, however, that the self renounce its agency and responsibility, paradoxically by assuming guilt or by representing itself as victim.

This subject is one that, in Levinas's words, "dissolves" in a wider horizon of being, playing a role in a drama of which it is not the author. In Badiou's terms, this subject has not broken with the law. Now, how can it be that this subject, born when the Enlightenment replaces religion with reason as a guarantee of intelligibility, is tragic? Why is it that this autonomous subject, a subject that claims to be self-legislated, can be considered controlled by someone else? Elsewhere I have claimed that accepting a transference of guilt and depicting ourselves as victims allows us (tragic modern subjects) to invoke an inexorable fate as an alibi ("it was inevitable, I was acting under control..."), and thus to disclaim responsibility for our actions.[3] Being responsible for one's actions implies being responsible before someone else, and if we deny our responsibility we also deny our accountability to other people. It is the receiving pole of action, the real people who suffer from our acts, that we blind ourselves to—that we obliterate, when we depict ourselves as victims. (It is in this way that when we claim we are victims we create real victims.) But perhaps even more pressing than refusing responsibility is the aspiration to preserve the social symbolic order that produces us as subjects. Only other people are real others who can question our way of life. Therefore, while the abstract otherness of fate, law, or the father configures the self as an intelligible subject, real people, with their presence and needs, question the centrality of the self. Paradoxically, the eagerness to embrace subjection, even at the cost of death, betrays a fear of leaving ourselves, an urge to preserve our integrity, and with it the preeminence of sameness that only a real person can disrupt.

Hence the paradox of our modern subjectivity: we represent ourselves as victims in order to preserve our autonomy. When compared to the uncertainty of the subject of the break, the death that reaffirms the symbolic order comes as a relief. Modern subjectivity, in sum, never abandons the paradigm in which guilt functions as evasion, as escape. As we shall see, the (ethical) heteronomy of the same [*le même*] that bears witness to the eventual interruption, which Levinas describes in terms of an "alteration without alienation and election" (*OB* 141/*AE* 221),[4] questions the (tragic) heteronomy in which the subject cooperates. This self-consenting victimization attributed to an essentialized and alienating otherness (fate, the past, the law) returns the self to itself by splitting it, by causing the internal division that premises identity as identification.

In Seminar VIII, *Le transfert*, Lacan suggests that if in classical tragedy the irruption of objective necessity in human life creates a kind of trauma, the trauma in modern times is that "destiny no longer applies" (VIII 358). In modern times, given the absence of a transcendental necessity that structures the social field, one runs the risk of having to do without guilt, without the refuge afforded by the awareness of being in debt. Since guilt provides the division through which we become subjects, and thus our position in the symbolic framework of society, lack of guilt precipitates us into the responsibility of acting with no guarantee. But in effect we are neither exposed, nor accountable, without destiny. We have managed to transfer destiny's power to control us onto other essentialized constructs that secure our place in the constellation of guilt. We may call these syntheses of authority the Father, the Law, or the state, but also the free market, advertising companies, or intelligence organizations that, we claim, structure our desires, and dictate our lives. In tragic style, we require other agencies to act on our behalf, even though we want to think of ourselves as free, autonomous agents. So destiny does apply after all, since we seem to have succeeded in preserving guilt by creating "necessary fictions" such as the Law, which enable the "necessary fiction" of the subject.

We could rephrase this in terms of Lacan's formulation that desire is the desire of the other: we construct the desire of the Other—of the symbolic order that through prohibition produces us as subjects—as a kind of "objective necessity" that we then adopt as our object of desire. In Badiou's terms, this "desire as automatism" is linked to being-towards-death, to the path of death that (according to Lacan) must be refused. "[O]nly the law fixes the object of desire," he writes, "binding desire to it regardless of the subject's 'will.' It is this objectal automatism of desire, inconceivable without the law, that assigns the subject to the carnal path of death" (*Saint Paul*, 79/83).[5] And he continues: "This figure of the subject, wherein the division lies between the dead Self and the involuntary automation of living desire, is, for thought, a figure of powerlessness. Basically, sin is not so much a fault as living thought's inability to prescribe action" (*Saint Paul*, 83/87). Badiou's description of this subject as the correlation between desire as "automatism" and death helps clarify the constraints of the subjective agency inaugurated in a symbolic debt. Although the law premises the possibility of agency by giving the self a position in the social order, subjective agency is radically constrained because it emerges in subjection, through prohibition. In fact, considered rigorously, subjective "agency" may consist in retrospectively accepting as voluntarily chosen what was inevitable in the first place. Let me anticipate that this desire linked with guilt that produces the modern subject differs from faithfulness to one's desire (Lacan) or from the heteronomy (Levinas) that inaugurates the subject of the break.

It is important to note that in this process representation enables subjectivity at the price of occluding something crucial. Why should this happen? Let me rehearse one of several possible explanations. Although the structure of desire is that of representation, that of the signifying order (of metonymical differentiation), desire aims at the dimension of the Real, which exists outside the constellation of content. In Lacan's words, "that which is signified in an act passes from one signifier of the chain to another beneath all the significations" (VII 322/371). As Alenka Zupančič explains, because the Real is inaccessible, the full satisfaction of desire is unattainable, and it is the function of the law to help us deal with this impossibility.[6] In other words, it is not exactly the case that prohibition suppresses our desire, but neither does it simply provoke, feed, and invigorate it, as we usually assume. What the law does, rather, is "to forbid something which is in itself impossible." It does so by naming—by giving signifying form to—what is nothing but an unrepresentable impossibility.[7] What one perceives as the law, as an explicit interdiction, is a signifier, a representation without content (empty) that blinds us to the impossibility to satisfy our true desire. In forbidding what was in any case impossible, the law protects us from the recalcitrant emptiness that constitutes its other side.

Ethics of the Break

The subject of an order (the tragic subject) has been interrupted by something unrepresentable that it cannot assimilate. As we shall see, the name that Levinas gives to this derangement of ontological being is "trace." And in "bearing witness" to this disturbance of order, to this trace that the event has imprinted in world and subject, the subject itself *becomes* the event.

But Levinas is better known for his earlier attempts to address the question of ethical motivation in *Totality and Infinity* (1961). In this text, the ethical demand comes from an absolutely exterior other, an other that cannot be represented because it exists outside of the constellation of content, which Levinas *names* with the figure of the face, *le visage*. But in evoking an other that is absolutely exterior, isn't Levinas already positing it? Would the "face" name a true absence, or does it represent just one more speculative thought, a presupposed other? This is the question that Jacques Derrida and Maurice Blanchot raise in the mid-1960's. In his 1964 response to Levinas, "Violence and Metaphysics," Derrida writes, "According to Levinas, there would be no interior difference, no fundamental and autochthonous alterity within the ego."[8] In other words, if the other is absolutely exterior, if it is separated from the self by an untraversable distance, how does one know that the other exists?[9] In positing an absolute exteriority that would interrupt ontological being, Levinas has not yet left the realm of ontology: he has not yet found the language and the performative gestures that would allow him to perform a break with ontology, not even a partial or momentary one. Though according to him the other that disrupts the self cannot be thought, positing something unrepresentable in terms of absolute exteriority to the self is still a way of representing it: in the end there can be no real disruption, and thus no proper bearing witness to the event. Levinas's attempt in *Totality and Infinity* to point to the unrepresentable event of the other ultimately does not succeed (and given that this is Levinas's most read book, many readings of Levinas miss important parts of his thought and of his mode of expressing it).

It is in the early 1960's that Levinas finds a "new modality" of *saying*, the performative expressions that would allow him to evoke the event—such as the "mode of the perhaps," as well as the trope of the trace.[10] The trace is the derangement of the "order of the world": "Someone has already passed. His trace does not *signify* his past, as it does not *signify* his labor or his enjoyment in the world; it is the very disturbance imprinting itself [we would be tempted to say *engraving* itself (*se gravant*)] with an irrecusable gravity."[11] As a derangement of an order, the trace is also the disturbance of being (one of whose historical embodiments would be the modern autonomous subject) provoked by the event of the other. With the trace, the alterity-relation no longer needs to be evoked in terms of exteriority. Thus *Otherwise than Being* refers to the alterity-relation as *l'Autre-dans-le-Même* [the Other-within-the-Same]: it is a being-disrupted-within-oneself.[12] The alterity-relation now happens within the skin of a subject obsessed by proximity and marked by the event, a subject that *responds* to it—that *bears witness* to it—as one responds to a trauma, without having decided to respond (deciding would still be the act of a noninterrupted subject whose agency depends on identification). And the subject itself is the one that "bears witness" to the disruption provoked by the event: " 'Here I am' (*me voici*) as a witness of the Infinite, but a witness that does not thematize what it bears witness of, and whose truth is not the truth of representation, is not evidence. There is witness—a unique structure, an exception to the rule of being, irreducible to representation" (*OB* 146/*AE* 229). By bearing witness without any actual knowledge to an event that does not appear to him, the subject itself becomes a trace of the event. Badiou's Saint Paul declares the event in a like manner[13]: "The apostle, who declares an unheard-of possibility, one dependent on an eventful grace, properly speaking knows nothing."

The event is "witnessed" in "a declaration and its consequences, which, being without proof or visibility, emerges at that point where knowledge, be it empirical or conceptual, breaks down" (*Saint Paul* 45/48). Since philosophical language in incapable of declaring the event, Badiou speaks of the need to invent "a new discourse and . . . a subjectivity that is neither philosophical nor prophetic (the apostle)," for "it is only by means of such invention that the event finds a welcome and an existence in language" (*Saint Paul* 46/49). For both Levinas and Derrida, the *saying* of the event would have to be done—supposing that such a *saying* were at all possible and could be expressed in the passive mode—in the mode of the perhaps and performatively: as a saying that turns into a *said* that then must be unsaid so that one can say again.

Yet, however crucial Levinas's account of witnessing may be to his description of subjectivity, such description is not yet complete: its political orientation, which has been repeatedly insinuated and performed along *Otherwise than Being*, becomes (more) explicit in the next section of chapter V, which Levinas titles "From Saying to the Said, or the Wisdom of Desire." In order to explore that political dimension, we will need to account for the "reintroduction" of representation in Levinas's text—though the term "reintroduction" will prove inaccurate, referring as it does only to the "linear" temporality of my own argument, but not to that of Levinas's, since at this moment his book has tirelessly *said, unsaid*, and *said again*; even less does my "reintroduction" refer to the temporality of the ethical break whose trace Levinas attempts to *say* (the "said" that "saying" turns into is itself a trace), since that is a diachronic temporality outside of chronological time. It is thus only *me* who will have to "reintroduce" representation, a representation that, as it will turn out (in the linearity of my argument), will have always already been there. We will soon see how Levinas's depiction/performance of subjectivity becomes more inclusive—which is to say: political—in representation, but first we will have to ask whether this ethical subjectivity would not ultimately collapse with the self-victimizing (and victimizing) subjectivity of guilt.

Witnessing introduces, moreover, a new emphasis into Levinas's description of subjectivity. The self bearing witness is a historical being, and bearing witness becomes an *act* in the world and in language. The one who bears witness expresses his/her engagement in an event of which he/she has no evidence. Bearing witness is the *act* of declaring something that exists outside of knowledge and representation (the event), of giving the derangement it provokes an existence in language. But what kind of action and of language are at stake here? If according to Levinas autonomous agency is interrupted, in what sense could witnessing be an *act*? How would witnessing as an *act* differ from the modern agency achieved by internalizing guilt? What would prevent witnessing from representing, from filling the void?

Politics and Representation

"Filling the void" by representing the command as a kind of inevitable destiny (such as the superego, Power, the Law, or the Past) is the operation at the center of tragic subjectivity, as I have argued elsewhere.[14] It is also the operation that secures the paradoxical nature of autonomous subjectivity: it allows the subject to assume guilt and depict itself as a victim in order to preserve its autonomy, at the price of creating real victims. However problematic it may be, this subject premised on internalizing guilt and depicting itself as victim constitutes the basis of democratic politics, since it is the locus of the rational principles of universality and equality. Therefore, the very egalitarian principles that found democracy, enabling constitutions, the rule of law, and courts of human rights, may result, paradoxically, in an inability to reach out to others, if not in their outright suppression. But this does not imply that we can renounce subjectivity, for it is a necessary creation constitutive of who we are. Even supposing that we could renounce it, with it we would give up agency (however precarious), the possibility of political struggle and of the rule of law (however imperfect). By renouncing subjectivity we would give up ourselves, that is, the very position from which such a renunciation is made.

Yet I have proposed that tragic subjectivity and the illusion of autonomy enabled by it evade an unbearable *ethical* obligation. There is something even more terrifying than the guilt induced by the superego, which is acting beyond the social rules that legitimate our actions. It is daring to decide what our duty is, to make it concrete, and then to act on it without any external confirmation. Though ethical obligation is unrepresentable, it demands a vertiginous and perhaps violent act of representation, and a radical investment (to use Laclau's term) in an action that must remain unsure of itself. One must take the risk of acting without the guarantee of success, expanding the space of political action beyond the safe realm of institutions and laws. This agent is not always militant and definitely not heroic, but rather uncertain and vulnerable.

Hence the relation between ethics and politics is often understood as a deadlock. For how can the radical responsibility demanded by the ethical break (as Levinas describes it) coexist with the social rules that enable political life, whose reliance on the autonomous subject may result in avoiding responsibility? To put this question in different terms: if autonomy constitutes an evasion from *ethical* heteronomy, what is the rapport between autonomy and heteronomy? It would seem that the distinction between tragic and ethical subjectivity is subtle but crucial, for in it lies the possibility of an ethical subjectivity that breaks with the paradigm of difference, victimization, and guilt. But how would ethical subjectivity ultimately differ from the very tragic subjectivity that it questions, disrupts, and exceeds? Is it possible to think of an autonomy that is not based on the superego and guilt?

In the last chapter of *Otherwise than Being*, Levinas refers to the experience of the event as "this way for a command to sound in the mouth of the one that obeys" (*OB* 147/*AE* 230), that is, as "inspiration" and "witness." To witness is to be inspired in the common sense of the word. Being inspired means finding in myself something that was not in me before. Inspiration is "the possibility of being the author of what had been breathed *unbeknownst to me*, of having received, one knows not from where, that of which I am author" (*OB* 148/*AE* 232). Because I find it in myself, I consider myself the author of an order of obedience that I receive from elsewhere, that is unheard of [*inouïe*] and unheard, that has "slipped in me 'like a thief,' " that has been heteronomously imposed. This order speaks, says Levinas, "by my own voice. The command is stated by the mouth of him it commands" (*OB* 147/*AE* 230). But I only find this order "exercised by the other in me over me" [*exercé par autrui en moi sur moi*] (*OB* 141/*AE* 221) in "this assignation to respond," in my "here I am" [*me voici*], in "saying with inspiration" (*OB* 142/*AE* 222), in bearing witness to the event.

Furthermore, in inspiration, in "the inscription of the law in consciousness," "autonomy and heteronomy are reconciled" (*OB* 148/*AE* 232), to our surprise. And no wonder we are surprised. For this reconciliation takes place when heteronomy, the core of Levinas's ethics as first philosophy, reverts into autonomy. As is well known, one of Levinas's (apparent) differences with Kant is that for him the other has priority over the self, whereas Kant privileges the principle of autonomy. When Levinas says that heteronomy reverts into autonomy, is Levinas implying that the very autonomy that is questioned by the heteronomous demand, by ethical interruption, is also the result of the demand? Isn't Levinas betraying the primacy of heteronomy for the sake of autonomy, as Kant does?

In alluding to inspiration and the reconciliation of heteronomy and autonomy, Levinas introduces in his account the birth of self-consciousness, which had been absent up to this point. The subject is both autonomous (persevering in itself) and heteronomous (exceeding itself, with another within), autonomy and heteronomy interact in subjectivity. We could say, in other words, that autonomy and heteronomy account for a similar experience from two different perspectives. From the limited perspective of the self-conscious rational subject, autonomy would constitute a perception of the derangement provoked by the event outside of temporality and of representation. Autonomy acquires the status of founding principle by occluding ethical heteronomy from the very self-consciousness it inaugurates.

Far from betraying the centrality of heteronomy as first philosophy, then, Levinas throws unprecedented light on Kant's idea of autonomy. When he refers to the "reverting of heteronomy into autonomy," Levinas points to the distancing of the subject from itself, or the suspended distinction between the "inside" and the "outside" that Lacan calls extimacy. This distancing (which in the Levinasian subjectivity becomes possible by recasting the unchosen derangement that is the trace as a decision made by the self) allows for self-consciousness. Although the self is indeed heteronomously obligated, autonomy emerges as the effect of looking at oneself from the viewpoint of consciousness and of representation, which is the only position we can occupy as rational subjects.

My creative response to the other who "orders me by my own voice" is political, also in the literal sense of political representation: I speak for the other. Politics emerges precisely in "the reverting of heteronomy into autonomy," that is, in "the possibility of finding, anachronously, the order in the obedience itself" (*OB* 148/*AE* 232). I am heteronomously obligated, but I believe I am autonomous when I believe myself the author of a decision made in me. Autonomy is therefore an illusion, the result of a narrowing of "perspective" that enables my perception of myself as self-conscious being. Could we refer to this autonomy, which is in effect an autoheteronomy, as ethical, to differentiate it from the "tragic" autonomy that recasts the other as an enemy, as a victim that demands our compassion, or as an other that one must respect (i.e., kept at a safe distance from me)? The difference is subtle but crucial and may be elucidated by discerning what kind of split constitutes the self. The tragic split that produces the subject's identity as unicity results from melancholic internalization (where the part of the self that identifies with the lost other marshals aggression against the other part), or from reducing ethical obligation to internalized authority or superegoic guilt. The interval that constitutes the ethical subject of the break is, in turn, opened by the other within (an other irreducible to the same), whose unrepresentable and unfulfillable order speaks by the voice of the one it commands. This subject is a failed unicity because its acts can never fill the ethical void, and because it is *plural*: as an other-in-the-same the subject is *at least* two.

The same is *at least two* because in inspiration, in the conciliation of heteronomy and autonomy—in autoheteronomy—the third comes into view in Levinas's text. The third was already there (and it was in Levinas's writings at least since the 1954 essay "Ego and Totality"; and the moment of its appearance in *Otherwise than Being*—OB 157 /AE 244—had been repeatedly cross-referenced from the beginning of the book's argument). The third was already there, in the alterity-relation, because it is a structure of the other that signifies that the other is not singular but plural. Though Levinas devotes most of *Otherwise than Being* to evoking the self's substitution for the other—for this is the sense of subjectivity as the "other-within-the-same," as the same with an other within—his account of the subject only becomes complete when the other appears as plural. The third was always already in the other, the other was always already plural, and so was the same as the one-for-the-other, but the third takes centerstage in Levinas's argument only *at this very moment*. At this moment too does the reader realize that the subject's response to the other that "orders me by my own voice" is (always already) political and has (always already) become an action in the world. As coming from the other, the subject's initiative also *bears witness* to the event: the subject speaks for the other and no longer for itself, or rather, the subject speaks for the other in speaking for itself. The subject acts for the other in acting for itself: a political "activity beyond activity" emerges from the "passivity beyond passivity" of substitution.[15] Ethical obligation, present only in terms of a lack (an empty presence or an absent fullness, in Laclau's terms) calls for concrete action, and thus for representation. But it also calls for the performative gestures (such as the affirmation of uncertainty performed in the mode of the perhaps) that signify the interval's excess over indispensable particular acts. The interval cannot be represented (though it could perhaps be *named*), nor can the ethicopolitical void be reduced.

Who or What is the Same?

As I hope to have suggested in evoking these ethics of the break, the derangement that disturbs the self's ontological order does not occur within the logic of identity, a logic that would encompass any temporary interruption. It is therefore not linked to the problem of alterity, if we understand "alterity" in terms of altruism (or "concern" for the other). Rather, the interruption of the self is related to the "enigma" of the same [*le même*], which Levinas describes as a "claim laid on the same by the other in the core of the same ... or inspiration, beyond the logic of *same* and *other*, of their insurmountable adversity" (*OB* 141/*AE* 221). One could in fact say that the "problem" of the other still belongs in the "logic of same and other, of their insurmountable adversity." Within this antagonism, the other's resistance—an ontic event—would oppose the self's powers by force, whereas ethical resistance suspends the freedom of a self who can no longer have power [*ne peut plus pouvoir*]. Although Levinas underscores the suffering inflicted on others by the self by virtue of the "violence of the encounter with the non-I,"[16] by virtue of the confrontation and struggle required by identity, this is not his main goal in *Otherwise than Being*. Identity presupposes difference between other and self—hence the inseparability of "ethics of difference" and "identity politics," hence the fact that altruistic concern for the other verges on its negation, on the assimilation of the non-I by the I. When Levinas speaks of subjectivity as "substitution offered in the place of another," he immediately clarifies: "Not a victim offering itself in his place, which would suppose there is a reserved region of subjective will behind the subjectivity of substitution" (*OB* 145/*AE* 228). So long as one remains within the logic of the autonomous subject, which is the logic of the antagonism between self and other of which altruism is only another expression, one misses the question of subjective constitution.[17]

Kant, Levinas, Lacan, and Badiou are not concerned with the difference between the self and the other, but rather with the gap opened within the same by an irreducible event. The other-event that constitutes the ethical subject is empty, and its trace is the interval that it opens within the same. In Levinas's words, this interval is the "undoing of the substantial nucleus of the ego that is formed in the same, a fission of the mysterious nucleus of inwardness of the subject by this assignation to respond, ... alteration without alienation or election" (*OB* 141/*AE* 221–2). The same is *l'Autre-dans-le-Même*, my being-disrupted-within-myself, that is, a same with an other within which is therefore not "one." But the "other" within is not an "other" in the singular, either: the other is not "one." "If proximity ordered to me only the other alone, there would have not been any problem. . . . A question would not have been born, nor conscience, nor self-consciousness" (*OB* 157/*AE* 245). If the other were singular, the problem of the political would not have emerged, but neither would have self-consciousness: there would have been no subject. Thus, it is neither just oneself's relation to the other-event that constitutes its subjectivity, nor one's becoming a sign of the eventual derangement. If the subject of the break is constituted as such, it is because the other-within is plural.

What is then the "problem" born with the self-conscious subject? Proximity "is troubled and becomes a problem from the entry of the third" (*OB* 157/*AE* 245) and of the need for justice. Proximity *has always already been* troubled, it *will have always become* a problem, because the entry of the third is not an empirical fact, but rather a structure of the other. The third *will always have been* there, in the same's orientation toward the other within ("the other in the core of the same," *l'Autre-dans-le-Même*), because the other is not singular, but plural: the third is the other in plural. Or, as Alenka Zupančič points referring to Lacan, we "should note that the Lacanian thesis that 'there is no Other (of the) Other' aims not at the exclusion of the third, but, on the contrary, at its inclusion. The Other (of the Other) is included in the Other—and this is precisely what makes the Other Other, not just a duplication or repetition (or complement) of the One.[18] Though "the Other" to which Lacan and Levinas refer is not exactly the same other, the structure is clarifying: precisely because the other is plural, the other is not the complement of the same. And the problem that emerges (that has *always already* emerged) with the third and self-consciousness is no other than the subject. And with the subject (have *always already*) come to light philosophy, knowledge, science, reciprocity, rationality, representation, and politics. "We have to follow down the latent birth of knowing [and of essence, and of the said, and of a question] in proximity" (*OB* 157/*AE* 245). Cognition and representation were there from the start, interrupted *and* demanded by the event of the plural other. If there is a subject at all, a subject that is an other-within-the-same, it is because the other-within is plural, and thus the subject is political. This ethical subjectivity is political through and through: the subject of the event-other, the subject as *same* (interrupted, exposed and uncertain) is no longer—or not only—the self-victimized subject of the law.

Notes

1. For an extensive account of tragic subjectivity, see Basterra, *Seductions of Fate*.
2. Moreover, that the modern self can experience itself as an agent depends, as Louis Althusser and Michel Foucault have shown, on occluding the state's agency in producing subjects through subjection (Althusser, "Ideology and Ideological State Apparatuses." 182; Foucault, "The Subject and Power." 212), and Butler, *Psychic Life of Power*.
3. See Basterra, *Seductions of Fate*. 9 and 96.
4. I have modified some of the translations from French. Where a reference to two pages is offered, the first one points to the English translation and the second to the French original. In those cases where a translation does not exist, the translation is mine.
5. Yet, remarks Badiou, "death is not a destiny but a choice" (*Saint Paul*. 73/77).
6. Zupančič, "Ethics and Tragedy in Lacan." 178.
7. Ibid.
8. Derrida, "Violence and Metaphysics." 109.
9. Badiou echoes this question in his *Ethics* (the chapter that includes his critique of Levinas is titled "Does the Other Exist?"). Does Badiou take into account the different subjectivity and writing that Levinas performs in *Otherwise than Being*?
10. See especially Levinas's essays "Meaning and Sense" (1964) and "Enigma and Phenomenon" (1965). When speaking about the trace and of witnessing, I am in conversation with Zeillinger (see note 12).
11. Levinas, "Meaning and Sense." 63.
12. Here I am in dialogue with three recent presentations by Peter Zeillinger: "Derrida's more-than-performative Saying the Event" ("Following Derrida: Legacies," U of Manitoba, Winnipeg, Canada, September 2006); " 'Femininity of the Other,' 'le moi viril,' and 'the Other within me': A Reading of Levinas Beyond Possible Critique"; and "Rethinking the Foundation of Theology: From Onto-Theology to Testimony in the late Levinas" (both in "First Philosophy, Phenomenology, Ethics" Radboud U, Nijmegen, September 2006). For a thorough study of the trace in Levinas, see his essay "Phänomenologie des Nicht-Phänomenalen. Spur und Inversion des Seins bei Emmanuel Levinas." I would like to express my gratitude to Peter Zeillinger for his insights and for this dialogue.
13. See, for example, *Saint Paul*. 42–47.
14. In "The Present Absence of Ethics and Politics," a plenary lecture given at the conference organized by Dillip Gaonkar, Robert Harriman, and Ernesto Laclau, "Trope, Affect and Democratic Subjectivity." Northwestern U, November 2–5, 2006.

15. I take this expression from Gillian Rose, who uses it to reinstate the risks of political action.
16. Levinas, "Philosophy and the Idea of the Infinite." 49.
17. Badiou writes: "[T]he real question—and it is an extraordinarily difficult one—is . . . that of *recognizing the Same*" (*Ethics* 25/*L'éthique* 43).
18. Zupančič, *The Shortest Shadow*. 137–138.

Works Cited

Althusser, Louis. "Ideology and Ideological State Apparatuses." *Lenin and Philosophy*, trans. Ben Brewster. New York: Monthly Review Press, 1971.
Badiou, Alain. *Ethics: An Essay on the Understanding of Evil*, trans. Peter Hallward. London: Verso, 2001.
———. *L'éthique: essai sur la conscience du mal.* Caen: Nous, 2003.
———. *Saint Paul: La fondation de l'universalisme.* Paris: PUF/Les essays du Collège International de Philosophie, 1997.
———. *Saint Paul: The Foundation of Universalism*, trans. Ray Brassier. Stanford: Stanford UP, 2003.
Basterra, Gabriela. *Seductions of Fate: Tragic Subjectivity, Ethics, Politics.* New York and Basingstoke, UK: Palgrave Macmillan, 2004.
Butler, Judith. *The Psychic Life of Power. Theories in Subjection.* Stanford: Stanford UP, 1997.
Derrida, Jacques. "Violence and Metaphysics." *Writing and Difference*, trans. Alan Bass. Chicago: U of Chicago P, 1978.
Foucault, Michael. "The Subject and Power," in *Michael Foucault: Beyond Structuralism and Hermeneutic (Second Edition with an Afterword by and an Interview with Michael Foucault)*, ed. Hubert L. Dreyfus and Paul Rabinow. Chicago: U of Chicago P, 1982. 208–226.
Lacan, Jacques. *Le séminaire, Livre VII. L'éthique de la psychanalyse 1959–1960.* Paris: Éditions du Seuil, 1986.
———. *Le séminaire, Livre VIII. Le transfert 1960–1961* (seconde édition corrigée). Paris: Éditions du Seuil, 2001.
———. *The Seminar of Jacques Lacan, Book VII. The Ethics of Psychoanalysis, 1959–1960*, trans. Denis Porter. New York: Norton, 1992.
Levinas, Emmanuel. *Autrement qu'être ou au-delà de l'essence.* Paris: Le Livre de Poche, 2004.
———. "Enigma and Phenomenon." *Basic Philosophical Writings*, ed. Robert Bernasconi, Simon Critchley, and Adriaan Peperzak. Bloomington, ID: Indiana UP, 1996.
———. "Meaning and Sense." *Basic Philosophical Writings*, ed. Robert Bernasconi, Simon Critchley and Adriaan Peperzak. Bloomington, ID: Indiana UP, 1996.
———. *Otherwise than Being or Beyond Essence*, trans. Alphonso Lingis. Pittsburgh: Duquesne UP, 1998.
———. "Philosophy and the Idea of the Infinite." *Collected Philosophical Papers*, trans. Alphonso Lingis. Pittsburgh: Duquesne UP, 1998.

———. *Totalité et infini: essai sur l'exteriorité.* Paris: Livre de Poche, 1990.
———. *Totality and Infinity. An Essay on Exteriority,* trans. Alphonso Lingis. Pittsburgh: Duquesne UP, 1969.
———. "The Trace of the Other." *Deconstruction in Context,* ed. Mark C. Taylor, trans. Alphonso Lingis. Chicago: U of Chicago P, 1986.
Zeillinger, Peter. "Phänomenologie des Nicht-Phänomenalen. Spur und Inversion des Seins bei Emmanuel Levinas." *Phänomenologische Aufbrüche,* ed. Michael Blamauer, Wolfgang Fasching, and Matthias Flatscher (Hg.) Frankfurt/M: Lang, 2005. 161–179.
Zupančič, Alenka. "Ethics and Tragedy in Lacan." *The Cambridge Companion to Lacan,* ed. Jean-Michel Rabaté. Cambridge: Cambridge UP, 2003.
———. *The Shortest Shadow: Nietzsche's Philosophy of the Two.* Cambridge: MIT Press, 2003.

Part II

ETHICS AND CULTURAL STUDIES

3

ETHICS AND CITIZENSHIP IN THE BLOGOSPHERE: ACADEMICS MEET NEW TECHNOLOGIES OF ONLINE PUBLICATION

Idelber Avelar

On the Internet one most often speaks and writes to an other that one does not really know. Ethical questions thus manifest themselves there in slightly different fashion than, say, in teaching, where one often has a fairly good sense of who one's interlocutors are. The fact that the composition of the reading public on the Internet may, and often does, change faster than one's ability to get fully acquainted with it, combined with the durability and dissemination allowed by electronic media, makes Web writing approach an experience rarely seen in strictly scholarly communication: that of *writing to a wholly other*, of addressing someone with whom one does not share even the most basic discursive premises and protocols. Academics are used to the idea that the basis of exchange and conversation is the existence of a relatively well-circumscribed set of assumptions that remain stable over some time. This is not so say, of course, that those assumptions are unchangeable, but one is expected to have a sense of what they are and how long each of them has been in effect—in order to *alter* them, you must have proven to be able to *share* them.

No such ethics apply to blogging or to most forms of Web writing. Due to the increasingly democratic access to the Internet, Web writing has often functioned on a fundamentally different principle: that of forming communities the entrances into which are filtered, at any given point, in ways unknown to the members of those communities.

The conversations around those criteria of entrance may be, in fact, the reason why the community has gathered in the first place—there is a metalinguistic thrust on the Internet that rivals that of any of modernist masterpiece. On the other hand, membership might change so quickly that the most cherished principles often vanish into thin air in a matter of days. This is not to say that Internet writers do not have information regarding themselves and their reading public, naturally. I will have a chance to quote a recent survey of bloggers that map the composition of that class in fairly accurate sociological terms. Similar studies are readily available for other groups of Web writers. The point is, rather, that over and above the sociological depiction of a public, there is the ontological fact of the constitution of a *subject*, that is, an inscription *not represented a priori in that sociological equation*. How radical, or interesting, or novel that subject, that irruption, that *event* turns out to be is a matter to be measured carefully—and Jon Beasley-Murray was correct in chastising an earlier version of this paper as too euphoric.[1] It seems undeniable to me, however, that Web writing confronts its practitioners with ethical imperatives rather different from those of other forms of writing. This difference has much to do with the perennial possibility of the arrival of *a wholly other*, an unanticipated foreign inscription not foreseen in the conversation. Foremost among the Web exchanges propitious to that arrival are the ones being propelled by blogs.

"Blog," as is known to most of us by now, is short for "Web log": a personal Internet page updated with some frequency and composed of entries organized in reverse chronological order, so that as you open up the page, you will always see the latest entry. These entries, called posts, are often accompanied by a comment thread where readers write in their responses (although several bloggers choose not to have a comment box). Posts may be as short as a word and as long as an essay, but their essence is the hyperlink, that better-than-a-footnote resource allowing bloggers simultaneously to comment on sources and to send readers to them. The endpoint of a link may be a piece of news, a post in another blog, an image, a song, a video, a podcast (as we call the homemade "voice posts"), or just about anything available on the Internet. On one side of their main pages, bloggers will usually include a blogroll, listing the blogs that they visit and with which they are engaged in conversation. In almost all blogs, each post will include, following the text, a "permalink," that is, a link that will permanently send the reader to that particular post, rather than the blog's main page. The permalink is the "memory" of blog writing and lies at the heart of the quickness and accuracy with which bloggers customarily refer readers to sources.

In the more widely visited blogs, the number and frequency of comments may cause engaging conversations to take place in the comment box. Their "truth effect" will depend on the existence of mutually understandable yet different enough arguments and, above all, on the perception that there is a "real time" dynamic presiding over the conversation: things grow old incredibly fast in the blogosphere. When the timing, diversity, and mutual understanding conspire, however, blogs can produce true exercises in civic debate. Not all excellent, canonical blogs manage to produce that kind of comment box: Brazil's foremost journalistic blog, by Ricardo Noblat (http://noblat1.estadao.com.br/noblat)—the only one that you will see regularly referred to by politicians and major journalists as a source of political news—elicits hundreds or thousands of comments per post, all rendered useless, however, due to the exchange of accusations and occasional insults by supporters of the government (Lula's Workers' Party, PT) and the opposition (Fernando Henrique Cardoso's Social Democratic Party, PSDB). Other widely read blogs such as Dan Gillmor's (http://www.bayosphere.com/blog/dangillmor), the pope of online journalism, remain influential but do not necessarily generate debate in their comment boxes. Important blogs such Michigan Professor Juan Cole's Middle East-focused *Informed Comment* (http://www.juancole.com), or *The Rude Pundit* (http://rudepundit.blogspot.com), a "punk" yet powerfully erudite critique of the American political establishment (particularly the Republican Party), do not have space for reader responses; their comment boxes would be unmanageable, the former because of its theme, the latter due to both theme and style. Predictably, in literary, photographic, or artistic blogs in general, comments tend to be less important to readers than in journalistic, essayistic, or political blogs, although they remain vital to the *writer*, as has been profusely reported by fiction writers who have taken up blogging.[2] At any rate, the interactive nature of blogs is of foremost importance for understanding how they have impacted culture in the past half decade. This can be attested with a visit to some of the hundreds of thousands of entries in the Daily Kos (http://www.dailykos.com), the successful collective blog run by Democratic Party activist Markos Moulitsas and visited daily by millions of left-of-center Internet users in the United States.

The first blogs emerged in the late 1990s, and in several countries today—United States, Brazil, France, Iran, China[3]—they have become an integral part of the experience of the Internet. According to Technorati, a site that tracks down links on the Internet, there were 60 million blogs worldwide in late 2005.[4] Every fourteen seconds, someone creates a blog somewhere. In countries such as Iran, in a context of severe censorship over traditional media, the blogosphere already is the main source of news. In countries such as the United States blogs have definitely been a force in showing how thoroughly servile, tendentious, and homogeneous corporate media have become. Something interesting has been happening, in fact, with journalistic blogs: many of them started simply by linking to, repeating, and commenting on news reported by the major media. Today, this movement has been reversed somewhat. Using Internet resources to reach information (what some major media have derisively called "journalism in pajamas"), blogs have begun to report news before the rest of the media and do so more thoroughly, in such a way that newsgroups are now often echoing pieces of news first reported in the blogosphere. All major Brazilian newspapers have devoted teams of reporters to tracking down what goes on in the blogosphere. The former editor of *Correio Brasiliense* and Brasilia-based journalist/blogger Ricardo Noblat recently noted that "going out in the streets" in search of news is no longer a time-effective choice, at least for the sort of political journalism he does (as it is now far more worth his time to work online all day, especially since opening a blog). Hardly a day goes by in the United States without a political piece of news coming out through blogs. It has become increasingly common for traditional media to be forced to go after or respond to pieces of news uncovered by blogs: recent cases include that of Jeff Gannon, the male prostitute who gained press passes to the White House, the unveiling of the Bush/Dan Rather forged document episode, and the very candidacy of Howard Dean for the Democratic presidential nomination in 2004, primarily catapulted and financed through blogs.

In the academy, blogging has been slower to take off than in other corners, although there is a very respectable English-language team of scientific and humanistic blogs. In the sciences, bloggers have worked actively not only to popularize scientific findings, but to also better frame the highly-politicized debates that have taken place regarding the teaching of science in public schools. The collective of academic bloggers gathered at "Science Blogs" (http://scienceblogs.com) has consistently written on scientific issues of general interest such as global warming, birth control, avian influenza, the current creationist crusade in the United States, and other topics. Among the blogs hosted at scienceblogs.com, *Pharyngula* (http://scienceblogs.com/pharyngula), by University of Minnesota biology professor PZ Myers, has gained prominence due to the author's erudition and his fiery arguments devoted to opposing the religious Right's hijacking of science curricula. A recent article in the respected scientific journal *Nature* listed *Pharyngula* as the top science blog in the world, appearing at a respectable 179th in Technorati's rankings (which essentially measure the number of links pointing to a blog).[5] Given scienceblogs.com's wide readership—between January and July of 2006, they have had close to 250,000 visitors—it is reasonable to assume that many Internet users are being exposed to high-level scientific material to which they would not otherwise have access. In the humanities, bloggers such as Penn State English Professor Michael Bérubé (http://michaelberube.com) have also made quite an impact with posts on everything from Literary Theory through the Iraq War to satires of the Republican Party. A Nobel Prize winner in Economics, University of Chicago professor Gary Becker has accepted the challenge of writing in intelligent *and* intelligible terms on politics and economics for a Web audience, and the blog he authors in partnership with Richard Posner (http://www.becker-posner-blog.com) ranks among the most successful and respected in the world.

According to a recent survey conducted by the Pew Internet and American Life Research project, 8 percent (or 12 million) of all Internet adult users in the United States keep a blog and 39 percent (or 57 million) read blogs. The report finds that "blogging is usually the first foray into authorship," as a full 54 percent of bloggers "had not published their writing or media creations anywhere else, either online or offline." To be expected are the statistics that reveal that bloggers are more likely to have broadband at home than Internet users in general (79 percent against 62 percent), more likely to get their news online as well (95 percent against 80 percent), and more likely to go online several times a day (84 percent against 64 percent). Bloggers are evenly divided between men and women and are, not surprisingly, overwhelmingly young. More than half (54 percent) are under the age of 30. Somewhat surprising perhaps is the finding that in the United States, bloggers are less likely to be white than the general population of Internet users: 60 percent of bloggers are white, 11 percent are African American, 19 percent are English-speaking Hispanics, and 10 percent identify as some other race; by contrast, 74 percent of all Internet users are white, 9 percent are African American, 11 percent are English-speaking Hispanic, and 6 percent identify as some other race. When asked what subjects their blogs address, the option "my life and personal experiences" came first with 37 percent, while "politics and government" ranked second with 11 percent. Overall, the survey shows that first-person writing continues to be the major force behind blogging; independent journalism and political commentary, however, have acquired a prominent position as well. The aforementioned academic blogs notwithstanding, scholarly communication still lags behind.

For scholars, the questions posed by the power of a medium such as the blog cannot but hark back to dilemmas regarding the location of intellectuals in the public sphere. How feasible and desirable is it for academics to write on a regular basis for an audience beyond the university walls? How prepared are we to operate in an environment where the rules for debating ideas and verifying truth are so far removed from the relatively consensual ones that preside over scholarly communication? These are questions that have been answered quite differently in the United States than in Europe and Latin America, where the figure of the "public intellectual" has been more central in civil society. In Europe and Latin America, intellectuals have traditionally been summoned to speak on topics of general societal interest and have at times been raised to the status of "conscience" of the collective. In the United States, in spite of a strong tradition of, for example, New York intellectuals who spoke strongly and consistently beyond their specializations, it has been more common to stigmatize academics who choose to write for broader audiences and intervene in civil society. One of the byproducts of the overspecialization of academic work has been an unspoken pact of adherence to a structure that allows scholars to operate with considerable freedom as long as they stay within safe disciplinary boundaries. However, severe suspicion is raised every time they venture beyond those walls. As attested by a recent piece in the *Chronicle of Higher Education* entitled "Bloggers need not apply," for junior faculty the act of stepping into the terrain of broader cultural discourse may turn out to be deadly, no matter how brilliant, prolific, and accomplished they happen to be in their fields.

In academia, *journalism* is the name reserved for this beast. The term is used in academic discourse in at least two different senses, in a *strictu sensu* to designate the set of practices that emerged and consolidated themselves around the institution of the modern newspaper in the nineteenth century, but also in a *lato sensu* to signify any and all discourses of knowledge, on any object, that do not conform to the boundaries proper to the modern, departmentally-divided research university. "Oh, his work is kind of journalistic," we tend to say with disdain about those who dare speak with a greater degree of clarity to an educated general readership. This is not to deny, of course, that there is stuff that passes for scholarship but is, in fact, journalism in the strict sense—a compilation of already produced knowledge that therefore should be called by its name. However, more often than not, the disqualification of journalism in academia works as a protective barrier to maintain the separation between academia and its outside. In the modern research university, very seldom will you be able to put yourself in a position to act as a public intellectual without confronting the charge of being "journalistic." Undoing the anxiety that belies that charge is itself one of the major tasks of intellectual work.

In a debate promoted by *The Nation* in 2001, Jean Bethke Elshtain mused that the problem with public intellectuals is that they tend to become more and more public, less and less intellectual: not necessarily less respectful academically, but "less reflective, less inclined to question one's own judgments, less likely to embed a conviction in its appropriate context with all the nuance intact." In finding a comfortable niche for him/herself, in establishing a voice from which a certain public already knows what to expect, the public intellectual runs the risk, at the limit, of becoming a paid publicist, a spinner, an ideologue. That is not, of course, inevitable. Jean-Paul Sartre and Susan Sontag could be mentioned as two examples of thinkers who maintained their full critical edge and rigor after a life-time of work in the public sphere. It was only after decades of engagement as a socialist intellectual, in fact, that Sartre wrote his monumental study of Gustave Flaubert, *The Idiot of the Family*, a work as rigorous as anything ever produced on the nineteenth-century French realist. For academics hoping to act as civic intellectuals, then, the reconciliation of a broad public discourse with the maintenance of the rigor inherited from academic work is perhaps the foremost challenge.

The figure of the politicized intellectual has always been closely connected with the space defined by Habermas as "public sphere"— *Öffentlichkeit*, the German term, brings with it the idea of openness and an essential relationship with the outside.[6] In the United States, the question of the very existence (or absence) of genuine public intellectuals has elicited a lengthy bibliography. Scholarly works such as Bill Readings's *The University in Ruins* or Peggy Kamuf's *The Division of Literature: Or the University in Deconstruction* have mapped the growing process of specialization undergone by the post-Fordist university, where an increasingly corporatized structure forces academics into ever-smaller corners of specialization. In this context, the figure of the intellectual in the European sense—or even in the New York sense, in which Edmund Wilson and Irving Howe may count as examples—seems to have been on sharp decline. Susan Sontag's death in 2004 may be taken here as a somewhat allegorical endpoint for a whole generational experience. For those of us who are not comfortable with the retreat into the safety of academic specialization and yet remain aware that the conditions are not conducive for a revival of the public intellectual of the universalist, Sartrean type, what is to be done?

There are several reasonable answers to this question, but my contention is that none is available without a reflection on the nature of new technologies that does not fall prey to the nostalgic belief that before the Internet we somehow had a truer and more authentic public sphere. This has been the tendency among thinkers associated with a defense of the heritage of the Enlightenment, most notably Jürgen Habermas himself. In a recent piece entitled "The Chaos of the Public Sphere," Habermas writes:

> The utilization of the Internet has simultaneously enlarged and fragmented communication channels. This is why the Internet produces, on the one hand, a subversive effect upon regimes that dispense an authoritarian treatment to the public sphere. On the other hand, interconnectivity in horizontal information networks weakens the conquests of traditional public spheres. ("Caos" 5)*

Habermas does not cite any serious studies that lend credence to the claim that the use of the Internet has "weakened" public spheres. Indeed he cannot, as there aren't any, even if one chooses to attach the qualifier "traditional" to the phrase, as though suggesting that there was such a thing as a "traditional" public space that somehow has been blocked, atrophied, or overshadowed by new technologies. For one, the public of the Internet is not "anonymous and dispersed," as Habermas affirms later in the piece. While it is true that the Internet is a medium that allows for *certain forms* of anonymity in *selected* contexts, it is far from certain that anonymity can be attached as a general qualifier of that public in *all* similar contexts. In fact, as a blogger and frequent writer for other Web sites, my experience—and that of millions of other users of active forms of online communication—has been precisely the opposite: the most fruitful, lasting, and relevant

---

* All translations from Portuguese to English, unless otherwise stated, are my own.

online experiences take place in communities where members do not choose to remain anonymous at all. As for the "dispersion" of this public, Habermas again falls prey to (an oversimplified version of) modernist myths. Most certainly, the nature of the World Wide Web—a massive network involving billions of virtual sites—favors distributions and assemblages of subjects that one might call "dispersed," if that were not such a vague term. However, this is a far cry from saying that the particular cultural and language acts performed by *specific online communities* could ever be characterized as "dispersed" at all, lest we give in to the laziest forms of thinking. Habermas proves to be unable to tackle the thornier question of the real effects of performances by specific online actors organized in communities, for he is way too concerned with passing judgment on the Internet as a whole, according to a reified, congealed concept of what the public sphere should look like.

Underlying Habermas's preoccupied verdict upon the Internet is the commonplace opinion—in fact an unproven platitude—that the multiplication of references (sites, sources) and the acceleration in production/distribution of electronic content has somehow been responsible for a presumed "impoverishment" of intellectual and civic life. Habermas repeats this platitude while giving all sorts of indication that he may not be familiar with much at all when it comes to intellectual-civic activity online: "The price to be paid for the positive increase in egalitarianism due to the Internet is the decentralization of access to non-written contributions. In these surroundings, the contributions of the intellectuals lose the necessary force to constitute a focus" (5). This may sound close to not being credible at all, but once the reader strips Habermas's argument of its convoluted rhetoric, s/he is left with an essay by a thinker who is staring a global/communicational phenomenon in the face and finds himself completely unable to make any sense of it. Two equally poor clichés about online life creep their way into his reasoning on the issue: first, the notion that the democratization of access to unwritten information is something to be lamented; second, the apocalyptic prediction that decentralization would presumably weaken intellectuals who, as a consequence, would find themselves deprived of "focus." This chain of unwarranted generalizations is sustained by Habermas's ignorance of a vast array of intellectuals who have *come to life as such* with the advent of the Internet, through activities—written, musical, filmic—that are inseparable from the medium that has made it possible.

Habermas theorizes about "intellectuals and the Internet" by committing a dramatic metonymic reduction, that is, taking his own experience as a venerable and erudite, but quite electronically illiterate, European philosopher, as if it were the experience of the whole of the intelligentsia as such. Again, while it may be true that earlier forms of universalistic intellectual interventions may be in decline (particularly in Europe, their historical home par excellence), it is far from warranted to confuse that fact with a supposed "loss of focus" of the social group known as "intellectuals" as such, as though a new type of intellectual had not already emerged with and through the Internet. When engaging in production of content online, Web intellectuals (bloggers are good examples here) are not simply "incorporating" the Internet as a tool, in a process that would leave those persons unchanged. On the contrary, the ethics proper to the medium becomes constitutive of those subjects themselves. They are, in that sense, not qualitatively different from intellectuals who have arisen out of other backgrounds such as journalism or the academy. Certainly, their ethic differs from previous ones, much as the latter differed from each other. But it is beyond arrogant and obscurantist (unenlightening, therefore) to follow Habermas in presuming to be able to theorize the *essence of the medium as such*, without demonstrating any significant engagement with it as an intellectual. After reading Habermas's essay, one cannot but wonder when and where was it, again, that "focus," "conquests of traditional public spheres," and his otherwise rosy picture of earlier civic life ever existed, and for whom.

While critiquing Habermas's apocalyptic version of online public sphere, I would strongly oppose any recasting of this debate along Umberto Eco's dichotomy between the apocalyptic and the integrated in *Apocalittici e integrati* (1964). While it is true Habermas sees the Internet according to the model of degeneration, the range of positions represented in the community of bloggers, online journalists, Internet activists, and other Web intellectuals cannot, by any means, be reduced to the terms outlined by Eco as characteristic of the "integrated." Several of these positions include thorough critiques of the power relations inherent in the medium and do not, in fact, celebrate modernization as a value in itself, the way *integrati* would. When it comes to the question of online citizenship, the real debate is not a Habermasian one on the pros and cons of the medium, or on the superiority or inferiority of the present vis-à-vis an idealized practice of pre-electronic enlightened public sphere somewhere in the past.

The debate that matters takes place, rather, among those who have *understood the inevitability of the medium and worked from that premise*. Habermas does not represent either side of the debate on the "virtual" public sphere but has instead chosen *to speak from a position external to the debate itself*, even as much of the debate is framed with reference to Habermas's concept. In other words, it is paramount to pose the debate in a way that acknowledges the essential, inevitable, and constitutive nature of online activity vis-à-vis most, if not all, original forms of citizenship to have emerged in the past decade. We need, then, an ethic of politicointellectual work on the World Wide Web that does not fall prey to comparing today's arrangement with some other, truer, more transparent form of public sphere. The debate in the blogosphere is not between Habermasians and *integrati* but rather among different groups who represent diverse nonapocalyptic approaches to the relation between new technologies of online publication and the broader, wider question of citizenship. We have seen that we cannot really count on defenders of the Enlightenment when it comes to thinking through that question.

In fact, the amount of scholarship devoted to the Internet in its relations with citizenship and to the role of the intellectuals has grown in so many directions that one is at a loss as to where to start refuting Habermas. After a decade of work on the Internet that led to his rather optimistic *Cyberdemocratie* (2002), French philosopher Pierre Lévy went as far as comparing the emergence of cyberspace with the invention of writing. Reviewing a mass of experiments in online citizenship and Web-mediated participatory democracy, Lévy concludes that while the earlier public sphere filtered its members "a priori," the process of selection in new online communities suffers no a priori restrictions (except, naturally, for the one that excludes anybody who does not own a computer or an Internet connection). Selection is carried out "through the number of links that converge to a site, the frequency of its connections, the references made to it in discussion groups or other sites, votes by readers or observations of users, etc." (Lévy 60). In that book, published in 2002 and probably written between 2000 and 2001, Lévy goes as far as to ask "what dictatorship would be left standing in a country where 25 percent of the population has access to the Internet?" (41).

Today, five years later, we could think of several authoritarian regimes that are alive and well in countries with over 25 percent of the population connected to the World Wide Web. That is to say, the technology has proven not to be necessarily a guarantee of democracy and openness, at any rate, not at the level and intensity predicted by thinkers such as Lévy. However, if we take into consideration the evolution of the blogosphere, among other Internet phenomena to have taken place in the past five years, it would be hard to avoid the conclusion that the French philosopher *has proven to be closer to the truth* than Habermas and his apocalyptic, nostalgic account of a coherent, organized public sphere later corrupted by the Internet. When it comes to the analysis of the circulation of informational goods, Lévy is indeed correct in envisioning online communities as a globally democratizing force. Today, after the "boom of blogs," Lévy's statements on the potentially democratic role of the Internet are even truer than they were when he wrote them, back in 2001, when the blogosphere was still being born. If some of Lévy's formulations may strike us today as overtly optimistic, he undoubtedly was on the right track in noting the remarkably democratizing potential of so many citizen initiatives that have coalesced on the Internet. One only needs to visit the sites recommended by Lévi in 2002 to notice how many of them are still active, having in fact improved and incorporated a number of other features, including many associated with blogging.[7]

Keeping at bay the temptation of facile analogies between the Internet (or the network of bloggers) and Derridean figures such as dissemination, I do contend that deconstruction is more equipped to handle the task of reframing ethics in the light of the experience of online communities. In a late piece written for a survey on "intellectuals," Derrida still claimed allegiance to a tradition that defined the intellectual by the ability to "analyze, critique, deconstruct guaranteed horizons and criteria" (212–13). He chastised the commonplace concept-turned-cliché *society of the spectacle*, a mantra with the allusion to which several people are presumed to be able to resolve the question of the relation between new technologies (particularly communicational ones) and the intelligentsia. In discarding that easy path and proposing another set of questions, Derrida positioned himself closer to a blogger ethic of a "hands-on" approach that refuses to venture to say things about the essence of a certain medium (much less without *experiencing* the said medium!) and chooses, rather, to ask *how and to what extent new media have affected the subjects, institutions, and discourses already in place* at the time of their arrival. That is to say, the focus should be on how venerable a set of problems such as the ones covered by terms such as "ethics" and "intellectuals" can or should be rethought in new arenas and media; the focus should not be on lamenting that those sets of problems no longer display the same structure. The first three sentences of Derrida's polemic against a certain "Debordianism" could be easily imagined (and in different words they have indeed appeared) in polemics by bloggers against a certain corporate journalism. After critiquing the enclosure of the discussion of new technologies into the cage of "the society of the spectacle," Derrida asks:

> Is it not more valid to do the utmost possible to work with professionals? With those who, among them, have at least competence, critical skill, and taste, so as to try and introduce the as of yet unregistered (*l'inedite*) into the contents and techniques of new media, particularly on the Internet . . . ? Is it not urgent to elaborate therein new international rights (*droits*) that, as much as possible, will not restore ancient powers of legitimation, sanction, and censorship such as those still ruling current media as well as publishing, the university, and other institutions—public and private, nation-bound and international? Will there be functions of the intellectual, should there be such functions in this other political space, in the new International that searches for its concept? (214–15)

The "New International" was a Derridean coinage that preceded the Internet, as the concept came into being as Derrida prepared *Spectres de Marx* (1993). In that book the phrase designated a "new form of community," one that wished to be beyond all partisanship and all identitarian groups, one that could gather its members in anonymity, in a promise of something that should never fully congeal into a fixed ideological edifice. In the terms outlined by Derrida in that book, the New International attempted to maintain something of the experience of the messianic without letting itself be trapped into any messianism (assuming, as Derrida does, that there is an irreducible difference between, on the one hand, the noun that alludes to ideologies and sets of beliefs, and, on the other hand, the adjectival construction that designates an *experience*).[8] On the eve of his death, Derrida returned to the phrase "New International" to designate the community that could, perhaps, "introduce the as of yet unregistered" [*l'inedite*] in the new media, "particularly on the Internet." In the massive and still relatively unexamined late writings of Derrida, one systematic concern was the thorny question of how to rethink "democracy," "ethics," "international law," and "citizenship," among so many other figures and concepts, in the light of new virtual, digital technologies. That chain of deconstructive concerns—particularly ethics—has something to profit, I would contend, from a more sustained reflection on blogging as a phenomenon.

The myriad ways in which blogging has redefined the experience of citizenship for millions of Internet users around the world still awaits a systematic study, but certain trends are apparent to those who follow the phenomenon. Bloggers have systematically overseen corporate media in ways that correct inaccuracies, parody their "balance," and unveil/critique tendentious reporting. In the United States, the experience of sites such as *Media Matters* (http://mediamatters.org), with their relentless daily analysis of big media, shows that technologies of online publication have allowed for a potentially greater citizen control over the veracity and "spin" of each piece of news. Although not technically a blog, *Media Matters* attests to the influence of a bloggers' ethic, in displaying features such as the permalink, the customary hyperlinking of its sources, and the presence of lively comment threads. If one could argue that major media in the past decade have become even more homogeneous, it is also true that their ultimate unreliability has been exposed more often and more thoroughly than ever before, to a greater and more organized group of citizens. Bloglike sites such as *Media Matters* have been a major part of that exercise in democracy and citizenship.

Blogs have not invented the hyperlinking of sources on the Internet, of course. That practice existed before the first blog was ever conceived. However, the accuracy and quickness allowed by the permalink, and the blogger ethic of always backing statements up by referring readers to sources, have led bloggers to resort to that practice more frequently and effectively than had ever been the case in the short history of the Internet. If I were to opine on what has been the main contribution of blogging to citizenship and "the public sphere," I would have to say that it is *the ethic of relentless citation through hyperlinking, including the citation of the one(s) who allowed you to get to that source*, something that was not invented by bloggers but has rightfully been associated with them, given its centrality in blogging. The linking of sources has proven to be particularly useful in the ever more common online polemics, where the resource of the permalink allows debaters to refer readers *directly, with one click, to the totality* of what opponents have said, in their own words. While this does not guarantee an ideal Habermasian community of dialogue, it brings interested parties to a position closer to it than any apparatus of the earlier public sphere had accomplished. When one compares this situation to political or cultural polemics of a few decades ago, decisively shaped by the access of each polemicist to printed or visual media, one has a clear sense of the positive effects of these technologies of online publication. Not to go back any further in time, we could mention the bibliography on one important arena in the recent history of intellectual citizenship in the United States, the "culture wars" of the 1980s and 1990s. That bibliography has clearly shown that the ferocity and quickness of media attacks upon higher education went largely unmatched due to the morose nature of the responses allowed by scholarly venues of publication as well as due to the limited access of scholars to major printed and televised media.[9] Blogs have not leveled the playing field, of course, but their tilting of the scale toward democratization has been undeniable.

To return to the question that opens this article, then, what does the blogosphere tell us that may be of interest to the rethinking of the ethics of intellectual work? It should be clear from the preceding pages that I do not see much value in another totalizing set of injunctions that would offer us the illusion of a readymade ethical philosophy for the electronic age. At a time when the "conventional definition of the intellectual . . . appears ever more questionable" (Derrida 212), the question is not whether intellectuals and their traditional "public spheres" have been strengthened or weakened by new technologies (i.e., the question that ultimately guides Habermas), but rather what are the new possibilities, ethical commitments, and forms of action opened up by new media. It is thus not a matter of how much weaker or stronger intellectuals now are; it is rather a matter of mapping *what has become of intellectuals* and understanding which new tasks have called them and which old ones are no longer valid. In that sense Derrida's late reflections have left a far more enduring legacy, as they turned our attention to the promise of a new genre, a new law, a new configuration altogether, one that could transform the figure of the intellectual in hitherto unthought ways.

In the transformation of intellectuals allowed by what Derrida describes, shorthand, as "new media," blogging has offered a number of unequivocal ethical signposts: in bringing to the forefront of online life a ceaselessly-attentive relationship with corporate media (one that has begun to reshape the way that even *nonreaders of blogs* approach corporate news), in turning hyperlinking and the referral of everything back to their sources into a true ethical obsession, in engaging in constant polemic but always respecting the principle of *linking back* to the one with whom you are polemicizing, in giving credit to the source of every piece of information in ways that create a true memory of electronic culture, and above all in disseminating a do-it-yourself ethic that has reached considerable proportions, as any minimally-literate Internet user can (and millions of them do) use one or another publication platform to become a blogger. It is well and good, certainly, to remain cautious against any overtly-optimistic celebration of online media as a necessary guarantor of greater democracy—and this chapter does suggest that the democratizing potential of personal online publication is something to be seen as given in advance. It seems clear to me, however, that the thorny question of the tasks and possibilities of citizen intellectuals can no longer be tackled without an engagement with the ethical lessons learnt from the recent experience of blogging—a paradoxical form of individualistic communitarianism that is perhaps in the process of creating a wholly new class of intellectuals out of subjects who had never thought of themselves as such.

Notes

1. Jon Beasley-Murray implicitly objected to phrases such as "amazingly innovative experience," which I used in that version to characterize blogging.
2. Fiction writers who have adopted the blog as a medium to communicate with their readers invariably point to the importance of feedback. The most recent example I witnessed was the roundtable on "Blogging and Literature," held at São Paulo's Primavera dos Livros in August 2006. At that event, fiction writers Indigo and Ivana Arruda Leite, former prostitute and current bookstore blockbuster Bruna Surfistinha as well as journalist Rosana Hermann all testified to the importance of reader feedback for their blogging.
3. For a realistic assessment of what the blogosphere has represented in the Islamic Republic of Iran, see Rahimi. For an interesting analysis of the emergence of online intellectuals among Chinese-Americans, see Melkote and Liu.
4. This is an impressive number but should be looked at more carefully. Technorati also tracks the updates done to each blog; they recently found the figure of 1.6 million new postings per day, an awfully low number when divided by the 50 million blogs, yielding an average of only 0.032 new posts a day per blog. As a blog would undoubtedly have to be updated more often than that in order to be considered *active*, the conclusion is that Technorati's figures for existing blogs is somewhat inflated and includes inactive as well as spam blogs. See Kevin Burton for an analysis of these numbers.
5. I thank South Korea-based Brazilian blogger scientist Lucia Malla (http://www.umamallapelomundo.blogspot.com) for referring me to the *Nature* article on scientific blogs.
6. Habermas's original formulation of the concept of public sphere is to be found in *The Structural Transformation of the Public Sphere*, where he deduces the concept from the hypothesis of a "separation" or "autonomization" of the three distinct realms of science, aesthetics, and ethics.
7. Each one of the chapters of Pierre Lévy's *Cyberdemocratie* includes a list of web sites that range from search engines or encyclopedias through citizen initiatives to global juridical or cultural endeavors. A number of them are still active and quite a few have incorporated blogger-type resources.

8. For an extensive treatment of the difference between messianism and the messianic, see Derrida's *Specters of Marx* and Jameson's remarkable engagement with it in "Marx's Purloined Letter." I have also written on this question in "El espectro en la temporalidad de lo mesiánico."
9. Foremost in that bibliography, see the work of Michael Bérubé, who not surprisingly later became a blogger. See his monograph *Public Access* as well as the volume he coedited with Cary Nelson, *Higher Education under Fire*.

Works Cited

Avelar, Idelber. "El espectro en la temporalidad de lo mesiánico: Derrida y Jameson a propósito de la firma Marx." *Espectros y pensamiento utópico*, Vol. 2 of *La invención y la herencia*, ed. Federico Galende. Santiago: ARCIS-LOM, 1995.

Beasley-Murray, Jon. "Blogging." February 10, 2006. http://posthegemony.blogspot.com/2006/02/blogging.html.

Bérubé, Michael. *Public Access: Literary Theory and American Cultural Politics*. London and New York: Verso, 1994.

Bérubé, Michael, and Cary Nelson, eds. *Higher Education under Fire: Politics, Economics, and the Crisis of the Humanities*. New York: Routledge, 1995.

"Bloggers need not apply." *The Chronicle of Higher Education*. August 7, 2005. Online version for subscribers: http://chronicle.com/weekly/v51/i44/44c00301.htm.

Burton, Kevin. "Technorati's Numbers Are Wrong." August 08, 2006. http://www.feedblog.org/2006/08/technoratis_num.html.

Carter, Stephen, John Donatich, Jean Bethke Elshtain, Herbert Gans, Christopher Hitchens, Russell Jacoby, and Steven Johnson. "The Future of the Public Intellectual: A Forum." http://www.thenation.com/doc/20010212/forum.

Derrida, Jacques. "Mas . . . , não mas . . . , jamais . . . , e no entanto . . . , quanto aos meios de comunicação (Os intelectuais. Tentativa de definição por eles mesmos. Enquete)." *Papel-máquina*, trans. Evando Nascimento. São Paulo: Estação Liberdade, 2004. 207–215.

———. *Spectres de Marx: l'etat de la dette, le travail du deuil et la nouvelle Internationale*. Paris: Galilée, 1993.

Eco, Umberto. *Apocalittici e integrati: communicazioni di massa e teorie della cultura di massa*. Milano: Bompiano, 1965.

Habermas, Jürgen. "O Caos da Esfera Pública." *Folha de São Paulo. Caderno Mais!* August 13, 2006. 4–6.

———. *The Structural Transformation of the Public Sphere: An Inquiry into a Category of Bourgeois Society*, trans. Thomas Burger with Frederick Lawrence. Cambridge: MIT Press, 1989.

Jameson, Fredric. "Marx's Purloined Letter." *New Left Review* 209 (1995): 75–109.

Kamuf, Peggy. *The Division of Literature, or, the University in Deconstruction*. Chicago: U of Chicago P, 1997.

Lévy, Pierre. *Ciberdemocracia*, trans. Alexandre Emílio. Lisbon: Instituto Piaget, 2002.
Melkote, Srinivas, and D.J. Liu. "The Role of the Internet in Forging a Pluralistic Integration: A Study of Chinese Intellectuals in the United States." *International Communication Gazette* 62.6 (2000): 495–504.
Pew Internet and American Life Project. *Bloggers: A Portrait of the Internet's New Storytellers*. July 19, 2006. http://www.pewinternet.org/PPF/r/186/report_display.asp.
Rahimi, Babak. "Cyberdissent: The Internet in Revolutionary Iran." *Meria: Middle East Review of International Affairs* 7.3 (2003): 101–115.
Readings, Bill. *The University in Ruins*. Cambridge: Harvard UP, 1996.
Sartre, Jean-Paul. *L'idiot de la famille; Gustave Flaubert de 1821–1857*. 1971. 2nd rev. edition, 3 volumes. Paris: Gallimard, 1988.
"Top Five Science Blogs." *Nature*. July 05, 2006. http://www.nature.com/news/2006/060703/full/442009a.html

4

MODERNIST ETHICS: REALLY ENGAGING POPULAR CULTURE IN MEXICO AND BRAZIL

Esther Gabara

Studies participating in the recent "turn to ethics" in the U.S. academy often draw a lineage to the modernist avant-gardes of the first decades of the twentieth century; literary and art historical scholars have taken them up as powerful inspirations in the quest for ethically engaged criticism and cultural production.[1] The protagonist of this century-old story of how cultural producers fuse ethics and aesthetics is often the artist or writer who breaks out of the ivory tower through his or her engagement with some entity termed "the popular."[2] Important interventions by scholars including Beatriz Sarlo, William Rowe and Vivian Schelling, and Nestor García Canclini have made it clear that Latin America's "peripheral modernity" in general, and alternative modernisms in particular, must be viewed through a theory of the popular. If the ethical substance of modernism, therefore, can be analyzed through its engagement with popular culture, two questions concern me: *which* popular and *what form* does that image of the popular take? In Latin American studies, the definition of "lo popular" has expanded and contracted throughout the last century; Jean Franco names its multiple valences, pointing to a broad spectrum of social spheres as diverse as mass culture, popular culture, folk culture, entertainment, media, communications, and the culture industry (5–6). The ethical theory of modernism itself, then, needs to be as highly articulated as the popular's varied modes. In what follows, I will develop the ethical ramifications of Latin American modernism's engagement with two faces of "lo popular": the first, termed *cultura popular* [popular culture] in Spanish and Portuguese, is a folkloric or ethnographic popular; the second is the *cultura de masas* [mass culture], the commercialized mass culture that emerged with the explosion of media during the 1920s and 1930s. Photography is at the core of this examination, for as a technology of representation it bridges both realms of the popular and repeatedly reproduces two key figures that came to incarnate the modern: the racialized and the feminized body.

The modernist avant-garde emerged across Latin America during the late teens and early 1920s: the Week of Modern Art in São Paulo (Brazil, 1922) featured readings, concerts, and exhibitions, Estridentistas posted manifestos in the streets and published experimental visual poetry in Jalapa and Mexico City (Mexico, 1921), and odes to the urban such as *Twenty Poems to be Read on the Tram* (Buenos Aires, 1922) by Argentine Oliverio Girondo peppered the literary landscape.[3] During the 1930s the number of manifestos diminished, but experiments with prose fiction and visuality still flourished and laid the groundwork for the international importance of the Latin American novel throughout the rest of the century. Brazilian modernist anthropophagy, which proclaimed a nation of cultural cannibals who consumed African, Indigenous, and European cultures, recurs in novels, theory, films, and fine arts throughout the twentieth and into the twenty-first century. The Estridentistas and the Contemporáneos, the two leading modernist avant-garde movements in Mexico, were publicly at odds over the character of modern art and of modernity itself. Nevertheless, they shared a focus on linguistic innovations, temporal discontinuity, and interdisciplinary collaborations across the arts. These authors, who are now canonical figures in the national literary traditions of Mexico and Brazil, looked at modern life through the camera in a variety of ways. Mário de Andrade, known as the "pope" of Brazilian modernism, published in photographically illustrated journals and also took hundreds of photographs as part of an experimental ethnography. This practice, which he called "apprentice tourism," took shape in an unpublished mixed media manuscript that he worked on over the last fifteen years of his life. Estridentistas Arqueles Vela and Manuel Maples Arce, and Contemporáneos Xavier Villaurrutia and Salvador Novo, published widely in photographically illustrated magazines, an early form of mass media that inspired reflections on the relationship between image and word, as well as modernist aesthetics and popular culture.

Perhaps the best known and influential of the Latin American modernist movements, Brazilian and Mexican artists and writers are most famous for their articulation of nationalism through images of the popular. While the Brazilian revolution was by no means so socially disruptive as the Mexican Revolution (1910–1920), it did proclaim a New Republic in 1930, and similar increases in state funding for education and culture were found following these political changes. In both countries, the State's iconographic production of an ethnographic popular existed alongside the mass popular of the illustrated magazine. Mexican muralism's particular composition of a popular national culture program, sponsored by the Ministry of Public Education under José Vasconcelos, provides only a partial view of popular modernism, which must be analyzed with the growing commercial sector that took shape in postrevolutionary Mexico. Brazil's national program of culture in the 1930s employed modernist intellectuals as ideologically distinct as Mário de Andrade and Cassiano Ricardo. The widespread professionalization of writers at the time led them to participate in the growing economic sector of mass media, as well as to the increasingly centralized state. As much as modernist intellectuals engaged popular culture through both mass media and the state, an examination of the particular form of their involvement in these two spheres reveals important tensions that constitute an ethics. Their engagement of popular culture and participation in a variety of practices were limited neither to a statist definition of nationalism nor to the cultural programs that the state funded during these decades. While they certainly participated in educational programs and university reform and placed art in public spaces through murals, they also dedicated journalistic publications to the question of how to bridge the vast distance between intellectuals and the masses who were to become the modern citizens of both countries. Mexican and Brazilian modernists did not simply mine the popular for exotic and scandalous images but rather actively located themselves within it, as producers and consumers of mass and popular culture. They were amateur ethnographers and folklore collectors, as well as contributors to and editors of popular illustrated weeklies published by the first wide-distribution magazines and newspapers. Examining these other engagements of the popular reveals an ethics of modernism, as much as a politics.

The modernist avant-garde's active engagement of both the ethnographic and the mass cultural popular reveals gender as much as race to be a defining category for modernist aesthetics, and to be critical to the articulation of ethics in modernism. Although what we might call the racialization of modernity in the Americas has been dealt with in studies of the ethnographic popular, its feminization has been less systematically explored.[4] Photography was the tool used to capture the object of ethnographic study, and exploded onto the illustrated pages of mass media during the modernist avant-garde experimentation of the 1920s and 1930s. The study of the interdependence of these two images of the popular in modernism—*cultura popular* and *cultura de masas*—permits a more sophisticated understanding of how these movements figured the popular as both raced and gendered. More than just coexist as two independent images of peripheral modernity, these figures are in fact broader analytics that existed in an intimate relationship. Examining two cases of popular modernism in Brazil and Mexico, I will build upon Jesús Martín-Barbero's theory of *mediación* [mediation] to show how the mutual dependence and conflict between the mass and the popular are characteristic of the ethics and aesthetics of modernism.

Mass *Vanguardias*

While significant scholarship exists about the importance of theorizing "the popular" in Latin American modernism, for the most part it has not addressed in depth the role of early mass media. Nestor García Canclini, for instance, argues for a distinctive economic and cultural context for the emergence of the Latin American modernist avant-gardes, and thus establishes a space for thinking their relevance to theories of the popular. He differentiates Latin American modernity from European and North American modernity precisely in the relationship between the literate, elite Creoles and the popular classes.[5] University reforms of the late teens of the twentieth century created a condition crucial to the development of Latin American modernism, in which,

> the constitution of those autonomous scientific and humanistic fields . . . confronted with the illiteracy of half of the population and with pre-modern economic structures and political habits . . . [create a context in which] literary practices are conditioned by questions about what it means to make literature in societies that *lack a sufficiently developed market for an autonomous cultural field to exist.* (García Canclini 47, emphasis added)

Latin American modernist movements—though hardly successful in their utopic goals of a shared nation, and still characterized by the vast divide of class and race that split the elite from the masses—created "new aesthetic trends within the incipient cultural field and . . . novel links that artists were creating with the administrators of official education, unions, and movements from below" (García Canclini 53).[6]

Despite their vastly different histories of press and graphic design, mass media began to emerge in the mid to late teens of the twentieth century in both Mexico and Brazil. While the best known manifestation of Mexican modernism's populist nationalism is the muralist movement, known both for its massive conversion of public spaces into revolutionary history lessons and for its masculinist rhetoric, these decades also saw an explosion of photographically illustrated journals. These *revistas ilustradas* included photographs and texts dealing with fashion, politics, health, arts, and culture. In what may seem a contradiction between "high" and "low" art, many of the most canonical modernists contributed to this early form of mass media. The two most influential literary movements Estridentismo and the Contemporáneos contributed to weeklies such as *El Universal Ilustrado* and *Revista de Revistas*, despite the groups' mutual antagonism and a scholarly history of treating them as radically different instantiations of peripheral modernism. The modernist works published in the illustrated journals, while sharing certain key characteristics commonly ascribed to modernism—linguistic experimentation, collage, and play with the visual character of printed words—do not separate themselves from the mass reader or consumer culture. These techniques introduced into the early mass media in Mexico generated glowing responses in letters from their readers, the very consumers that theories of high modernism insist must have been alienated and thwarted by them. Similarly, Mário de Andrade and several of his influential cohorts contributed to illustrated journals including *S. Paulo* and *A Cigarra*.

Recent interventions in the field of Art History have challenged the defining separation between "high" and "low" art.[7] Thomas Crow has led this shift, emphasizing the "continuing involvement between modernist art and the materials of low or mass culture" (3). Rather than requiring modernism to reject mass culture in order to achieve the kind of criticality to which Frankfurt School philosophers Max Horkheimer and Theodor Adorno aspire, Crow productively argues that

> one need not assume that it somehow transcended the culture of the commodity; it can rather be seen as having exploited to critical purpose contradictions within and between distinct sectors of that culture ... The most powerful moments of modernist negation have occurred when the

two aesthetic orders, the high-cultural and the subcultural, have been forced into scandalous identity, each being continuously dislocated by the other. (25–26)

Although this vision of the involvement between mass and elite restages European modernism's critique of the despairing mood of modern culture, it does not surrender it entirely. Crow draws out a kind of attack and retreat strategy of culture, such that the moment of scandal and disturbance of the encounter with the popular does not last. Modernism, it seems, has a quick and notorious fling with mass culture and then retreats into its protected walls. Modernist artists are "mock conspirators" with mass culture, and do so when they are unable to produce a sense of novelty within the realm of high culture (Crow 27); they make raids into the terrain of the popular in times of desperation. Crow thus locates the avant-garde in what we could term a colonial relationship to popular culture, as "low-cultural forms are time and again called upon to displace and estrange the deadening givens of accepted practice" (4).[8] Mass culture plays the same role as the primitive in primitivism, which brings exotic energy to the decaying ennui of European modernity. Both the primitive and the mass cultural appear to imbue an exhausted elite with new life. The two faces of "the popular," the ethnographic and the mass, thus show themselves to be conceptually linked, such that a theory of modernism that seeks to address one must necessarily engage the other.

I will be concerned with precisely how the "involvement" to which Crow refers took place: how the modernist literary avant-garde *actively participated* in the early forms of mass media in Mexico and Brazil. Their active participation is crucial, because, unlike Crow's modernists, these writers did not just mine the popular for inspiration, picking out a newspaper clipping for a Cubist collage, but rather were editors and regular contributors to the popular publications introduced above. It is difficult to overstate the strange and varied participation of the Mexican modernist avant-garde in popular media. One fascinating example is a series of monthly publications (sponsored by a beer company) called *Boletín Mensual Carta Blanca*, which ran for six years between 1933 and 1938. Edited by Salvador Novo, it included short essays by Jorge Cuesta, Villaurrutia, Jaime Torres Bodet, Novo, Manuel Toussaint, and Samuel Ramos to name but a few. These contributors wrote about contemporary and historical works of art from Mexico and Europe, and also offered touristic recommendations to both Mexicans and foreigners ("Places That Should

Be Visited"). The pamphlets included high quality, color photographic reproductions of art works, alongside recipes for dishes that included Carta Blanca beer. Building upon Martín-Barbero's now classic theory of *mediation*, I propose an expanded vision of the meaning of modernism's popularity. *Mediation* presents a vision of culture as a conflictive field that is made up of different and unequal but nevertheless committed actors, all of whom, I will go on to suggest, contribute to the creation of popular modernism. The "involvement" of modernism with popular culture does not emerge from an authenticity or closeness, nor is it limited to a quick and scandalous fling with an exotic or debased "other." Instead, I understand modernism as a set of cultural practices which included active participation in the production and circulation of popular culture, and which thus constituted an ethics as much as an aesthetics.

Mediations

Martín-Barbero's landmark book *De los medios a las mediaciones* (1987) represented a major shift in studies of popular culture in Latin America, away from a more rural focus to an urban one.[9] In the history of cultural studies among Latin American scholars, it might appear that studies of popular culture as "folkloric" are an outdated practice that have given way to more contemporary studies of cities and mass culture. However, Martín-Barbero defines urbanism as always already in contact with the rural. His central proposal, which I find to be still extremely relevant and generative, is that the rural popular continues to exist within and outside of the urban masses: they exist in a relationship of mutual dependence and conflict. The very groups that had been enclosed in folkloric images of the popular and were therefore forced outside the unfolding of political, economic, and cultural history make up what has been called "the masses." Rowe and Schelling, relying heavily on Martín-Barbero, point to the limits of a notion of cultural pluralism based in liberal theory, which allows the State the ultimate power of mediating this plurality of interests. They instead argue in favor of a "notion of dispersed sites [of the popular]" that are not entirely homogenized, despite the state's interest in the process (10). These dispersed sites include social actors and media that participated in the articulation of Latin American modernity through newspapers, *folletines*, and photography. Building upon Martín-Barbero, we shall see that these groups are not only victims of the manipulative power of mass media. While the cost of the fusion of mass and popular was borne by communities with the least political and economic means, they were not culturally bankrupted by the process.

The roots of Martín-Barbero's influential theory of the popular and the masses are lodged in the period of modernist experimentation in the 1920s and 1930s. He even briefly refers to Mário de Andrade's studies of Afro-Brazilian music as an approach that conjoins the aesthetic avant-garde with the urban-popular and reveals the existence of the mass in the popular: "el gesto negro se hace popular-masivo" [the Black gesture is made mass-popular] (Martín-Barbero 189). Martín-Barbero points out that the 1920s and 1930s were transitional years of mass media, which permitted greater openness in the conflictive negotiation between popular and elite cultures, and between masses and nation. Mário de Andrade wrote in *The Slave Who Is Not Isaura* (1925), his classic articulation of modernist theory, "Pelo jornal somos omnipresentes" [Through the journal we are omnipresent] (*Obra imatura* 265). I propose that this reference reaches beyond familiar journals such as *Klaxon* and *Verde e Amarelo*, which resemble the short-lived, limited circulation "little magazines" that generally appear in modernist studies; the omnipresence of modernism is more apparent and powerful in the authors' collaboration with mass media illustrated journals. As much as in-between media such as the *folletín* and *literatura de cordel*, which Martín-Barbero calls hybrid cultural spaces that open up literature to multiple readings, the explosion of magazines and newspapers of the period opened modernism to new audiences.[10] Even more, I suggest that thinking these mediations of culture, rather than the dominant discourse of cultural *mestizaje*, is critical to understanding the ethics of modernism.

Mário de Andrade's research into Afro-Brazilian culture is just one of many examples of how modernists engaged popular culture through and as racialized bodies. Martín-Barbero does not erase race from his analysis but frames it as only part of the broader conflictive process of *mediation*. However, the first statement of his theory of mediation does not entirely replace the classically modern racial concept of *mestizaje* with this new figure of modernity:

> la *verdad cultural* de estos países: el mestizaje que no es sólo aquel hecho racial del que venimos, sino la trama hoy de modernidad y discontinuidades culturales, de formaciones sociales y estructuras del sentimiento, de memorias e imaginarios que revuelven lo indígena con lo

rural, lo rural con lo urbano, el folklore con lo popular y lo popular con lo masivo. Fue así como la comunicación se nos tornó cuestión de *mediaciones* más que de medios, cuestión de cultura y, por tanto, no sólo de conocimientos sino de re-conocimiento. (Martín-Barbero 10, emphasis original)

[the *cultural truth* of these countries: of a *mestizaje* that is not only that racial fact from which we come but today's story of modernity and cultural discontinuities, of social formations and structures of feeling, of memories and imaginaries that mix up the indigenous with the rural, the rural with the urban, the folkloric with the popular and the popular with the massive. It was thus that communication became a question of *mediations* rather than media, a question of culture and therefore, not only of knowledge (cognition) but of re-cognition.]

There is no avoiding the problem here of treating race as a "fact," rather than as a discourse lodged in colonial history, which was made factual by the violence it rationalized.[11] Nonetheless, I would emphasize that Martín-Barbero here begins to think mediation rather than *mestizaje* and imagines culture as a strategic space for negotiation between the unfairly matched pair of the hegemon and the popular. This shift is crucial because it undermines *mestizaje*'s foundational threat of homogenization through racial fusion and suggests a way to analyze the reality of racial differences as they are lived in the Americas.[12]

While trained alongside other members of the highly influential generation of Latin American social scientists of the 1960s, Martín-Barbero argues for a modified, culturalist approach to theorizing the popular and the massive. This method takes into account recognizable hegemons such as the State, as well as the influence and power deployed by mass media. As much as Horkheimer and Adorno help Martín-Barbero to analyze the systematic production of (consumer) desire in mass media—we want what we see reproduced over and over again—he argues that Walter Benjamin's analysis of the process is more relevant to modernity in Latin America. Martín-Barbero appreciates that the systematic culture industry that Adorno theorizes makes impossible a purely culturalist position and its concomitant division of high and low; the danger he detects, though, is that it reproduces the same reading of every cultural text or object it encounters. The result is the "atrofia de la actividad del espectador" [the atrophy of the activity of the spectator] and a "pesimismo cultural" [cultural pessimism] (50–51). Martín-Barbero argues that this is an error based in the confusion between a *mode of historical use* and a *technological rationality*, an error that produces a form of cultural elitism that denies the possibility of a plurality of uses of culture and a multiplicity of aesthetic experiences. In contrast, Benjamin addresses the conflictive nature of mass culture, finding the popular to be not the negation of culture but rather its production.

The term "aesthetic experience" is crucial, although it runs as a rather subtle current within Martín-Barbero's broader argument for the study of culture as a conflictive site of mediation. He writes that his goal is to contribute to an anarchist aesthetics, which is based on the premise that art resides in experience and thus actively blurs the division between art and life (24). Through this anarchist aesthetics, Martín-Barbero asserts culture as a space not of the manipulation of the masses, but rather of productive conflict and heterogeneous practices.[13] The aesthetics of experience also comprises artistic (re)production in a series, and thus returns us to photography. Benjamin's cultural theory is important here, especially his vision of how photography transforms the manner in which art is received and functions, for it shows how mass image reproduction coexists with art as experience. Following his now canonical writing on art in the age of mechanical reproduction, Benjamin's concept of culture shifted from being a conception of the work of art as *total* to a theory of *multiple* works, practices, and most of all, *experiences* of those works. Whereas Adorno's vision of the work of art is that of one person immersing himself in the work, Benjamin pictures a mass of people in which the work is immersed. Adorno still relies on the concept of the individual reading or viewing the work, whereas Benjamin imagines a collective experience that makes the circulation and reception of the work(s)—henceforth always plural in their hermeneutics—as important or more so than their made objectness.

Photography: "The Popular Medium *par excellence*"[14]

This dispersion of the work of art is closely tied to practices of photographic montage and reproduced images, which were employed by the seemingly ideologically opposed projects of modernism, advertising, and mass media. However, Benjamin's vision of the work of art is made possible by his deep interest in the "minor arts": caricature, pornography, and especially photography, cultural practices linked to a history of "una iconografía para usos plebeyos" [an iconography for plebian uses] (Martín-Barbero 119). Martín-Barbero's subsequent proposal that the visual is a discourse accessible to a largely illiterate population is absolutely relevant, given the dismally high rates of illiteracy in Mexico (and most Latin American countries) in the first decades of the twentieth century.[15] If visual iconography and visual culture in general are a highly charged field, characterized in the twentieth century by increasing degrees of state intervention, I find that photography plays an especially complex role. One need only think about the importance of the medium for criminology and late nineteenth-century "sciences" studying aberrant human behavior to begin to understand photography's utility for the State. Yet photography also brought the art of portraiture to the popular classes and filled the pages of new mass media in the early decades of the twentieth century. Indeed, within his theory of mediation, Martín-Barbero encounters a promise of resistance in the visual in particular, not as a rule but as a possibility that appears at certain moments in history.

Photography played a central role in the modernist production of both images of popular culture—the folkloric and the masses—welding together these two faces of the popular and revealing their powerful influence on the formulation of literature, art, and theory. In the 1920s and 1930s, the boundaries between artistic, journalistic, and ethnographic photography were relatively undefined, and the same images illustrated experimental literature in mass media publications and political journals, and appeared in new art galleries and museums. Since its inception, photography has been a medium that has bridged the professional and the amateur, the artistic and the everyday, making "the popular" central as an aesthetic question as much as a question of the theme to be represented and its mode of production. Both engagements with the popular took place, in a sense, through the lens of the photographic camera: in the capture of racialized ethnographic subjects with the new, handheld Kodak, and through mixed media essays and texts that pictured femininity over and over in an explosion of photographs.

As much as the history of modernist writers and artists has made them appear as the heroic leaders of cultural production during these decades, they were in many ways at the mercy of the growing power of both commercial and ethnographic photography. Mário de Andrade took photographs that revealed the medium to be both the tool and the enemy of the modernist artist: the camera offered a means to research, document, and integrate Afro-Brazilian and Indian cultures into modern artistic practice, but yet it always already undermined the authority of the Brazilian modernist who held it.[16] It is clear, however, that photography was closely linked to his idea and image of "the popular." While Mário de Andrade's images of rural populations avoided a folkloric idealization of a foundational (and therefore necessarily past) autochthonous race, all of his work from poetry to music to photography made images of the popular central to the Brazilian modernist project. Similarly, in his groundbreaking "Manifesto Pau Brasil" (1924), fellow modernist Oswald de Andrade wrote:

> Advertisements producing letters bigger than towers. And new forms of industry, of transportation, of aviation. Gas stations. Gas meters. Railways. Laboratories and technical workshops. Voices and tics of wires and waves and flashes. Stars made familiar through photographic negatives. The correspondent of physical surprise in art . . . *See with open eyes* . . . , Barbarous, credulous, picturesque and tender. Readers of newspapers. The forest and the school. The National Museum. Cuisine, ore and dance. Vegetation. Pau-Brazil. (186)

Photography appears at the center of a proclamation that intersperses both images of the popular, joining jungle with school, and readers of journals with barbarians. The medium contributed to modernism's active engagement with popular culture, in part due to its mass reproducibility and increasing circulation during these decades. In photographically illustrated journals, the "popular" appeared as a mass media audience, a population defined by its participation in a rapidly expanding circulation of images, ideas, people, and goods.

Similarly, a radical Estridentista manifesto in Mexico simultaneously proclaimed Charlie Chaplin as "la posibilidad de un arte nuevo, juvenil entusiasta y palpitante" [the possibility of a new art, youthful, enthusiastic, and palpitating] and was published on a poster with a large photograph of Manuel Maples Arce dominating the right side of the page. The proclamation ended with the famous concluding line, "Viva el mole de guajalote!" [Long Live Turkey *Mole*!] (Maples Arce et al. 170–171). By naming mole, the indigenous sauce made of chile and chocolate, and employing the Nahuatl word "guajalote" rather than the Castilian "pavo," the Estridentistas produced a visual, international modernity that also contained an idea of traditional culture belonging to the nationalist rhetoric of *indigenismo*. Francisco Reyes Palma emphasizes the group's simultaneous focus on pre-Columbian cultures and interest in the industrialized graphic press, particularly in *El Universal Ilustrado* and *Revista de Revistas*. In what follows,

I examine these two cases of modernist popular culture, focusing in particular on race and gender as the mediation of the mass and the popular.

Case 1: S. Paulo, Brazil

Mário de Andrade's poem "Toada" was first published in 1932 and reprinted in August 1936 in the large format publication *S. Paulo* (figure 4.1). "Toada"—the name of a dance from Parintins, which can also be translated as "rumor" or "sound"—presents a photographic experience of the city of São Paulo.

> Busquei São Paulo no mapa,
> Mas tudo, com cara nova,
> Duma tristeza de viagem,
> Tirava fotografia...
> E o meu cigarro na tarde
> Brilhava só, que nem Deus.
> Fiquei tão pobre, tão triste,
> Que até o olhar se fechou.
> No outro lado da cidade
> O vento me dispersou. ("Toada" n.p.)
>
> [I looked for São Paulo on the map,
> But everything, with a new face,
> Of a sadness of travel.
> I took photographs . . .
> And my cigarette in the evening
> Shined alone, without even God.
> I remained so poor, so sad,
> That even my gaze closed up.
> On the other side of the city
> The wind scattered me.]

If the consolatory practice of photography described in the poem results in the simultaneous location and dispersion of the poetic self in the modern city, its reprint in *S. Paulo* explicitly shows the circulation of people and products associated with modern life. The pages in which the poem is printed flip out and unfold, so that the placement of the poem appears to change, and like all of the pages of the journal, they are filled with dramatic photographs, photomontages, and experimental graphic design. A portion of the folded page on which "Toada" appears offers "A trip around São Paulo" and presents a

Figure 4.1 "Toada," *S. Paulo*, August 1936. Biblioteca, Instituto de Estudos Brasileiros, Universidade de São Paulo.

photographic collage showing sailboats and a futuristic building in the background. The bottom half of the extended page is divided between de Andrade's evocative poem and cartoon-like drawings of the diverse tourist attractions of the city: from the Horto Florestal to the modern urban vista of Ypiranga. Viewed with the other page unfolded, the same sailboats meet a dynamic photomontage of men loading and carrying coffee beans ready for export.

From more efficient agricultural production to building constructions, railroads, public health, and the very publication of journals and newspapers, *S. Paulo* displays the city's triumphant entry into modernity in photographs. The journal's pages are overrun by photo-essays and photomontages that portray the rapid industrialization and growth of the city, and its editors sought to demonstrate the state's investment potential to both a domestic and international business readership. Employing the popular new technology of rotogravure, the journal celebrated the burgeoning achievement of modernity in São Paulo as a "Renaissance" of commerce, industry, and culture. Proclaiming a new generation of Paulista Bandeirantes, the journal's editors unapologetically revive the image of the rapacious explorers from São Paulo who were responsible for conquering and claiming the mine-rich lands in the interior of Brazil in the seventeenth and eighteenth centuries. They write, "Este mensario, orgão documental das realizações paulistas, nasce da propria logica deste instante, como um espelho necessario a fixar nossa pujante vitalidade. Seu valor residirá apenas nas imagens que nelle se reflectem, si bem que tudo seja pequeno para poder reproduzir a acção e o pensamento de uma 'raça de gigantes' " [This monthly, documentary organ of Paulista achievements, is born of the very logic of the moment, like a necessary mirror to fix our powerful vitality. Its value will barely reside in the images that are reflected in it, though everything may appear small in reproducing the action and thought of a "race of giants"].[17]

The first issue of the journal explicitly reflected on its own function in this process in a photograph of a young boy selling newspapers in the fast moving street traffic of the city (figure 4.2). The growth of a national mass media was a point of pride in Brazil's modern status, and journals both popular and experimental emphasized the crucial connection between print and modernity that Benedict Anderson revealed to be central to the imagination of nation.[18] A journal published in Rio de Janeiro and contained in de Andrade's archive proudly proclaimed that the city with only two million inhabitants, and São Paulo with one million, produced more journals and magazines than

Figure 4.2 "The Paulista Sense of Brazilian Life Means:" *S. Paulo*, January 1936. Biblioteca, Instituto de Estudos Brasileiros, Universidade de São Paulo.

New York with a population of thirteen million people. While these numbers are likely inaccurate, the claim itself is important, as the author explains that throngs of Brazilians were so eager to publish their own literary production that the periodicals were cropping up "like mushrooms."[19]

The editors of the eclectic pages of *S. Paulo* were well-known modernist collaborators Cassiano Ricardo and Menotti del Picchia, as well as Leven Vampré.[20] What is more, these editors argue that cultural experimentation goes hand in hand with economic development and governmental modernization projects:

> O extraordinario avanço economico de São Paulo é acompanhado pelo seu admiravel surto cultural. O actual goberno encara o crescente desenvolvimento do ensino como um dos problemas cardeaes da administração publica... como luminosa cupula de um monumento de instrucção e de cultura, alteia-se a Universidad de São Paulo, creação do actual governo. Nella pontificam luminares das ciencias e das artes.[21]

> [The extraordinary economic advance of São Paulo is accompanied by its admirable cultural boom. The current government views the growing development of teaching as one of the cardinal problems of public administration... the University of São Paulo, the creation of the current government, rises like a luminous cupola of a monument to teaching and culture. In it teach luminaries of the sciences and the arts.]

They note Claude Lévi-Strauss's contributions to the renewed Bandeirante spirit during his stay in Brazil (1934–1937) and insist on the importance of the governmental Department of Propaganda and the Department of Culture for the advancement of the city and the nation. The Week of Modern Art of 1922 and the modernist movement in general are credited for replacing writers with "feet in Brazil and heads in Europe" with those who seek to reveal Brazil to itself. They define the new intellectual: "Bandeira Intellectual quer dizer: pensamento em acção" [Intellectual Bandeirante means: thought in action].[22] The image presented in *S. Paulo* is of a national modern renaissance fueled by three key forces: the state, the media, and the modernist movement.

This type of developmentalist rhetoric has fueled critiques of modernism as a coconspirator in the preparation for Getúlio Vargas's repressive dictatorship. Yet this editorial voice that directly addresses its readers, explaining the journal's *bandeirante* function, is only one of the multiple voices contained within *S. Paulo*. Despite its celebration of the cooperation between industry, state, and culture, the contributions by modernist writers and the images with which they engaged reveal a contradictory vision of São Paulo's modernity. In addition to the few texts that appeared in *S. Paulo*, de Andrade published regularly in the *Diário Nacional*, the opposition journal of the Partido Democrático that initially supported the Revolution of 1930 but later opposed Vargas's increasingly oppressive government.[23]

Even *S. Paulo* itself did not present a flawlessly progressivist ideological stance; instead, its mixture of photographs, text, and modernist poetry mediates the conflicts of Brazilian modernity. Cassiano Ricardo, later branded as an apologist for the Vargas regime, published a poem entitled "Girl Drinking Coffee" in the illustrated journal, which presents a strong critique of the very systems of modernization and global capital celebrated in the earlier editorial essay.[24] The poem leads the reader from the image of a happy young girl in Paris drinking her coffee, across the ocean, through a Brazilian port, on a train to the *sertão*, to a laborer covered with dirt who works the land to produce the coffee. The laborer dreams richly at night but awakens poor everyday, only to face the back-breaking task of "derrubou sósinho a floresta brutal" [destroying all by himself the brutal jungle] ("Moça" n.p.). The riches of the coffee plantation in Brazil are described as a promise never meant to be kept, a burnt wedding veil, a dream torn from the hands of the laborer. Ricardo's poem begins and concludes with the repetition of the question "Quedê?" [What of?]. It asks in a redundant fashion about what happened to the worker, who toils planting coffee, and then about the coffee itself, thus tracing the movement of one of Brazil's most important exports from the site where it is grown to the site of its consumption. The poem answers back that the coffee was drunk by a girl, and concludes with a final, slightly altered question: "Mas a moça onde está?/ está em Pariz./ Moça feliz" [But the girl, where is she?/ She is in Paris./ Happy girl] ("Moça" n.p.). Thick with irony, the poem contradicts the celebratory claims for modernization by the editors—by Ricardo himself—and reveals the sinister edge of the photomontage of a bright-eyed girl of European descent drinking coffee, surrounded by a backdrop of a burgeoning urban landscape (figure 4.3). As much as the collage celebrates the growth of São Paulo due to the globalization of the coffee industry, the poem indicates the cruel limits of who benefits from this process. What is more, the poem and the photograph reveal the necessary links between the two faces of the popular: the feminized mass cultural and the racialized rural worker. Reading the *mediation* of Ricardo's work

Figure 4.3 *S. Paulo*, September–October 1936. Biblioteca, Instituto de Estudos Brasileiros, Universidade de São Paulo.

reveals the profound and unresolved ethical contradictions of a modernism simultaneously grounded in these two forms of the popular.

The ideological position of the journal appears yet more contradictory when this poem is read alongside "Canto da Raça" [Song of the Race] also by Ricardo and published in June 1936. This slightly earlier poem is an unapologetic celebration of the urban success of São Paulo and revels in "batalha violenta e sonóra que é São Paulo construindo tres casas por hora!" [the violent and sonorous battle that is São Paulo constructing three houses per hour!]. The poem shares the page with a photomontage of construction workers, showing them high above the growing urban landscape of São Paulo. As much as the image of industrial São Paulo was crucial to the ideal of a Brazilian modernity and the rate of urban growth surged incredibly during this period, the owners of the land that cruelly awoke the worker from his dreams of riches continued to exercise economic and political power. The montage of photographs and the interplay of images and text in *S. Paulo* create pages that underline both the cooperation and the battles between the forces that sought to picture modernity in Brazil during these decades.

Modernist intellectuals participated both in these popular illustrated journals and in the state's attempt to define Brazil through its popular culture.[25] The question of what ethics a modernism indebted to Vargas's Estado Novo might contain appears not only in figures such as Ricardo, but even in Mário de Andrade, long associated with a less authoritarian current of modernism. In addition to his educational and media jobs, de Andrade held several positions in the early years of Getúlio Vargas's regime. He served as director of the Department of Culture and Recreation for the city of São Paulo in 1936 and was later asked by Gustavo Capanema, Vargas's infamous minister of press and propaganda, to draft a proposal for a Serviço de Patrimonio Artístico Nacional [Service of National Artistic Patrimony] (Williams 98). In his draft of the state-sponsored design for cultural patrimony, de Andrade attempts to put into practice the theory of modernist nationalism seen in his creative work and clarifies the multiple definitions of "the popular" at its core. He defines national artistic patrimony broadly as "all works of pure and applied arts; popular or erudite art; art produced by nationals and foreigners; and, art owned by public entities, independent organizations, private individuals, and foreigners residing in Brazil" (see Williams 100).

In addition to the more ethnographic engagement with "folkloric" popular culture seen in *O Turista Aprendiz* (1927–1929, published 1978) [The Apprentice Tourist]—a mixture of travel diary, ethnographic study, and experimental novel—and *Danças Dramáticas do Brasil* (1959) [Dramatic Dances of Brazil], de Andrade includes a broad reach of popular cultural practices in this plan for a national patrimony, including gardening, regional dress or costume [*indumentaria*], and fashion [*moda*].²⁶ Most fascinating and relevant to this theory of popular cultural expression is the logic by which he links "indumentaria regional" [regional costume], specifically "o cavaleiro, o vaqueiro, a baiana" [the horseman, the cowboy, the Bahian woman], with upper- and middle-class fashion. He writes: "Outro processo ainda, e utilissimo, pra por em prática esta parte movel do programa social seria o lançamento duma Revista da Moda Nacional, ou criação duma seção dirigida pela Sociedade, numa revista já lançada (*Vanitas, Cigarra*), de combinação com os directores dela" [Yet another process, and very useful, to put into practice this mobile part of the social program, would be the founding of a Magazine of National Fashion, or the creation of a section directed by Society, in a magazine already launched (*Vanitas, Cigarra*), in accordance with its directors].²⁷ Here the "ethnographic" collection of regional uses of skins (one example he gives) would operate parallel to and within the new, photographically illustrated women's magazines that show samples of the newest styles from Rio de Janeiro, London, and Paris. De Andrade himself published frequently in *Cigarra*, which like *S. Paulo* included photographic collages but was directed primarily at a female audience. The national popular expressed through clothing is both the ethnography and "apprentice tourism" seen in de Andrade's photographs, and the fashion and cinematic photography published in popular women's magazines.

Perhaps predictably, de Andrade's expansive definition of the national was substantially altered after the outline was submitted to Vargas's propaganda minister. It became instead a proposal for a Serviço do Patrimônio *Histórico* e Artístico Nacional (SPAHN) [Service of *Historical* and Artistic National Patrimony], and the insertion of this single word reflects a crucial shift of focus from contemporary popular culture to a historical definition of patrimony.²⁸ These changes allow Daryle Williams's interpretation that during the first Vargas regime, "cultural patrimony would be synonymous with high art" (101). This was not, however, de Andrade's vision of this patrimony. As his experimental photography and ethnography were erased from the SPAHN's structure, so also was the conception of an equally important and contemporary urban popular culture that bridged *cultura de masas* with *cultura popular*. De Andrade's unexpected and suggestive proposal that fashion magazines be a central location of the creation of a national patrimony stands out as a bizarre and defining combination of indigenous skins and Parisian furs.

Leonel Kaz describes the importance of these illustrated magazines of "varieties" for the earliest careers of many writers and artists responsible for the modernist movement and points to this period as a major transition in the function of graphic design and illustrated publications. Emiliano di Cavalcanti, likely the creator of the Week of Modern Art in São Paulo that launched *modernismo* in 1922, got his start in the women's magazine *Fon-Fon* in 1914 and contributed artwork for the covers of the widely popular *O Cruzeiro*. This magazine was a leader of the illustrated publications, with news as well as "sport, politics, art and spectacles, consumption, ways of life" (Kaz 22). These variety publications were explicitly designed for a female audience and addressed the many interests and concerns of their public. What is more, Kaz describes a twentieth-century process during which mass media publications "se feminizaram" [were feminized], as women left the privacy and intimacy of the home to enter into the public sphere of paid work and politics (158). The widespread popularity of these illustrated magazines is quite impressive, given the literacy rates cited above: the magazine *Revista Feminina*, which was founded in São Paulo in 1914 and began publishing photographs in 1916, apparently sold more than 20,000 copies per month (Kaz 162).

The explosion of a mass media sphere in Brazil, as in Mexico, was characterized by photographically illustrated magazines for women, in which the contradictory nature of modernity was drawn onto the figure of the modern woman. The "transmutation," as Martín-Barbero terms it, of popular into mass takes place in specifically gendered spaces—the pages of popular illustrated magazines filled with variety pieces and photographs of Hollywood stars as well as experimental poetry and photomontage. Despite the clear address to their women readers, it is important to be clear that the politics of such journals cannot easily be termed feminist. While a section of the *Revista Feminina*, entitled "Vida Feminina" [Feminine Life], reported on women's movements around the world and defended women's right to vote, it condemned the aggressive actions of foreign suffragettes and tended toward a conservative, moralistic tone based largely on the importance of women as mothers. These journals nonetheless played a crucial function in *mediating* the popular, the mass, and the modernist avant-garde.

The impact of this process of mediation can be seen not only in the works published by modernists in journals such as *S. Paulo*, but also in some of their most canonical literary works. De Andrade's classic text *Hallucinated City* (*Pauliceia Desvairada* 1922) addresses the city as:

> Mulher mais longa
> que os pasmos alucinados
> das tôrres de São Bento!
> Mulher feita de asfalto e de lamas de várzea,
> toda insultos nos olhos
> toda convites nessa boca louca de rubores! . . .
> E serás demore, morrente chama esgalga,
> meio fidalga, meio barregã,
> as alucionações crucificantes
> de todas as auroras de meu jardim! (63)

> [A woman taller
> than the hallucinated awe
> of the towers of São Bento!
> Woman made of asphalt and marsh mud,
> all insults in the eyes,
> all invitations on that mouth mad with blushes! . . .
> And you will always be, dying flame growing thin,
> half lady, half whore,
> the crucifying hallucinations
> of all the dawns of my garden!]

In this early poem, images of the conjoined marsh mud and urban asphalt prefigure the two faces of the popular that are so crucial to the ethics as well as to the aesthetics of modernism. As is clear from the terms that admire and denigrate modern São Paulo as a lady and a whore, the resulting (feminized) modernism is grounded in an ethics. Further, it is no coincidence that the inviting mouth of Lady Pauliceia tops a body painted the dark brown color of mud and the black color of asphalt. Like Ricardo's "happy girl" drinking the coffee produced by the brutal labor in the interior of the land, the woman of asphalt and mud who represents industrializing São Paulo is both an intimate of the modernist writer and his terrifying hallucination.

Case 2: El Universal Ilustrado, Mexico

Martín-Barbero argues that Mexico functions as an important case for understanding the urban popular in all of Latin America, for its vision of revolution, of popular struggle, and mass social movements. As in Brazil, these masses appeared in a feminized mass media, in which the modernist avant-garde actively participated to fascinating and contradictory results. The decades following the massive social disruption of the Mexican Revolution (1910–1920) were defined by tensions between the media and the state, as the federal government simultaneously centralized bureaucratic power using a revolutionary, nationalist rhetoric and reaffirmed private capital. The growing bourgeois class increasingly took control of radio and the press out of the hands of French, English, and U.S. owners, as much as they operated under the watchful eyes of the revolutionary *caudillos* who successively passed through the presidential seat of power (Corral Corral 57). The postrevolutionary government paradoxically depended upon this new urban mass media and upon a nationalist discourse grounded in the image of a populist, rural revolution. During the 1920s and 1930s, the illustrated journals that were owned and run by this bourgeoisie displayed their resistance to the populist discourse of the revolutionary government but also sought to diversify the political sphere and to create some version of civil society in the aftermath of a decade of militarization. Both the media and the state, mutually intertwined but not with identical interests, staked their claims to the definition of a national popular culture.

In addition to these powerful, competing interests in the sphere of popular media, new social actors appeared on the scene. Julieta Ortiz Gaitán argues that this process began with the Constitution of 1917 and continued with major changes in social structures and labor organization during the Revolution and the strengthening of working classes and *campesinos* following it:

> La presencia de estos sectores medios y populares fue el factor clave para el surgimiento de una nueva actitud social, determinada en buena medida por un mayor poder adquisitivo, por la consciencia de su papel protagónico y de manera fundamental, por nuevos aparatos ideológicos de gran fuerza como son los medios masivos de comunicación. Se prefiguran así los perfiles de la llamada cultura de masas y la sociedad de consumo de nuestros días. (180)
>
> [The presence of these middle and popular classes was a key factor in the emergence of a new social attitude, determined in large part by a greater buying power, by a consciousness of their leading role and fundamentally, by powerful new ideological apparatuses such as communication mass media. The profile of the so-called culture of masses and consumer society of our days are prefigured here.]

In her excellent study of Mexican comic books, Anne Rubenstein similarly insists that:

> Mexicans in the postrevolutionary era used mass media . . . as the best available space for dissent, negotiation, and accommodation. As surprising as students of Antonio Gramsci may find it, the interpretive communities gathered around popular culture *were* Mexican civil society in this era. By producing, distributing, and interpreting words and pictures, citizens could and did consent to the general structure of the relationships that formed the state, while also, at times, commenting on and even changing specific government policies. (3)

Mexico's "reasonably broad middle class" participated in the discussion about the use of public space and the role of the postrevolutionary government, in the form of debates in public spaces from the streets to auditoria. These debates were real struggles grounded in a core set of issues: postrevolutionary transformations of the household and workplace, masculinity and femininity, and religion. Rubenstein moderates that the state operated as mediator and instigator to manipulate cultural conflict to its advantage, even as national media sources sought to gain ground by turning the state's resources against its interests. This process imagines another logic of the popular, one that was impure, conflicted, and a mixture of urban and rural.

The weekly illustrated magazines to which both Estridentistas and Contemporáneos contributed were affiliates of daily newspapers, the largest of which were founded in the late teens of the twentieth century and operated until the close of the century. Among the first and most influential of these newspapers was *El Universal*, which was founded in 1916 and pronounced to be independently owned and operated. There is tremendous debate in the historiography of this period of mass media, especially regarding *El Universal*—debates that range between accusations of its complete obedience to President Venustiano Carranza, whose support launched the paper, and its own proclamations of total financial independence. In one collection of essays dedicated to the history of Mexican journalism, Silvia González Marín criticizes *El Universal* as the instrument of the middle and upper class, financed by advertising and too critical of the revolutionary government (159), while Blanca Aguilar Platas denies the claims of owner and founder Félix Palavicini about the newspaper's independence from governmental support, stating that "sus afiliaciones a los sucesivos regímenes a partir de Carranza eran un secreto a voces" [its affiliations with successive regimes following Carranza were an open secret] (134). Archival evidence shows that the Secretaría de Hacienda y Crédito Público [Ministry of the Treasury] provided money to pay for the paper given to *El Universal* on March 12, 1917; in fact, control over access to paper was for many years the federal government's best means of control over the press.[29] Thus in his very entertaining and melodramatic autobiography, *Mi vida revolucionaria* (1937) [My Revolutionary Life], Palavicini is not entirely honest when he writes:

> Me dediqué a organizar una empresa privada para editar un diario, pues mi propósito era dedicarme al periodismo político, creando una gran empresa para hacer un diario revolucionario independiente . . . Es oportuno declarar que el Gobierno del señor Carranza no proporcionó un solo peso para la fundación de este periódico. (353–4)
>
> [I dedicated myself to the organization of a private business to publish a daily paper, well my intention was to dedicate myself to political journalism, creating a great business to make an independent, revolutionary daily paper . . . It is opportune to declare here that the government of Mr. Carranza did not provide a single peso for the foundation of this periodical.]

In fact, Carranza put Palavicini in charge of the management of newspapers of the Revolution, and he was responsible for the creation of the Publications Department within the Ministry of Public Instruction (Loyo 299).

Governmental support was not ongoing, however, and *El Universal* and its illustrated weekly survived many dramatic political shifts during these decades. Despite his reliance on the federal government, Palavicini describes his own view of the limits of the state: "El Estado puramente político decae en nuestra época. . . El industrialismo, en cambio, es dueño del mundo moderno: difunde el bienestar, consolida la democracia" [The purely political State is weakening during our era . . . Industrialism, in turn, is the owner of the modern world: it spreads well-being, it consolidates democracy] (363). He states that laws and taxes are not sufficient to resolve real social problems, but instead Mexico must distribute "los medios de acción" [the media of action] to alleviate the country's immense social inequalities and fulfill its revolutionary promise.[30] As much as *El Universal* relied upon the federal government for funds (at times) and even at times deployed its revolutionary discourse, it is clear that from the earliest days of mass media there was a goal to differentiate its politics from those of the state.[31]

Juan Manuel Aurrecoechea and Armando Bartra's history of the genre of the *historieta* (a form of comic) offers a balanced description of the relationship between modernist avant-garde, the state, and the media: "En este contexto de efervescencia cultural, que abarca tanto al Estado como a la naciente industria del entretenimiento; que se extiende desde las vanguardias *más o menos elitistas*, hasta las aún irredentes masas populares y que combina el nacionalismo exacervado con el plagio gozoso y creado . . . " [In this context of cultural effervescence, which the state as much as the nascent entertainment industry founds, extends from the *more or less elitist avant-gardes* to the still unredeemed popular masses and combines an exacerbated nationalism with a joyous and created plagiarism . . .] (200, emphasis added). While the authors stress the "precarious autonomy" of the press, calling it Mexico's "doubtful fourth power," the strange mixture of a "more or less" elite avant-garde with the popular masses must give theorists of modernism pause. These weeklies sought to broaden their readership, to integrate the entire family as a "reading public" through the inclusion of the colorful illustrations and a section of *historietas*. While it has proven impossible to confirm the figures about the numbers of journals and newspapers that circulated at the time and their readership, these authors provide important details. In the 1920s, the web of distributors and the number of street sellers of periodicals increased notably, the Unión de Expendedores, Voceadores y Repartidores de la Prensa [Union of Vendors, Criers and Distributors of the Press] was founded, and when the vast open market at La Lagunilla began in the 1930s, the weekly illustrated supplements were sold alongside second-hand books. Aurrecoechea and Bartra state that these new publications were not simply vehicles of political parties, nor the mere products of cultural elites such as their nineteenth-century predecessors.[32]

The Brazilian concern with the "feminization" of the press was shared by similar characterizations of the mass media in Mexico.[33] Carlos Noriega Hope was the director of *El Universal Ilustrado* during the height of its engagement with the modernist avant-gardes, from March 4, 1920 until his death in 1934. In his *Director's Commentary* in the journal that was subtitled "Semanario Artístico Popular" [Artistic Popular Weekly], Noriega Hope states:

> El ideal de esta revista es un [foro] . . . frívolo y moderno, donde las cosas trascendentales se ocultan bajo una agradable superficialidad.

> Porque es indudable que todos los periódicos tienen su fisonomía y su espíritu, exactamente como los hombres . . . . Los hay frívolos y aparentemente vacíos, pero que guardan, en el fondo, idea originales y una humana percepción de la vida. Quizás este semanario, dentro de su espíritu frívolo, guarda el perfume de una idea. (Noriega Hope 34)
>
> [The ideal of this journal is to be a (forum of) . . . the frivolous and the modern, where transcendent things are hidden under an agreeable superficiality. Because it is doubtless that all periodicals have their physiognomy and their spirit, exactly like men . . . There are those that are frivolous and apparently vacuous, but that hold, at their base, original ideas and a human perception of life. Perhaps this weekly, within its frivolous spirit, contains the scent (perfume) of an idea.]

This mixture of frivolity and innovative thought is expressed in mixed codes of silly femininity and modernist avant-garde. In the history of *El Universal*, published by the newspaper itself in celebration of 75 years in print, the ideological and aesthetic confusion still had not ended. The authors write that the page of *El Universal* regularly dedicated to film reviews, "Del arte silencioso" [On the silent art], which Noriega Hope coordinated before becoming director of the weekly cultural supplement, "era una anárquica plana ilustrativa de las diferentes corrientes artísticas; no llevaba en realidad coherencia alguna ya que sus temas eran tan disímbolos que una plana era insuficiente para darles orden" [was an anarchical illustrative plane of different artistic currents; in reality it had no coherence whatsoever since its themes were so dissimilar that one sheet was insufficient to give them any order] (Castro Ruiz and Maya Nava 21). *El Universal Ilustrado* under Noriega Hope's leadership served as a fascinating and contradictory meeting ground for the discourses of nation articulated by the state, the increasingly powerful bourgeoisie, and avant-garde artists and writers. It reported on the educational programs of Vasconcelos, included fiction and poetry by both of the major groups of the *vanguardias*, and even reflected a conservative, Catholic voice frequently associated with middle-class women of the time. The mixture of frivolity and avant-garde originality in this mass media made possible a nondogmatic ethics and a strangely mass cultural modernist aesthetic.

Like de Andrade's woman of asphalt and mud, the ethics of popular modernism in *El Universal Ilustrado* appears at the intersection of race and gender, specifically through a revamping of modernism's familiar obsession with masks. Internationally favored by artists from Hannah Höch and Pablo Picasso to de Andrade himself, the "ancient and modern" practice of masking weaves through a 1926 issue of *El Universal Ilustrado*. This issue contains two photo-essays about masks, printed one after another, as well as an article on the topic by Contemporáneos poet Xavier Villaurrutia. The first photo-essay, titled "Masks" and signed with the pseudonym "El Caballero Puck," shows a variety of masks as examples of an ancient art. Here *El Universal Ilustrado* provides a familiar, racialized image of the mask that appears to satisfy the same primitivist desires associated with European modernism. "Puck" praises Estridentista artist Germán Cueto's colorful terra-cotta mask of Germán List Arzubide for its mixture of "the prehistoric memory of carnival" and the modern art of caricature. However, his article is followed directly by the anonymous "Our Artists in Masks," which presents the masked faces of the stars of the day from screen and stage—the *mujeres nuevas* [New Women] of Mexico (figures 4.4 and 4.5).[34] The similar, circular graphic designs of "Masks" and "Our Artists in Masks" present them as mirrored faces of the same modern city, faces that mediate between the mass and the popular. "Our Artists in Masks" examines each of the numbered photographs of the women, describing their characters and citing poems by Estridentistas about them. The author states that the pictured women are "Artistas. Mujeres que tienen la celebridad pasajera del éxito, que exhiben su belleza en el frívolo tablado de la farsa. Almas incógnitas que hacen gráfico el símbolo de "La Señorita Etcétera": UNA, DOS, TRES, CUATRO, CINCO, SEIS, SIETE, OCHO . . . " [Artists. Women who have the passing celebrity of success, who exhibit their beauty in the frivolous stage of farce. *Mysterious souls that make graphic the symbol of the "Señorita Etcétera"*: ONE, TWO, THREE, FOUR, FIVE, SIX, SEVEN, EIGHT . . .].[35] The mixture of traditional masks and these popular stars of cinema and theater is the photographic image of the Estridentistas's modernist aesthetics, for the "Señorita Etcétera" refers to a novella by that name by Estridentista Arqueles Vela.[36]

While this discussion of masking resonates with the renovatory function of European primitivism, Villaurrutia's essay in this issue of *El Universal Ilustrado* elaborates a crucial difference in his understanding of masks: their simultaneous status as artistic and functional object. While primitivism's basic operation is the extraction of an object from its (religious or secular) function and its insertion in an artistic sphere, in "The Mask" Villaurrutia writes that masks are the connection between the quotidian and the significant, the artistic and

Figure 4.4 El Caballero Puck, "Masks," *El Universal Ilustrado*, March 4, 1926. Hemeroteca Nacional, Universidad Autónoma de México.

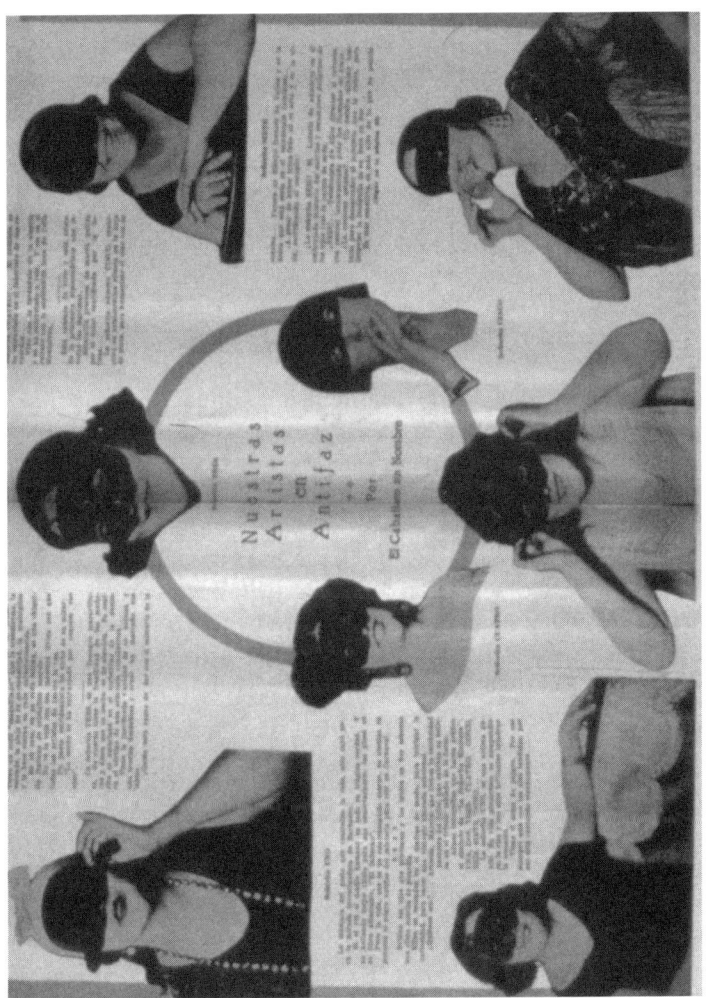

Figure 4.5 "Our Artists in Masks," *El Universal Ilustrado*, March 4, 1926. Hemeroteca Nacional, Universidad Autónoma de México.

the utilitarian (figure 4.6). He states that in this sense, the mask operates like language, which can be used either to communicate a simple message or to write poetry:

> El nacimiento de la máscara dibujó, siquiera imprecisamente, los límites entre el espectáculo ideal y la diaria faena ideal. Antigua como la palabra, tan semejante a ella en cuanto pretende fijar en estrecho y definitivo gesto la expresión de una realidad significativa; en cuanto se le destina a la vez que a mostrar algo, a ocultar algo también, es como ella un modo de puente tendido hacia un reino puro.[37]
>
> [The birth of the mask drew out, if only imprecisely, the limits between the ideal spectacle and the ideal daily task. Ancient like the word, so similar to it in terms of trying to fix in a narrow and definitive gesture the expression of a meaningful reality; as far as it is destined at the same time to show something, to hide something also, it is like it [the word] a kind of bridge stretched toward a pure realm.]

Villaurrutia explains that masks are neither quotidian nor sublime, but rather a bridge that belongs to neither side. When the mask functions simply as sculpture (as art) or only to hide a face (as a tool), it loses its unique means of creating meaning; in its aesthetic and utilitarian quality, as both image and word, the mask articulates a modernist aesthetics. Villaurrutia goes on to describe the mask as "senda medianera entre la representación mecánica del rostro y la pura misión artística" [a mediating path between mechanical representation of the face and pure artistic mission]. The mask is the mechanical reproduction of the face and yet, because it has a real function, cannot be reduced to the mimetic representation of a face. Here he seems to offer a theory of photography as much as of the mask, for descriptions of the mechanicity of the medium and arguments for its artistic potential were already proliferating in Mexico. The layering of (photographic) mass cultural and ethnographic popular images therefore contains a vision of a functional modernist aesthetics.[38] The direct movement from the pages of ethnographic masks to the pages of masked mass media stars in *El Universal Ilustrado* makes this useful art possible.

The very notion of a utilitarian modernist aesthetic goes against the grain of most modernist theory by introducing both an ethics and an aesthetics of the popular. While I do not wish to repeat reductive versions of Clement Greenberg's articulation of modernism, it is nonetheless clear that Villaurrutia's aesthetic differs substantially from his conception of medium specificity in which, "turning away from subject matter of common experience, the poet or artist turns it

Figure 4.6 Xavier Villaurrutia, "The Mask," *El Universal Ilustrado*, March 4, 1926. Hemeroteca Nacional, Universidad Autónoma de México.

in upon the medium of his own craft" (6). Greenberg's essay can in no way accommodate the three discussions of masks discussed above, for in addition to the turning in of the art object, he also defines the avant-garde in opposition both to mass cultural *kitsch* and genuine folk (popular) culture. In contrast, these pages join the mass popular photographs of women with the racialized image of the mask, and the two with a modernist theory by Contemporáneos poet Villaurrutia. The unlikely combination—like de Andrade's skins and middle-class fashion—produces a useful, and thus ethical, modernist aesthetics. It is important to note here that the photographic mask's utility does not provide a direct political content or function. Popular modernism does not instruct the viewer on how to wear the mask, how to be modern, or even how to be Mexican. Instead, modernist language and art themselves, as much as the mask, stretch between representation and communication. They are grounded in the reach, the *mediation*, between art and tool, popular and avant-garde.

Villaurrutia's logic of a useful aesthetics, formed jointly by mass and popular culture, is an ethics of modernism defined by modernist writers' and artists' active involvement in popular culture. This participation in popular culture by the modernist avant-garde is not limited to the important cases of Mexico and Brazil. In other places in Latin America as diverse as Argentina, Chile, and Puerto Rico, the rapid growth of a national mass media similarly opened up an important new cultural space whose character was marked by the remarkable inclusion of experiments with photography and design. Jorge Luis Borges, perhaps the most-read Latin American writer inside and outside the region, published regularly from 1936 to 1939 in the popular illustrated magazine *El Hogar* [Home].[39] As with *El Universal Ilustrado* and *A Cigarra*, the intended audience were women who, while certainly belonging to a cross-section of working, middle and bourgeois classes, nevertheless were new social actors. The most engaged of the modernists, like Mário de Andrade, learned from their own research into indigenous and Afro-Latin American communities, such that they were shown to be vibrant and active producers of modern culture. The same must be said about the women who read and appeared in the illustrated journals. I began this essay with the story of the modernist intellectual leaving the ivory tower in search of an ethical aesthetics. This story must include these new actors, for the ethics of popular modernism certainly did.

Notes

1. Lawrence Buell's article in the *PMLA* is a prime example of the association of the avant-garde with ethical art.
2. Here I will limit my discussion of ethics to the question of the modernist's relationship with the popular. It is, however, just one part of a larger phenomenon I call *ethos* in my book, *Errant Modernism: The Ethos of Photography in Mexico and Brazil* (forthcoming, Duke UP).
3. In Lusophone Brazil, the avant-garde movements of the 1920s and 1930s are called *modernismo*; in Spanish America, they are *vanguardias*. In this article, I will refer to both as "modernist avant-gardes" and modernism. For excellent critical surveys of the Latin American avant-gardes, in Spanish, see Schwartz, *Las vanguardias latinoamericanas*, and, in English, see Unruh, *Latin American Vanguards*.
4. See in particular Poole, *Vision, Race and Modernity*; and Natalia Majluf, "El indigenismo en México y Perú: Hacia una visión comparativa," in *Arte, historia e identidad en América: Visiones comparativas*, Mexico: UNAM, Instituto de Investigaciones Estéticas, 1994: 610–628.
5. Angel Rama's *The Lettered City* presents a history of these *letrados* [lettered men], who penned both literature and law in the Americas from the Conquest to the revolutions of the twentieth century.
6. The defining function he grants to these connections between high and low art provides a striking contrast to the theory of the (European) avant-garde established by Peter Bürger, in which these movements fundamentally relied upon the "autonomous status of art within bourgeois society" (Bürger 24).
7. Much of this work followed the criticized exhibit at the New York Museum of Modern Art, "High & Low: Modern Art and Popular Culture" (1990–1991).
8. Crow does grant certain modernist artists a different status, allowing them a less cynical relationship to mass culture. Turning to Maurice de Vlaminck's *Houses at Chatou* (1904–1905), he writes: "A child of the suburban working class, Vlaminck in these paintings was no tourist, and this set him apart from his colleagues" Braque and Picasso (31). Vlaminck is exempted from the guilt of elitism for having been raised in a certain class. Crow may well be correct that Vlaminck's paintings more sympathetically or even more accurately engage the experiences of the working classes they represent, but this purely bio-graphical explanation of class identification leaves crucial aesthetic and ethical questions about the form of representation of the ethnographic or primitive "popular" unanswered.
9. Translated by Fox and White as *Communication, Culture and Hegemony*. The translations that follow, however, are my own.
10. *Folletines* are cheaply published pamphlets, and *literatura de cordel* are booklets that hang from a piece of string [*cordel*] in the stands where they are sold. They tend to be long narrative poems with woodcut illustrations on the cover, often done by the poet himself.
11. The bibliography about the discursivity of race is large, notably by the group of scholars examining the "coloniality of power" including Aníbal Quijano, Walter Mignolo, and Immanuel Wallerstein.

12. Critiques of *mestizaje* have rejected its erasure of contemporary indigenous peoples, cultures, and languages, and argue that Vasconcelos's vision of a slightly bronzen cosmic race extends nineteenth-century racist ideologies into the twentieth century. For a trenchant critique of representations of *mestizaje* in Mexico, see Lund, "They Were Not a Barbarous Tribe." See also Tenorio, "A Tropical Cuauhtemoc."
13. This definition of aesthetics also brings in Michel de Certeau's strategies, tactics and *uses* or practice of everyday life.
14. Described by Ehrenberg in his essay "La desobedencia como método de trabajo" as "[el] medio popular por excelencia."
15. Although figures vary from source to source, in 1921 approximately 70% of Mexico was illiterate, and by 1940 that number had fallen to 45%. It is important to note that the illiteracy rate for the capital city in the same year was by contrast only 25%, in comparison to states such as Chiapas (80%), Querétaro (78%), and Guerrero (82%). Moreno y García surveys data from the other Latin American countries, and compares it to the United States. In 1920, 75% of Brazil was illiterate, while in 1930, the United States only had a rate of 4.3%. He notes, however, that African-Americans and immigrants in the United States suffer from much worse access to education and higher rates of illiteracy (Moreno y García 40–41).
16. For more on this, see my "Facing Brazil."
17. Editorial, *S. Paulo* 1.1 (1936): n.p.
18. Anderson made this argument about print media for the nineteenth century, and has been roundly criticized for ignoring the specificity of nationalist discourse and the history of independence in the Americas (See Castro-Klarén and Chasteen). As much as Anderson's chronology is to be debated, in this volume Beatriz González-Stephan argues that nationalist discourse truly appeared in Latin America in the early twentieth century, precisely during the movements and moments under discussion here. Anderson's general observation about the importance of print culture is relevant, therefore, if not attuned to the specific histories of the Americas.
19. *Base* 1: 2 (September 1933): 25.
20. For a description of the journal as political propaganda and more details about its graphic design innovations, see Mendes, "A revista S. PAULO."
21. Editorial, *S. Paulo* 1.1 (1936): n.p.
22. *S. Paulo* 1.6 (1936): n.p.
23. The newspaper was forced to close in 1932.
24. Described as an "Estado Novo ideologue" (Johnson 8). For a sophisticated analysis of Ricardo's major poetic work *Martim Cererê* [1928] in relation to Vargas's dictatorship, see Luiza Franco Moreira, "All Silent . . . Only One Singing: Contradictions in the Brazil of Cassiano Ricardo's *Martim Cererê,*" *Cultural Critique* 38 (1997–1998): 107–135.
25. Mário de Andrade worked for the government and as a correspondent from *Diário Nacional* because he did not enjoy the financial security of his fellow modernist, Oswald de Andrade. Space constraints preclude a full discussion of certain modernists as professional writers, but it is important to emphasize that their participation in the popular was not purely due to an ethical stance

but also the need to pay their bills. I do not think that this diminishes the aesthetic and theoretical importance of these works, and in fact underwrites the discussion of the "utility" of modernist art at the conclusion of this article. On the differing class backgrounds of Brazilian modernists, see Miceli, *Intelectuais e classe dirigente no Brasil, 1920–1945*.

26. *The Apprentice Tourist* was never published in de Andrade's lifetime. The manuscript combined elements of a travel diary, ethnography, folkloric collections, poetry and fiction, and included photographs that were both experimental and documents of his travel up the Amazon River, and the people and cultures he encountered.

27. Esboço dum *Programa Geral de Cultura Artistica Nacional*, found in the Arquivo Mário de Andrade, Instituto de Estudos Brasileiros, Universidade de São Paulo (MA-MMA-59 Manuscritos Mário de Andrade).

28. The importance of this change in name might be considered in comparison the famous Museo Nacional de Antropología e Historia in Mexico City, which similarly makes the implicit argument that the diverse indigenous groups belong to the country's past rather than its present. Given the fact that according to the 1990 census more than 5 million Mexicans over the age of five speak indigenous languages—a number more likely to err on the low rather than high side—the insertion of the word "history" in these titles is quite powerful.

29. Archivo General de la Nación, Período Revolucionario, Gobernación, Caja 206 Exp 12 Fs 2: On letterhead from the Secretaría de Hacienda y Crédito Público, to the Departamento de Pago: "Con referencia al atento oficio de esa Secretaría No. 5836, girado el 8 del actual por su Sección 1/a., tengo la honra de manifestar a Ud. que hoy ordeno a la Tesorería General de la Nación, abone a la cuenta de esa propia Secretaría, la suma de $3,247.00 (tres mil doscientos cuarenta y siete pesos oro nacional), que importó la operación de la venta hecha a la Empresa Editorial de 'El Universal,'—de cincuenta rollos de papel, con peso de 9.550 kilos, al precio actual de plaza de $0.34 kilo"; signed "Por orden del Secretario, El Oficial Mayor en funciones de Subsecretario," March 12, 1917.

30. This liberal economic model in no way precludes a racist attitude, which appears in his hispanophilia and proclamation that "autochthonous elements" have not sufficiently developed the country, and Mexico needs new immigration. This statement only slightly veils Palavicini's desire for the kind of ideal of "blanqueamiento" [whitening] by means of the recruitment of European workers that took place in countries such as Brazil and Argentina.

31. Certainly politics took their toll on these publications, as individual editors were fired, exiled (including Palavicini himself from 1927 to 1929), or had their newspaper shut down as a result of critiques of the current *caudillo*.

32. In addition to *El Universal Ilustrado*, *Excelsior*, founded in 1917 by the businessman Rafael Alducin, "appealed to all sorts of populist recourses to create a public: promotion of Mother's Day, competitions for babies' photographs, etc." (Aurrecoechea and Barta 202). When the director, Rodrigo de Llano, supported the rebelling *cristeros* (a religious uprising in Mexico, 1926–1929), the government bought the newspaper and installed its own director.

33. For more on the feminization of illustrated journals in Mexico, see my "Engendering Nation."
34. "El Caballero Puck" was a pseudonym for Manuel Horta (Ruiz Castañeda and Márquez Acevedo 396).
35. Horta, "Nuestras artistas en antifaz," emphasis added.
36. First published in 1922 as the weekly novel of *El Universal Ilustrado*, *La señorita etcétera* has since been canonized as a classic (elite) avant-garde text.
37. Villaurrutia, "La máscara," 35.
38. It is important to keep the social context in mind with this idea of "function." The women stars who are pictured here, like so many other women, literally went to work during and after the Mexican Revolution.
39. While several books containing these texts have been published, they tend to downplay his investment in them, and do not analyze them as serious sites for literary experimentation. Enrique Sacerio-Garí and Emir Rodríguez Monegal state from the beginning that they will ignore the question whether the housewives who were the readers of *El Hogar* appreciated the texts. María Kodama reveals that Borges published in the magazine between 1925 and 1962, and even reproduces images of the mixed media, photographic design that filled the pages, but does not analyze their impact on his avant-garde aesthetic. See Borges, *Textos cautivos. Ensayos y reseñas en "El Hogar" (1926–1939)*; and Kodama, *Borges en El Hogar, 1935–1958*.

Works Cited

Aguilar Platas, Blanca. "1917–1934: los caudillos," in *Las publicaciones periódicas y la historia de México (ciclo de conferencias)*, coord. Aurora Cano Andaluz. Mexico: UNAM, 1995. 129–138.

de Andrade, Mário. "A escrava que não é Isaura." *Obra imatura*, 3rd edition. Belo Horizonte: Livraria Martins Editora, 1980. [1925].

———. *Paulicea desvairada. Hallucinated City. A Bilingual Edition*, trans. Jack E. Tomlins. Kingsport, TN: Vanderbilt UP, 1968. [1922].

———. "Toada." *S. Paulo* 1: 8 (August 1936): n.p.

———. *O turista aprendiz*, ed. and comp. Telê Ancona Lopez. São Paulo: Livraria Duas Cidades, 1978.

de Andrade, Oswald. "Manifesto of Pau-Brasil Poetry." Stella M. de Sá Rego, trans. *Latin American Review* 14.27 (1986): 184–187. [1924].

Aurrecoechea, Juan Manuel, and Armando Bartra. *Puros cuentos. Historia de la historieta en México*, Vols. 1–3. Mexico: Grijalbo, 1994.

Borges, Jorge Luis. *Textos cautivos. Ensayos y reseñas en "El Hogar" (1926–1939)*, ed. Enrique Sacerio-Garí y Emir Rodríguez Monegal. Barcelona: Marginales Tuquets Editores, 1986.

Buell, Lawerence. "Introduction: In Pursuit of Ethics." *PMLA* 114: 1 (1999): 7–19.

Bürger, Peter. *Theory of the Avant-Garde*, trans. Michael Shaw. Minneapolis: U of Minnesota P, 1984.

Cano Andaluz, Aurora, coord. *Las publicaciones periódicas y la historia de México (ciclo de conferencias)*. Mexico: UNAM, 1995.

Castro-Klarén, Sara, and John Charles Chasteen, eds. *Beyond Imagined Communities: Reading and Writing the Nation in Nineteenth-Century Latin America*. Baltimore: Johns Hopkins UP, 2003.

Castro Ruiz, Miguel, and Alfonso Maya Nava, dir. *Historia de El Universal: El Gran Diario de México*. Mexico: El Universal Compañia Periodística Nacional S.A. de C.V., 1991.

Corral Corral, Manuel. *La ciencia de la comunicación en México: orígen, desarrollo y situación actual*. Mexico: Editorial Trillas, 1986.

Crow, Thomas. "Modernism and Mass Culture in the Visual Arts." *Modern Art in the Common Culture*. New Haven: Yale UP, 1996. 3–38.

Ehrenberg, Felipe. "La desobedencia como método de trabajo," in *Aspectos de la fotografía en México*, ed. Rogelio Villarreal. Mexico: Editorial Mexicana, 1981. 94.

Franco, Jean. "What's in a Name? Popular Culture Theories and Their Limitations." *Studies in Latin American Popular Culture* 1 (1982): 5–15.

Gabara, Esther. "Engendering Nation: *Las bellas artes públicas* and the Mexican Photo-Essay, 1920–1940," *Yearbook of Comparative and General Literature* 49 (2001): 139–154.

———. "Facing Brazil: The Problem of Portraiture and a Modernist Sublime," *CR: The New Centennial Review* 4.2 (2004): 33–76.

García Canclini, Nestor. *Hybrid Cultures: Strategies for Entering and Leaving Modernity*, trans. Christopher L. Chiappari and Silvia L. López. Minneapolis: U of Minnesota P, 1995.

González Marín, Silvia. "La prensa y el poder político en el gobierno del general Lázaro Cárdenas," in *Las publicaciones periódicas y la historia de México (ciclo de conferencias)*, coord. Cano Andaluz: 157–168.

Greenberg, Clement. "Avant-Garde and Kitsch." *Art and Culture. Critical Essays*. Boston: Beacon Press, 1989 [1939].

Horta, Manuel ("El Caballero Puck"). "Las máscaras." *El Universal Ilustrado* IX: 460 (March 4, 1926): 28–29.

———. "Nuestros artistas en antifaz," *El Universal Ilustrado* IX:460 (March 4, 1926): 29–30.

Johnson, Randal. "The Institutionalization of Brazilian Modernism." *Brasil/Brazil* 3.4 (1990): 5–24.

Kaz, Leonel. *A Revista no Brasil*. Editorial director Thomaz Souto Corrêa. São Paulo: Editora Abril, 2000.

Kodama, María. *Borges en El Hogar, 1935–1958*. Buenos Aires: Emecé Editores, 2000.

Loyo, Engracia. "Lectura para el pueblo, 1921–1940," *Historia mexicana* 33.3 (1984): 298–345.

Lund, Joshua. "They Were Not a Barbarous Tribe," *Journal of Latin American Cultural Studies* 12: 2 (2003): 171–189.

Maples Arce, Manuel, Germán List Arzubide, Salvador Gallardo et al. "Manifiesto Estridentista Num. 2," in Jorge Schwartz *Las vanguardias latinoamericanas*. 170–171.

Martín-Barbero, Jesús. *Communication, Culture and Hegemony: From the Media to Mediations*, trans. Elizabeth Fox and Robert A. White, introduction by Philip Schlesinger. London: SAGE Publications, 1993.

Martín-Barbero, Jesús. *De los medios a las mediaciones. Comunicación, cultura y hegemonía*. Barcelona: Editorial Gustavo Gili, 1987.

Mendes, Ricardo. "A revista S. PAULO: a cidade nas bancas," *Imagens* 3 (December 1994): 91–97.

Miceli, Sérgio. *Intelectuais e classe dirigente no Brasil, 1920–1945*. São Paulo: DIFEL, 1979.

Moreno y García, Roberto. *Analfabetismo y cultural popular en América*. Mexico: Editorial Atlante, 1941.

Noriega Hope, Carlos. *Carlos Noriega Hope, 1896–1934*. Mexico: INBA, 1959.

Ortiz Gaitán, Julieta. *Imágenes del deseo: Arte y publicidad en la prensa ilustrada mexicana (1894–1939)*. Mexico: UNAM, 2003.

Palavicini, Félix F. *Mi vida revolucionaria*. Mexico: Ediciones Botas, 1937.

Poole, Deborah. *Vision, Race and Modernity: A Visual Economy of the Andean World*. Princeton: Princeton UP, 1997.

Rama, Angel. *The Lettered City*, ed. and trans. John Charles Chasteen. Durham: Duke UP, 1996.

Reyes Palma, Francisco. "Arte Funcional y vanguardia (1921–1952)." *Modernidad y modernización en el arte mexicano, 1920–1960*, ed. Olivier Debroise and Graciela Reyes. Mexico: CONACULTA, 1991.

Ricardo, Cassiano. "Canto da Raça." *S. Paulo* 1.6 (1936): n.p.

———. "Moça tomando café." *S. Paulo* 1.9 (1936): n.p.

Rowe, William, and Vivian Schelling. *Memory and Modernity: Popular Culture in Latin America*. London: Verso, 1991.

Rubenstein, Anne. *Bad Language, Naked Ladies, and Other Threats to the Nation: A Political History of Comic Books in Mexico*. Durham: Duke UP, 1998.

Sarlo, Beatriz. *Una modernidad periférica: Buenos Aires 1920 y 1930*. Buenos Aires: Nueva Visión, 1988.

Schwartz, Jorge. *Las vanguardias latinoamericanas. Textos programáticos y críticos*, Portuguese texts trans. Estela dos Santos. Madrid: Cátedra, 1991.

Tenorio, Mauricio. "A Tropical Cuauhtemoc: Celebrating the Cosmic Race at the Guanabara Bay," *Anales del Instituto de Investigaciones Estéticas* 65 (1994): 93–137.

Unruh, Vicky. *Latin American Vanguards: The Art of Contentious Encounters*. Berkeley: U of California P, 1994.

Villaurrutia, Xavier. "La máscara," *El Universal Ilustrado* IX: 460 (March 4, 1926): 35, 66.

Williams, Daryle. *Culture Wars in Brazil: The First Vargas Regime, 1930–1945*. Durham: Duke UP, 2001.

Part III

The Limits of Literature

5

A FEW NOTES ON CONSTRUCTED WORLDS: THE CONTRADICTORY LEGACY OF PAST DECADES

Sergio Chejfec
Translated by Heather Cleary

In addition to the dissolution and complex reconstruction of thought regarding the social and the cultural, divergent ways of thinking about literature have long existed in Latin America. These currents touch upon its methods, its character and, above all, its relevance to social discourse. Literature has lost its density, aesthetically as well as ideologically—at least, the density that we are or were accustomed to finding in it has changed. Through an examination of several Latin American narratives from the 1960s and 1970s, I seek to describe both the anticipation of these (future) modalities and the moments of explicit resistance to the aesthetic mandates of the time. Their gestures of resistance rendered these texts, in a sense, illegible, reinforcing not only a dominant strain of critical representation but also a mode of reading, both of which tended to reduce the aesthetic scope visible in Latin American literature. This scene is further complicated when one considers its variable "ethics," in the sense bestowed upon the word in recent decades: the ethics of writing, of action, of politics. It is impossible to ignore the sense of transformation inherent to these offerings, or the contradictory conclusions that can be drawn from terms considered so diffuse. This tension defined schools and modes of representation that form, in a contemporary reading, an unexpected constellation: worlds at once central and cast aside.

By way of introduction, it is my hope that the following passage will illustrate the ways that literature was able, decades ago, to present itself as a dialogue with the outside world and was able to do so with energy and spontaneity. I chose, then, to begin with this quote in order to situate it half-way between the epigraph and the document.

No hay acontecimientos en los cuales podamos participar, ni aquí ni en ninguna parte del mundo. Él dice que los dos estábamos hechos para acontecimientos del futuro y que nacimos antes de tiempo, y que de todos modos no habrá futuro y que por lo tanto no vale la pena hacer nada. (Rodríguez 47)

[There are no events we can take part in, not here, not anywhere. He says we were created for future events and that we were born too early, but that there won't be a future, anyway, so there's no point in doing anything.]

These words are taken from a 1963 Venezuelan novel; they are spoken in Paris, where much of the story takes place. Through the location of Paris, we can infer one possible meaning of the sensation of abnormality and pessimism felt by the youths of this time, at least within the context of European literature and cinema. The young men of Godard's early films, little brothers of those in Pavese and Camus, relatives of the youths in Latin America penned by Juan José Saer, were all then as little known as his characters. Suffering is perceived as a passing feeling because the events of the future, whatever they may be, will either displace or negate it. And all the while life goes on, breeding rebellion and disillusionment.

Read in a Latin American context, however, these words become enigmatic in another sense. Contrary to the vast majority of the literature of its time, as well as to that which preceded and followed it, one does not find in this passage the desire to settle accounts with history. It seems, instead, to be the manifesto of individuals who choose to exist at the margins: at the margins of their country, from which they are physically distant, at the margins of the city they inhabit, in which they struggle to survive and, as will be discussed shortly, outside the literature that had supposedly provided them the form, or medium, to cultivate experience.

These words, then, are uttered in opposition to the incipient dominant perception of Latin American literature as a vehicle of social meaning, which requires expression in order to be made real, and of the union of art and politics. They are spoken near the end of the book and epitomize, perhaps, the capricious ventures and claims laid out in it from the start. The novel is called *Al sur del Equanil* [South of Equanil], and it is Renato Rodríguez's first. Equanil is a well-known sedative and muscle relaxant, common in France and other countries. In the novel, this name carries a number of valences: it is a cipher and a plotline, a medicine and an identity. Beginning with its title, the novel brings spatial relations into play: the South as latitude, of course, but at the same time as a relative position, something placed beneath something else. Equanil also represents an emotional state, it is the suffering from which one cannot rise to the surface; it becomes an indirect reference to the geographical origins of the author and his travels in Colombia, Ecuador, Peru, and Chile. This "little white pill," as it is called in the novel, is also obviously a medicine and, above all, a commercial brand. We see, therefore, in this title a trace of the culture of that time, albeit indirectly: the pop era and the incorporation of brand names, mass consumption, labels and serials that are used in this case not playfully, or as criticism or celebration, but rather as a site of irony—mental degeneration has been co-opted by the commercial market, which attaches its name to the decline in order to define the space of the experience, as it would any other product.

I also chose this passage because it is a statement that appeals to a sense of history (of events, the world, the future) from a point of extreme subjectivity—in this case, unfulfilled. It is an outcry à la Sorel, in which traces of the Stendhalian gaze, suspended between the first person and the external world (forging the way for the modern novel), can be seen. Parts of this mandate were taken up in Latin American literature, sometimes too literally: it meant the conquest of France, or Europe, and that those who were charged with the task were artists and writers, at once the inheritors and the precursors of this sensibility, according to whom the attributes of modernity and nationality were defined. By the early 1960s, these designs had been shattered or reduced to rhetorical avatars: the theme of the Creole intellectual taking Paris by storm was reduced to a leitmotif oscillating between the picaresque and the melodramatic, preserving (at times) its past symbolic weight, yet transforming it into a false measure.

A short work by Sebastián Salazar Bondy will serve to illustrate the devaluation of the above themes: *Pobre gente de Paris* [The Poor of Paris] (1958) underscores the physical struggle of the poor Latin American (youth, student, artist or parvenu, or, perhaps, bohemian—like the characters of Rodríguez) in Paris, that is, the losing battle against poverty, hunger, and cold, the frustration of facing a woman in whom he discovers something he would rather not know. This work is unusual and deserves a specialized reading, although the tendency is to view it more as a signpost of lingering social problems than as a literary object unto itself, due to its proliferation of certain clichés. It should first be noted that the work presents a surprising counterpoint to another by the same author, published six years later and much better known, *Lima la horrible* [Lima the Horrible]. Both cities, Paris and Lima, serve as a backdrop for the staging of this Latin American fatalism: the failing struggle with the mundane in one and the impossibility of history in the other. Taken from another perspective, we can see the text as evidence (yet another example in an extensive inventory) of a mode of representation that has lost its illustrative capacity, showing itself to be the contentious parody of models reproduced in excess, and not only in literature. In this sense, Salazar Bondy would be the antipode of Rodríguez: he is pleased that Paris has ceased to be a Mecca.

Rodríguez is one of the various (who knows if there are many or few—imprecise terms, in any event) ex-centric Latin American writers, not only because he chose to distance himself from standard literary behavior, determined by the needs of the publishing industry, but because he constructs his narratives with pointed unconventionality. With the exception of his most recent work, his books were generally funded by friends, appearing as hushed emanations from a life far removed from the urban sphere and the cultural-institutional protocols so pronounced in Venezuela. His denunciation of the literary establishment (publishers, foundations, critics, academics, awards, etc.), an extension of his tirade against institutions in general, expresses a resistance to a form of media that was, due largely to rapid urbanization and population growth, undergoing an opulent and engulfing period of modernization. Rodríguez is one of the first generation of intellectuals from the interior without extensive formal education who begin to replace those of aristocratic, metropolitan origins such as Juan Liscano and Arturo Uslar Pietri. But unlike, for example, Oswaldo Trejo, Salvador Garmendia or Vicente Gerbassi, all with similar trajectories to his own, Rodríguez chooses to reject the institution. This tension between the notion of art founded in spontaneity and voluntary action and that of its professionalization by the State (and occasionally by the market) has existed for decades in Venezuela, shaping aesthetic ideologies, and remains present even today. Rodríguez's work can be seen as an icon of this persistent tension and as a model of its points of intersection, one that illustrates the many ethical and political ramifications of its possible articulations.

Essentially speaking, *Al sur del Equanil* conveys a literary formation and, simultaneously, modes of both its adoption and its rejection. The moment of its rejection and that of its adoption are, it would seem, one and the same because literature, in order to be such, must strive to be less literary. The compositional style adopted by Rodríguez is similar to that of his later books: a narrative develops and dissolves according to the flow of anecdotes and associations. The story at its center is maintained, but is elaborated through the interposition of accounts and characters, many of whose names frequently change, mainly because these characters pertain to a different tier of the narrative: interposed accounts that document the staggered progress of a developing writer. It is a means of representing experience, in which chance is ever-present. What we have, then, are unfixed identities and ambiguous plotlines; a testimonial quality (in this case the verist cachet of the diary as literary utopia) combined with a system opposed to any illusion of realism, and half-disguised allusions that suggest an extensive yet disorganized library.

Given this basic description, we may move on to more notable aspects of the matter at hand, such as the uncertain aesthetic status of the work and its problematic position with regard to its own intentions. The year is 1963, and we are faced with an author who, on one hand, writes without literary discretion and, on the other, idealizes the construction of imperfect books as a means of uncovering the falsities of the intellectual world. And yet, the themes mobilized to this end are not outside literary tradition; on the contrary, they are acutely adherent to it. *Al sur del Equanil* can also be read as a cross-section of the phantoms and preoccupations of Latin American writers from the nineteenth century on: professionalization, fame, the relation between experience and truth, the mythos surrounding the author and the creation of the work, the rebellion against institutions. We see, then, in Rodríguez an oppositional stance, albeit one marked by undertones of acquiescence. He offers a reading of something that was in the air, although it dealt with a different aspect of the times: 1963 is also the year of *Rayuela* [Hopscotch]. In this work, Cortázar gives rise to, among other things, the professionalization of the Latin American writer during the 1960s and the following decades. Into this web of literary and political strategizing, in which Cortázar will establish himself as the conductor of his own private orchestra for the remainder of his life, Rodríguez asserts himself (one might say meddles) by writing, in Paris, a book that could not quite be called contrary (for that, he would have had to have known of *Rayuela*) but instead, simply inimical—irreconcilable, yet existing within the same sphere. In this sense, we can read Rodríguez's novel as the account of an intellectual disappointment, or betrayal, and the need to refute the literary using only the weapons of the literati. The sociological backdrop of apocalyptists and conformists could likely account for the setting and some of the driving forces behind the novel; but I wish to point out that this, being given, does not address the strange aspirations of the text, which seeks not to create a rupture, but rather a murmur: a subterranean literary existence wavering like a whisper.

At the time of its publication, *Al sur del Equanil* garnered very little attention, and the notice it did receive was due almost exclusively to its bizarre composition. Nevertheless, years later, as we attend to the gradual diminishment of literature witnessed in the recent past, that is, as a discourse in which the ideologies and truths of our communities collide, works such as Rodríguez's engage the critical imagination and tend to rearrange both our conceptions of the literary and our libraries. On one hand, there is the issue of taste: Latin American literature has moved away from the canon of the 1970s in a relatively ambivalent way, and in this sense these books, read today, are able to bring to the fore from their position at the margins the incipient extinction of the so-called Boom and its related movements. On the other hand, there is a cultural sensibility inclined toward the hybrid, the less generalized. A new edict for books, authors, and subject matter is at issue; we will therefore need to consider different interpretive genealogies, ones that might shed some light on these questions.

This is not to say that in this pursuit we have at hand only unknown, unpolished, or unfinished works. There are also enigmatic works, those silenced as a result of a lack of proper conditions for them to be read. An example of this is *El apando* [The Cell], written in the late 1950s during José Revueltas's final incarceration. The author's biography is relatively well-known: militant and communist intellectual, autodidact from a catholic upbringing, author and screenwriter, among other things. Unlike Renato Rodríguez, whose works inscribe themselves within the 1960s avant-garde, Revueltas entered that era with a body of work that was already formally developed and somewhat well known, with strong realist leanings and a focus on economic injustice and political and social criticism. His books are, generally speaking, structured around rather predictable symbolic systems and tend to feature schematically portrayed characters and themes.

In the case of *El apando*, however, these standard elements are arranged in a new way, producing a surprising effect. The card catalog has been shuffled. The story is only fifty-four pages long and might be read as a soliloquy on dissociation that depicts, as though it were a myth or fable, the primal actions of fallen characters who have no past, no spiritual being, no moral virtue, and certainly no political identity. They are simply anonymous sociologists; poor and imprisoned—even those that are not behind bars could not be said to be free. Yet this anonymity makes them, paradoxically, all the more singular. Psychological depth is also diminished (and in this instance of narrative restraint, we see faint traces of socialist literature's mistrust of this brand of profundity). One might be tempted to say that the text conveys the essential without embellishment, yet this is not the case, as Revueltas employs a style grounded in redundancy, in the damning tone of a religious litany, and in abundant punctuation. What, then, causes the effect of austerity, of narrative economy? The concentration and economy of action, for one thing, and the mystery behind these events, suspended only in the moment of their description. Let us examine a passage that I feel illustrates this point:

> Meche no podía formular de un modo coherente y lógico, ni con palabras ni con pensamientos, lo que le pasaba, el género de este acontecer enrarecido y el lenguaje nuevo, secreto y de peculiaridades únicas, privativas, de que se servían las cosas para expresarse, aunque más bien no eran las cosas en general ni en su conjunto, sino cada una de ellas por separado, cada cosa aparte, específica, con sus palabras, su emoción y la red subterránea de comunicaciones y significaciones, que al margen del tiempo y el espacio, las ligaba a unas con otras, por más distantes que estuviesen entre sí y las convertía en símbolos y claves imposibles de ser comprendidas por nadie que no perteneciera, y en la forma más concreta, a la conjura biográfica en que las cosas mismas se autoconstituían en su propio y hermético disfraz. (Revueltas, 29–30)

> [Meche couldn't formulate, either in thoughts or words, a logical and coherent means of expressing what was happening to him, a definition of this unusual occurrence, this new language, secret and of unique, intrinsic qualities, utilized by all things in their expression, although perhaps it wasn't things in general or collectively, but rather each thing individually, each unto its own, specific, with its words, its emotions, and the underground network of communication and signification, which, at the limit of space and time, joins them, one to another, no matter how distant they might have been, and turns them into signs and symbols impossible for anyone not belonging, in a very substantial way,

to the biographical conspiracy in which these very objects constitute themselves within their own, hermetic disguise, to understand.]

It is a complex and abstract passage, the importance of which resides not in the information it conveys, but in the figuration of experience that it sets forth. It exists on the verge of analogy, and this is most likely why it closes with the recognition of the impossibility of expressing that which it had intended; and yet it manages that very thing, as if with a "mission accomplished." The experience is an erotic one, and it is associated with the physical offences suffered by the girlfriend of one of the prisoners as she enters the jail. I propose, however, that we may also read it as an example of the tone of this story, of its musical register and its mode of representation: objects come into contact in this state of dispersion and are unified only in passing, in the moment they describe one another, because before and after that moment they belong to the murky realm of the undefined.

Indeterminacy is a tangible potentiality that threatens the substance of the narrative; one might say that it is its very essence, wrought from anonymity and vulnerability. Revueltas rescues the text from this indeterminacy with a binary gesture, adopting a distant and cultured approach, as seen in his mythological and biblical references, and juxtaposing baroque language and appeals to linguistic naturalism. Not only do the characters speak according to their circumstance, the narration is also peppered with colloquialism, generally toward the end of enumerations, in order to emphasize the harshness of what is being described. I believe that *El apando* calls into question, in a subtle way, some of the dominant literary concepts of its time. The most important of these, perhaps, would be the degree of truth attributed to literature. Although the text does not contradict this belief, the use of a compositional style based on distance and complexity, yet without resorting to exoticism, to depict this sordid narrative must have made it highly unlikely that anyone at all would read it. The fact that this text was written by Revueltas makes it all the more surprising and, in a way, incendiary, because it comes not from a member of the avant-garde, but rather from a member, almost literally, of the rear-guard. It is possible, also, that this text announces the ideological resurgence of the author's final years, which becomes more and more complex as a breach of or response to the so-called Boom.

It is worth mentioning that, in 1969, another story in the form of a parable was published, this time a work of political pornography called *El fiord* [The Fjord], written by Argentine author Osvaldo Lamborghini. It is a relatively well-known book, and I wish to draw attention to it now as another example of the various acts of disobedience to the literary precepts issued by politicians, while forms such as the "Boom" were homogenizing a literary landscape that was already increasingly uniform. These precepts were, generally speaking, ideological and engaged not only aesthetic concerns, but the moral stature of the artists as well. Today we can see that the literature of the 1960s and the 1970s was a relatively conventional response to these tensions and that the price of this conventionality was to render invisible much that, in those years and before, had defied it.

How should we approach these texts today? On one hand, as I mentioned earlier, contemporary literary sensibilities are somewhat less transparent. Many authors and critics tend to eschew aesthetic pleasure and intellectual concord in favor of thematic analysis and textual rupture. At the same time, literary criticism—particularly throughout the academy—has focused its energies on something like a literature of diminishment, in which content is hidden or made implicit by various abstractive techniques. We see that these modalities are not necessarily anything new and that, as we have seen at other times, they both demand and suffer from their own genealogies. One of the greatest problems surrounding the boom has been its treatment at the hands of critics, who isolate it from other Latin American literary movements, rendering opaque its strategies, continuities, and disjunctions. It would be disheartening to see this gesture repeated on the eclectic and sinuous literature of today.

At the same time, no consideration of the Latin American literary canon should overlook the progressive, or leftist, ideological landscape with which these works aligned themselves. This landscape was tied up in the historical. Although we can assume that political regulation ultimately saturated or co-opted aesthetic articulations (producing, at times, antagonistic texts such as those described here), this would not disallow the possibility—for some, the necessity—of literature's aligning itself with the progressive, redefining existing notions of its commitment to and engagement with the social. This is in large part because, as I suggested earlier, we live in a time in which socioeconomic conditions have, generally speaking, not gotten better but instead have either deteriorated or been fundamentally altered. These outdated works, therefore, speak to us of an antiquated understanding, obsolete in many ways, yet authentic in its transitory moment: this pact offers both a promise and a threat to contemporary literature. It suggests that engagement with the social and the political is possible, but that the realization of this desire is inherently imperfect.

Works Cited

Lamborghini, Osvaldo. *El fiord*. Buenos Aires: Ediciones Chinatown, 1969.
Revueltas, José. *El apando*. México: Ediciones Era, 1999.
Rodríguez, Renato. *Al Sur del Equanil*, 4th edition. Caracas: Libros RAR, 1985.
Salazar Bondy, Sebastián. *Lima la horrible*, Ediciones Era, México, 1964.
———. *Pobre gente de París*. Lima: Librería Editorial Juan Mejía Baca, 1958.

6

SAYING THE UNSAYABLE: SAER, OR FOR AN ETHICS OF WRITING

Gabriel Riera

> Sociological criticism tends to exaggerate the features of unreality it finds in literature. It reduces the data it extracts from literature to sociological criteria, while the fragments that resist this simplification are often declared of no value. In this sense the sociologist behaves not unlike the common reader, a mere consumer: if it is true that the former does not skip pages while reading, he certainly interprets what he reads by passing them over and thus shapes an abstract context for the work, which is thus endowed with a fundamental unreality.
>
> Juan José Saer, El concepto de ficción, 254

> Language would exceed the limits of what is thought, by suggesting, letting be understood without ever making understandable (en laissant sous-entendre, sans jamais faire entendre) *an implication of meaning distinct from that which comes to signs from the simultaneity of systems or the logical definition of concepts. This possibility (vertu) is laid bare in the poetic said*...
>
> Emmanuel Levinas, Otherwise than Being, 170

In this chapter, I pose the question of the *otherwise* and its *reading*, that is, of the *ethical potentialities* of literary language, and how reading can be up to the task of preserving it. Two preliminary remarks are in order: the term otherwise [*autrement*] in this volume's title partially translates the expression that Emmanuel Levinas coins in *Otherwise than Being, or Beyond Essence* to refer to what, in language, exceeds the imperialism of the same, the violence of the order of discourse, not without leaving the inscriptions of its proper density and alterity. The complete form of Levinas's expression is the barbarism "otherwise than being," in which the adverb "otherwise" does not modify any entity or action (it does not indicate another modality of doing the same), but rather the adverbial character of "the otherwise than being," the modality by which the other comes to language beyond any ontological manifestation or epistemological determination. Levinas refers to what, without belonging to discourse, can only be said in terms of the order of discourse and which, consequently, supposes a form of betrayal: an unsayable saying that without exhausting itself in the contents or themes of the utterance (the said), in the values it expresses, defies the order of communicative reason and the imperialism of the concept.

It is precisely this unheard-of adventure of meaning that preserves the traces of the other, an *intrigue* beyond any ontological plot, on the reverse side of discourse (the same) that Levinas calls *ethics*.[1] This means that ethics does not refer to set rules preestablished by the content of previously defined agendas, but rather to the very density of what exceeds the order of being and discourse. It will therefore be a question of *reading the otherwise* such as it comes into the ethical horizon just outlined, as ex-position to the other of discourse *in* discourse: exposition to what exceeds the "simultaneousness of systems or the logical definition of concepts" (AE 262/ OB 170).

The object of this paper is to read the ethical potentialities of literary language ("the otherwise than being") without reducing them to the order of discourse.[2] I am *not* proposing a Levinasian reading of a literary text, but rather a reading of the "otherwise than being," of its modality and density, through the lens of a literary project. My aim is to make explicit a praxis of writing that exposes itself to the real, to the unsayable other, that manages to inscribe and preserve existence's inprescriptive fragments and that, therefore, compels us to elaborate protocols of reading capable of accounting for such ethical potentialities.

The focus of this chapter is the work of the Argentine writer Juan José Saer and in particular his novel *La pesquisa* [*The Investigation*].[3] I present the Levinasian problematic of "the otherwise than being" in terms of what Saer calls "the (literary) *fragments that resist the simplification*" that sociological and cultural criticism often perform upon literary texts. Where Levinas speaks of the order of discourse (totality), I speak of the State and Market (and of the social sciences that tend to prop up that order): these are the two targets of Saer's narrative poetics. Where Levinas speaks of the said as the dimension of the same, I speak in terms of the detective genre's conventions, and of the Oedipal metanarrative (the concomitant *fantasma* [fantasy] that sustains it). Where Levinas aims to bring to discourse the "otherwise than being," Saer aims to configure encounters with the real. And finally, where Levinas speaks of the saying that subtracts itself from the said, I speak in terms of a writing of the affects [*grafía de los afectos*] that has to be situated "on this side" of the symbolic or discursive order.

The reader will note that I recast the field of the "otherwise than being" in terms of a psychoanalytic problematic; this is demanded by the subject matter of Saer's text. It is important to keep in mind that the real in question also characterizes itself for being impossible and for resisting the symbolic order, for manifesting itself as its excess, as a saying that must unsay the said.

Anomaly, or for an Ethics of Writing

Characterized by an uncommon coherence and rigor, Juan José Saer's writing defies simple categories. In both his fictional and essayistic writing, Saer defamiliarizes the reader by questioning some of his most cherished certainties, especially those having to do with the role ascribed to Latin American literature, the uses of prose and poetry in the present, and the relation between language and the mass media. In the 1970s, European critics saw the novel's future in the Latin American literature then being produced[4]; this was a future epitomized by the novel of the Boom and magical realism, where novelistic intrigue still played a central role and there was an unproblematic contiguity between reality and language. To this view Saer responded by declaring that the novel is a historically finished genre.[5] And if Latin American intellectuals enthusiastically endorsed the Baroque as a way of characterizing the continent's permanent modernity, constructed out of the cultural debris from the centers of power,[6] Saer posited a "literature without attributes."[7] Critics have hardly begun to assess the implications of a project such as Saer's that places itself against the grain of dominant cultural discourses and refuses to subordinate literary writing to any preexisting agenda.

Neither "Latin American" à la Boom, nor "Baroque" or even "regional," Saer's literature is precisely "without attributes" and it is also so because of its "eccentricity" with respect to the Argentine literary canon. It therefore cannot be considered the expression of a particular personality trait or the endorsement of a reactive ideology, but rather the mark of literature's loyalty to its own postartistic condition.

Saer's is not an idealistic gesture that seeks to preserve the purity of the literary against the invasive threat of more popular cultural manifestations that are, perhaps, better equipped to survive in a neoliberal market economy. A literature without attributes speaks of the *anomaly* that literary writing has become and, in this sense, it is also an affirmation of fidelity to a historical mutation that, by a movement that is both internal and external, has deprived literature of any certainty, of any essence able to justify its right to exist. This is a complex process through which literature, stripped of its classical attributes, exposes itself to an absence of norm—what here we will call *anomaly*.[8]

Illegitimate, orphan, and *entenada* [bastard], Saer's literary writing is loyal to its own historical regime; it is the survivor of a double disaster that put an end to the notion of writing as a social endeavor guided by an essence or regulative Idea ("Art," "Revolution") and whose legacy has been a multiplicity without figure, law, model, or canon. Without subject or object, this survivor that Saer aptly calls "writing without attributes" arranges the ruins of traditions (the center/periphery hierarchy) and genres (novel, story, poem) without covering up the void that is precisely its impossible condition of possibility (*anomaly* or lack of norm). According to its own means and procedures, it also resists the ravages of a new regulative Idea that critical discourse wishes to install in that very void: the Market. This is a regulative Idea that bars any access to what Saer's writing aims to produce: encounters with the real.

The question that guides my reading is how writing can encounter the *real*. Let me state from the outset that the prospects seem to be disheartening: the novel genre (the most regressive forms of detective fiction of the historical novel, of the family romance, and of autobiographical texts), as well as the movies of the big studios and TV (the products of the "culture industry"), provide the schemas that shape our thoughts and emotions. These schemas respond to only two criteria: gratification and profitability, thus their need for "happy endings," since they tend to affirm a general feeling of nothing really happens here. In the era of televised simulacra (embedded journalism and its symmetrical twin, reality TV), "reality" is a byproduct whose *veracity* is simply affirmed by marketing techniques and by the debris of novelistic discourses still shaped by nineteenth-century conventions, as if the achievements of the avant-gardes and neo-avant-gardes had no currency whatsoever. "Reality" is the collective of novels and discourses shaped on nineteenth-century novelistic "realist" codes; they not only condition the stereotypical roles we play in our lives, but also their low affective level of investment.

If we adapt one of Lacan's formulations, it is possible to claim that "reality" is structured like a fiction.

This fiction is held together by language and by a particular mode of speech, prose, which according to Saer is "the instrument of the State."[9] However, Saer's position consists in implementing narrative prose in opposition to the State's use, against the "reign of the communicable" and against the reductive assimilation of prose theory and that of the novel with which:

> se busca siempre cuando se la interroga... la coincidencia de texto y referente. En música, en artes plásticas, en poesía, la ausencia de referente es, por distintas, razones toleradas. La novela no goza de ese beneplácito: *está condenada a arrastrar la cruz del realismo*. A decir verdad, nadie de un modo claro sabe qué es el realismo, pero se exige de la novela que sea realista por la simple razón de que está escrita en prosa. Casi que me atrevería a definir el *realismo como el procedimiento que encarna las funciones pragmáticas generalmente atribuidas a la prosa*.
>
> [the theory of prose and the theory of the novel are confused together: what is being sought through it is the correspondence between text and referent. In music, in the plastic arts, in poetry, the absence of the referent is tolerated. The novel does not enjoy that benefit; *it is condemned to carry the cross of realism*. To be honest, no one really knows for sure what realism is, but it is demanded that the novel be realist for the simple reason that it is written in prose. I would even venture to define *realism as the procedure that embodies the pragmatic functions generally attributed to prose*.] (NO 58, emphasis mine)

If realism is threatened by a double colonization (the State and the Market) that transforms the historical critical force of this procedure into a deadweight capable of fitting in within a pragmatic economy, how can the conditions for encountering the real be created? This is the recurring question that each of Saer's texts puts into play. As one of my basic hypotheses, I posit that Saer's texts compose the "fiction" *of* this fiction ("reality") and that through this splitting they "soften" their solidified imaginary formations. This softening makes it possible to touch a point of the real in which the sense of *experience* (death, finitude, desire, joy) keeps "speaking" at a time in which nobody wants to hear or know anything of the real. The impossible and unsayable *real*, the indelible remainder, is what maintains Saer's writing in permanent tension.

The latent poem allows Saer's writing to subtract prose from the instrumental role that the state assigns it and to change its *function*.

He does so by treating the language of prose with a series of *poetic* procedures (the rectification or isolation of certain words, the intensifying expansion of a recollection, the lengthening of the phrase or the phrasing of variations, the comic's sudden outburst), in an attempt to say what exempts itself from the instrumental realism of the state and the market: the unsayable. Two additional procedures must also be added: a limited and recurring repertoire of characters and a highly circumscribed setting (the "zone," the Paraná River's coastline, but also the *pampas*). Saer's writing gives density to what subtracts itself and he does so in the realm of the prose poem. By introducing the term "unsayable," my aim is not to make Saer a mystic or a romantic. What matters here is to signal Saer's relation to a modern regime for which language's power of presentation folds itself around an enigma whose "mystery is precisely that all poetics have at their center what cannot be represented."[10]

Saer's *arte de narrar* [art of narration] refers to the very *limit* of realist prose; a limit that the poets of the "alchemie du verbe" (not only Rimbaud, Mallarmé, and Lautréamont, but also Vallejo, Darío, and Juan L. Ortíz) had to confront: "*the unsayable* is what has neither been thought nor said before the advent of the poem; it is also not the product of an intellectual and logical discovery."[11] The poem's *unsayable* becomes the point of resistance of a prose that aims to subtract itself from the prosaism of the state and the market. If the destiny of the modern poem occurs in its *becoming prose*, for Saer the destiny of prose is played out in the proximity of the prose poem, of the becoming poem of prose. This explains why Saer's writing (its rhythm, syntax, and connections) resembles more the modern poet's inhumanity than the *vraisemblance* of the "realist" novelist.

Saer is a strange poet, it is true, since his subjects do not come from the "great" lyric tradition; in his work horror, death, terror, madness, orgies, and the menace of the feminine body are all prevalent. However, his way of implementing a set of neuter directives ("neither *melancholic* nor *nostalgic*")[12] on the current situation of a writing that has left behind the "time of the promise" and knows that "here nothing is promised but the power to be faithful to what is to come"[13] allows us to speak of Saer as a (post)modern poet. Consequently, Saer's writing must be placed within the lineage of great modern literature, since in a world deprived of the promise of the Other; it consists of a descent into the very foundations of the symbolic universe. *El entenado* [*The Witness*] is a good example of how fictional writing draws the fragile frontiers of the speaking subject and touches the scene of primary repression, the bottomless point of the real. In this experience "subject" and "object" reject and confront each other so as to delve into the limit of what can be thought and said.

There is an ethics of writing in Saer since the change in the function of narrative prose shows that the writer "does not give up on his desire," to quote Lacan's famous phrase, but that on the contrary it operates under the maxim make room for your desire.[14] His loyalty to the event called "literary writing" (a writing "without attributes") is a wager against both the deadly simplifications of mediatic pragmatism and the realism that seeks to please the taste of the mass public (recall the aesthetics of the theater troop in *El entenado*). Also, his texts not only "soften" the imaginary formations of "reality" but also shape a series of scenarios that narrate the (impossible) encounters with the real. And although the subject matters Saer chooses may not seem conducive to an "elevated" aesthetic feeling, his poetic prose composes momentary clusters of beauty that render the intensity of existence's imprescriptive fragments.

Encountering the Real

> *The real? It is what resists, insists, exists irreducibly and manifests in subtracting itself as enjoyment, anxiety, death or castration.*
>
> Leclaire, Démasquer le réel, 11

In *The Investigation* (*La pesquisa*, 1994) the reader once again finds familiar signs of Saer's fictional universe: the story unfolds in the "zone" and focuses on Pichón Garay, who after a twenty-year absence returns to his birthplace and recounts the crimes that occurred at the Leon Blum Square in Paris, as well as the investigation that Inspector Morvan conducted to solve them. It is telling that in what appears to be a detective story (the crimes, according to Pichón, "occurred in my neighborhood" and "appeared in all the papers"), there is an abundance of commentary regarding Parisian society:

> bien al abrigo en los anocheres de invierno . . . los que en otras épocas habían nacido para ser personas y ahora se habían transformado en meros compradores, en unidad de medida de los sistemas trasnacionales de crédito, en fracciones de los puntos de audiencia de la televisión y en blanco sociológica y numéricamente caracterizados de las tandas publicitarias . . . confundían el mundo con un archipiélago de representaciones electrónicas y verbales. (P 32)

[Snug and cozy on winter nights . . . those who in other eras had been born to be persons and had now been transformed into mere consumers, into units of measurement of transnational credit systems, into fractions of points of television audiences and a numerically defined social target of advertising campaigns . . . confuse the world with an archipelago of electronic and verbal representations.] (I 32)

Morvan's investigation takes place on Christmas Eve, a date that foregrounds the question and search for meaning (the incarnation of the Word in man), so even if that date motivates Pichón's criticism of consumer society and the society of the spectacle, the tenor of his statements have little to do with the conventions of the "classic" detective story.[15] Pichón, the narrator, sets the coordinates with which the story seeks to give an account of the *"impenetrable depths (fondo impenetrable)* in which the ephemeral days that civilizations endure are rooted" (P 81/ I 80, my emphasis) and to which one remains "deaf and blind" (P 81/ I 80). The text establishes an oppositional relation between the social situation (that Pichón signals intradiegetically) and the situation of three characters of *The Investigation* (Pichón, Tomatis, and Soldi), for whom, according to the external or extradiegetic narrator,

> únicamente *la conversación los ha hecho olvidarse* un par de horas del calor enbrutecedor, *del tiempo inquietante y oscuro* que los atraviesa, continuo y sin cesuras, *como un fondo constante y monocorde* . . . durante un par de horas han obligado a *las fuerzas que tiran hacia lo oscuro* a quedar fuera de sus vidas, sin dejar de saber ni un solo instante que, en las inmediaciones, dispuestas como siempre a arrebatarlos, esas fuerzas *palpitan todavía*. (P 171–2, my emphasis)

> [Conversation alone has made them forget for a few hours the mind-numbing heat, the disquieting, dark time that traverses them continuous and unbroken, *like a constant, monotonous background accompaniment* . . . for a couple of hours they have obliged *the forces pulling down toward darkness* to remain outside their lives, while at the same time never ceasing for a moment to know that, all around, close at hand, ready as always to carry them off, those *forces still throb*.] (I 179)

There is an opposition here between a refusal of the *real*, characterized by a saturation of images and representations, and that of an opening, whose privileged, although precarious vector, is language (the conversation and the story that begins to be told). The text establishes its cultural coordinates: it speaks in the present, in the context of a disillusioned contemporary world that is caught between the inexpressive *ennui* of media illusions and the desire for a fragile word that could offer some protection from the outside and is willing to run the risk of encountering the real (even in its less attractive manifestations). Against the pale brightness of stereotypical and pacifying images that fail to shield us from the violence that inhabits them, *The Investigation* posits the *resplandor apagado* [dim splendor] of a vision (P 69/ I 66). This vision detaches itself from the "society of the spectacle's" sadomasochistic roots and functions as a barrier against its violence, while at the same time allowing us to see the "distorsión sin nombre que pulula en el reverso mismo de lo claro" [*"nameless distortion* that teems on the other side of what is clear"] (P 82/ I 131). How can writing today encounter the *real*? This is the question that underlies all the evaluative utterances of the internal or intradiegetic narrator (Pichón).

The Investigation provides valuable clues as to how Saer's writing encounters the real. First, because it utilizes literary forms that do not seem to fit well within its project, such as the detective story in its classic and closed form: the filling in of an initial void produced by the supposed narrative ordering of partial information, the reduction of an enigma to an explanation that supposes a transparent and intelligible universe, and the elimination of all ambiguity or opacity through the intervention of the Great Detective who imposes his absolute, final, and true word.[16] Although detective fiction presents a series of formal problems, *The Investigation* allows us to see the sadomasochistic side of the "happiness" that the "society of the spectacle" promises. The historical novel is another form included in *The Investigation*. Titled *En las tiendas griegas* [In the Greek Tents], an outline of the novel's plot is recounted by another character to Pichón, who does not make it part of his own narrative at first but later introduces it in the context of a debate over the "truth of fiction" and the "truth of experience." One should not overlook that *En las tiendas griegas* refers to the homonymous poem by César Vallejo and therefore inscribes the interplay between the poem and prose. It also ciphers the singular affective dimension that I call "the writing of the affects."

In *El río sin orillas*, an autofictional text written in the same period as *The Investigation*, there is an explicit reference to Vallejo's poem that occurs in a significant context: when Saer reflects on the effects that names have on reality and the "realist reduction" that is at the heart of official state rhetoric. In this context the quotation from the poem has a double function: it breaks the link between prose, realism, and the State and gives testimony to the remainder that resists assimilation. Saer calls this remainder "la más oscura terminación nerviosa" [the darkest nerve end], which he elaborates on with the following quote: " *'Allí en el desfiladero de mis nervios!'* como se queja dulcemente César Vallejo comparando sus estados de ánimo con un campamento griego antes de la batalla" ["There in the cliff of my nerves!" as César Vallejo gently complains comparing his mood with a Greek camp before the battle] (RO 112–3).[17] We will see that these "estados de ánimo," to which I refer as the "writing of the affects," are a central concern in *The Investigation* and frame Pichón's story.

In its desire to explore the *"impenetrable depths [fondo impenetrable]* in which the ephemeral days that civilizations endure are rooted" (P 81/ I 67), I will also show that *The Investigation* exhibits the place of the subject ("Place") and its concomitant pain and horror; the site through which and in which it seeks to differentiate itself from the chaos, "las fuerzas que tiran hacia lo oscuro" ["the forces exerting their pull toward darkness"] (P 179/ I 81). Here it is a question of an incandescent, unbearable limit, between inside and outside; the "I" and the other on this side of fantasy (the reality and violent drives that subtend it) that only "art" (or what is left of it) can find and preserve in a fragile *vision*.

The Investigation is a highly structured story whose narrative plot is constantly threatened with dissolution by the "the forces pulling down toward darkness." Within a narrative representation, the themes of pain and sorrow are a testament to the affects that come from layers deeper than symbolization or narrative representation itself. The latter stages a perverse theater, plotted as an Œdipal story with interpretative clues included (although outwardly frustrated). Saer's story is a machine that puts the reader's desire to work; what must be determined then is the scope of this work of desire, what its law is and what limits it transgresses.

Saer's writing belongs to the tradition of modern literature since it performs a descent into the foundations of the symbolic universe in a world devoid of the promise of the Other. *The Witness* is a good example of how the writing of fiction (understood as a speculative anthropology) retraces the fragile frontiers of the speaking subject and touches that bottomless point of the real that is primary repression. In this experience "subject" and "object" reject and confront each other in order to relaunch themselves, inseparable and contaminated, toward the very limit of what is sayable or thinkable. *The Investigation* unfolds at the limit where writing seeks to encounter the real. In what follows, I will make explicit the articulation of desire that this machine puts into effect. First, through an analysis of the story's construction, in order to then show that, if a detective/Œdipal story (Œdipus could be read as the first detective) exhibits the roots of the phantasm proper to our contemporary "reality," the text inscribes an inassimilable margin that I call the writing of the affects, a *"regia* (albeit fragile) *victoria,"* on this side of fantasy.

By fantasy, I understand an imaginary scene in which the subject takes himself as object in order to exhibit his unconscious desire and, by so doing, to block the anguish that *jouissance* causes him. By writing of the affects, I understand the remainders of formations that are older than the symbolic order that survive it and which the Œdipal story cannot totally assimilate. While the phantasm is trans-subjective because it is structured by the order of language as well as by the Œdipal metanarrative, the affects and its figure (the vision) exceed the Œdipal metanarrative and are singular. It is only in terms of this "writing of the affects" that it is possible to elucidate the main features of Saer's ethics of writing.

Construction (on the "Object-Narration")

There is no anguish over the blank page in *The Investigation*. A voice assumes the function of narrator and we are introduced to his story *in media res*: "Allá, en cambio, en diciembre, la noche llega rápido. Morvan lo sabía" ["There, however, in December, night comes on swiftly. Morvan knew it"] (P 9/ I 2). This sentence elliptically condenses the beginning of the traditional realist story: where, who, and when. Even though it is not until twenty pages later that certain details about that narrative voice appear, for the moment, it is possible to establish some parameters in relation to the pragmatic context: a voice establishes a gap between the here of the enunciation and the there of the utterance, between the now of the enunciation and the night in December of the story; between the night of the act of telling and that of the intrigue told. It is not until after the three nuclei of the incipit are expanded and filled in that Morvan, the detective, and his "family romance" are clearly framed and localized and the narrative voice makes its appearance: "ustedes se estarán preguntando qué posición ocupo *yo* en este relato" ["you must be wondering what place I occupy in this story"] (P 22/ I 15).

The incipit that functions both as the beginning of the story and also as a story of beginnings consists of only one sequence in Morvan's history (which comprises around thirty-two pages) and expands only one narrative nucleus: the scene in which Morvan returns to his office after lunch, looks out the window, observes the coming snowstorm, and sees the bare sycamore trees. This scene introduces the mythological reference to Zeus's rape of Europe through the mediation of an illustrated mythology book. The reference to the mythological story—"porque fue bajo un plátano que en Creta el toro intolerablemente blanco, con las astas en forma de medialuna, después de haberla raptado en una playa de Tiro o Sidón . . . violó, como es sabido, a la ninfa aterrada" ["because it was beneath a sycamore tree in Crete that the unbearably white bull, with half-moon shaped horns, after having abducted her on a beach in Tyre or Sidon . . . raped, as is common knowledge, the terrified nymph"] (P 9/ I 2)—becomes the generative cell of the detective story and the axiom of Morvan's fantasy.[18] The story is centered on Morvan and the search for a serial killer who is characterized by his horrific treatment (rape, murder, and mutilation) of twenty-eight elderly Parisian women [*viejas*].[19]

The first part of *The Investigation*, which consists of three parts, closes without the reader knowing the identity of the speaking voice, where it is uttered and for whom. And it will not be until well into the second part that the principal narrator, who encompasses the narrator of Morvan's story, introduces the second investigation (concerning the identity of the author of *In the Greek Tents*). Focusing on Pichón, this principal narrator establishes the basic pragmatic situation on which Morvan's story depends: "quienquiera haya sido el autor—hasta ese mismo momento en que están sentados a la mesa tomando la primera cerveza de la noche con Soldi y Tomatis . . . no se le ha ocurrido [*a Pichón*] ningún nombre . . . " ["whoever the author may have been—until this very moment when he (Pichón) is sitting at the table drinking the first beer of the night with Soldi and Tomatis, no name has come to mind"] (P 63/ I 60). This second part is the responsibility of an omniscient heterodiegetic narrator with multiple focalizations (although the focalization on Pichón's affective state is the central one) and in contrast to the first part there is an abundance of direct transcriptions of dialogues. This narrator establishes the basic pragmatic situation: those present at a beer garden in the city of Santa Fé—Pichón, the narrator of Morvan's story; Tomatis, his old friend; and Soldi, a new character who belongs to a different generation than the others and who will link the plots of the two investigations.

The sequence is a long analepsis: after a morning boat trip to Washington's house (in order to investigate the identity of the author of *In the Greek Tents*) and the return trip from Rincón Norte at sunset, "once they got out of the boat at the Yacht Club they decided to go to dinner to the beer house where they now are . . . it was past nine when they met again in the beer house" (P 170–1/ I 176), they pass by the house (and by the location of Saer's other text *Nadie Nada Nunca* [*Nobody Nothing Never*]), which years before belonged to Gato, Pichón's twin, who has since disappeared along with Elisa. One could argue that *The Investigation* is a long semidiegetic analepsis constructed out of Pichón memories and appropriated by the heterodiegetic narrator.

The first narrative sequence of this second part corresponds to the "moment" immediately following the return from Rincón Norte, when the three characters briefly separate and then meet again for dinner. This means that the story told by Pichón, Morvan's investigation of the serial killer's identity, should actually be framed by the investigation of who wrote the historical novel. But in fact it is "unframed" and enjoys certain autonomy, since it is not until the third and final section that Morvan's story appears explicitly included in the basic narrative (hypodiegetic narration):

> Pichón sacude de un modo enigmático la mano por encima de su vaso de cerveza y continúa. Sin hacer ningún gesto Morvan esperó que Lautret se decidiera a hablar. (P 86)
>
> [Pichón shakes his hand enigmatically above his half-empty glass of beer and goes on: *Not making a single gesture, Morvan waited for Lautret to make up his mind to speak.*] (I 85)

In the absence of quotation marks, this transition is marked by the chiasmus gesture/voice.

The Investigation, in the singular, unfolds into two investigations whose common characteristic is "who?"—a question of authorship and of identity.[20] On the one hand, there is a detective story (a *whodunit*) that seeks to find the identity of a serial killer, on the other, there is a text that narrates Pichón's return to Santa Fé after a twenty-year absence (his return is due to the sale of family property that is his last and only link to his place of birth) and deals with the authorship of *In the Greek Tents*. In the singular, *The Investigation* is a double-edged, unframed story, given that if Pichón's return contains Morvan's story, as told by Pichón, the reader will not know this until he has read half the book.

This peculiar structure or variation on the traditional framed story (metadiegetic narration) forces the reader to focus on another investigation that now concerns the identity of the narrative "source." The narration itself becomes the object of the investigation ("object-narration") and questions the function of Pichón's story (what it evades or includes). Given that the detective story is first in the order of reading, the "investigation" names one of the components that structures the traditional detective story, which includes the story of a crime and the story of its investigation.[21] The title, in singular form, names a part of the whole but, according to the peculiar temporality of the detective story, comes after the (always vacant) story of the crime.[22] The "investigation" encompasses the two stories of what *The Investigation* in turn encompasses, links, and juxtaposes, not without eroding the logic of the frame and what is framed.[23]

It is highly significant that both the boat trip to Rincón Norte and the visit to Washington's library frame the knot of the intrigue of Morvan's story and that the two come first in the order of reading. This sequence is centered on the "zone-place": the text rewrites *Nobody Nothing Never*, as Saer himself states in *La narración-objeto*, and produces a transformation of the "zone-birth place" into "Place."[24] Taking the presuppositions of hyperrealism and the *nouveau roman* as its point of departure, *Nobody Nothing Never* had already made use of the detective story plot by inserting it in a text that rejected intrigue, psychological and revealing dialogue, as well as the significant anecdote. If the differences between *Nobody Nothing Never* and *The Investigation* are obvious, they nevertheless share a common characteristic: the interplay between writing and discourse in which form plays a critical function. The form becomes the "criticism" of discourse because it is a philosophy *of* narration and not because it proposes a philosophy *in* the story. *Nobody Nothing Never* postpones the outcome of the detective story and unfolds only after a multiplicity of repetitions and multiple conflictive versions of what happened; this dilutes its cognitive power and dissolves the closed form that subtends it. In *The Investigation*, on the other hand, the detective story props up a writing of the affects that is not totally absorbed by it.[25]

The Investigation's temporal unity comprises twelve hours and the spatial frame includes the city of Santa Fé, the Paraná River, and Rincón Norte (the "zone"). These unities of place and time are integrated into a peculiar structure: an "un-framed" story imbued with a series of figures that hold together its formal coherence. Two paternal deaths organize two "family romances," Morvan and Julia's, Washington's daughter. These in turn serve as the front for an undisclosed death, the cause of Pichón's trip, and the two authorial investigations, which are themselves also investigations about origins. Two kidnappings (Europa's by Zeus and Helen's by Paris, which according to tradition is a restitution of the first) not only link the story told by Pichón and the summary of the plot of *In the Greek Tents*, as told by Soldi, but also serve as a front for the "kidnapping" (disappearance) of Gato and Elisa (a couple that is ghostly doubled in the sporadic disappearances of Francesito, Pichón's son and Alicia, Tomatis' daughter) and the *failed investigation* of their whereabouts that has left "scars" in Pichón and Tomatis' friendship. Finally, the snow and the rain of white papers (the letter shredded by Lautret) in Pichón's story and the white butterflies that closes the basic story function as metonymic or diegetic metaphors that take their vehicle from the narration itself (or from the text) and not from a preexisting referent.

A story told by Pichón and the summary of an unpublished text related to him by Soldi make up the narrative structure of *The Investigation*. Pichón brings the story from Paris and, thanks to the correspondence he maintains with Tomatis, he also knows of the existence of an unpublished novel in Washington's archives. Pichón has access to the manuscript and from its perusal the heterodiegetic narrator states that

> lo que le ha llamado antes que nada la atención [a Pichón] es que la novela empieza con puntos suspensivos, y que en realidad la primera no es una frase sino el miembro conclusivo de una frase de la que falta toda la parte argumentativa: " . . . *prueba de que sólo es el fantasma lo que engendra la violencia* . . . " (P 62, my emphasis)
>
> [what has, above all else, attracted (Pichón's) attention is the fact that the novel begins with ellipsis dots, and that the first sentence is not really a complete phrase but, rather, the concluding clause of a sentence, all of whose supporting arguments are missing: " . . . *proof that it is only fantasy that engenders violence.*"] (I 58–9, translation modified)

If the beginning of *In the Greek Tents* can be read as a *mise en abîme* of Pichón's story and of *The Investigation*[26], it is significant that in the order of reading the epigraph comes before the oral summary of the plot related by Soldi. The epigraph is a floating supplement of meaning that by an *après coup* effect re-semantizes the detective story told by Pichón (which according to the order of reading Pichón *has been telling* even before his visit to Rincón Norte).[27] If *el fantasma* [fantasy] is what engenders violence, what is Pichón doing when he formulates a fantasy that does *precisely* what it says (engenders violence)? What happens between the acts of *engendering through narration* and formulating a fantasy that *engenders narration?*

"In the Cliffs of My Nerves": The *Writing of the Affects* or *On This Side* of the "Originary Fantasy"

> Y el General escruta volar siniestras penas
> allá..
> en el desfiladero de mis nervios! (César Vallejo, "En las tiendas griegas.")
>
> [And the general scrutinizes flying
> sinister sorrows
> there...
> in the cliff of my nerves!]

> Identifying a literary fantasy [*fantasma literario*] in a literary text and designating it by its name has no value as recognition ... The analysis of unconscious phenomema in literature never touches the drive's raw reality but constructs or models a representation which the reader imagines from the viewpoint of his unconscious. (Pierre Glaudes, "Après coup," 240)

> When dealing with fantasy [*fantasma*] it is above all a question of trying to see what is behind it. This is not an easy task since behind it there is *nothing*. However this is a nothing that can assume a variety of aspects. (Jacques-Alain Miller, "Dos dimensiones clínicas: síntoma y fantasma,'" 13)

> No hay, al principio, nada. Nada. (Saer, NNN 1)
>
> [There is, in the beginning, nothing. Nothing.]

The Œdipus complex founds the Law and Desire in which the father figures as support of the former and the mother is the prototype of the object (first object of desire and of the signifier).[28] In Morvan's story, the Œdipus complex is overcodified and a sadistic scene is played out. The sadism that Saer's texts often display can be read as a defense from the maternal—elements that pre-date the process of symbolization and that survive it: affects or energies—and is linked to a desire for self-generation. There is an unresolved Œdipus complex in Saer's works: a fusion of the writer with the work, of which he would be the creator and the work his offspring. A sort of perfect incest, the work being, in turn, the mother, the offspring, and its own entrails, born of itself. However, it is not convincing to treat the Œdipus complex, the modern myth par excellence, as a hermeneutic key that allows one to identify and name Saer's fantasy, as recent critics would claim.[29] And this for two reasons: first, because his writing can be read as "consciously" illustrated with symbols and psychoanalytic structures (as if it were Morvan's illustrated mythology book) and with an anecdote that has a psychoanalytic-mythical base. Second, because the work guarantees its own (partial) decoding by making use of the discursive intertext provided by Freud: the mystery and the clues are given to us "almost" simultaneously.[30]

Psychoanalysis teaches us that the Œdipus complex is the first narrative that tentatively provides the frame for processing and reconstructing an individual's past experience. The materials of this narrative are elements pre-dating symbolization that, although sifted through the order of language, are ruled by desire. The narrative is a signifying structure that corresponds to the unification of the subject with respect to an actantial pole of the Œdipal triangle; this in turn results from the desire and castration articulated within that structure. This structure, overdetermined by the family triangle, filters and translates the unconscious energy flux or rests (*affects*) that remain outside of the Œdipus narrative. A fictive story repeats the constitution of the subject in the Œdipus complex inasmuch as it is a subject *of* desire and subject *to* castration, but the fact that it introduces what the Œdipal subject has repressed, what we call affects, is a clear indication that the repetition of the Œdipus story that Saer's fictions occur in plain consciousness of its cause—cause of the Œdipus complex and the Œdipal cause of the fiction and, therefore, of the desiring and narrating subject. By representing and by putting into play what exceeds it, the "object-narration" *traverses* the Œdipal complex or, in what amounts to the same movement, the "object-narration" exhibits the limit of the Œdipal complex and for that reason transgresses it. And this is so only because it posits it *as* a limit and *not* as an end in itself.

Saer's themes are linked to a perverse sexual fantasy. The display of the maternal body and its possession exist in a latent and obsessive form and are frequent in his writing. However, it is important to clarify what we understand by fantasy, how his fictions treat that structure, and whether it has the last word in those desiring machines that are his stories.

Fantasy is a clinical term that points to an imaginary scene in which the subject figures, in a more or less deformed manner, the satisfaction of a desire that is ultimately sexual. Additionally, it covers the field of particular imaginary formations whose comforting role was noted by

Freud. Fantasy is at the same time the effect of an unconscious archaic desire and the matrix of actual desires, conscious and unconscious.[31] Following Freud, Lacan posits that fantasy functions like a machine to turn *jouissance* into pleasure, because if left to itself the former would result in unpleasure. Lacan distinguishes three dimensions of fantasy: its imaginary aspect, which corresponds to what a subject can produce as images, and its symbolic aspect, since it consists of a short story that responds to certain linguistic rules of construction. Only when its profusion, the "dense forest of the fantasy,"[32] decants itself completely, do we obtain its axiom (a phrase with grammatical variations). Finally, Lacan distinguishes the fundamental dimension of fantasy: the real. To say that fantasy is a real in the analytic experience is equivalent to saying that it is a remainder that cannot be modified.

The life of a subject is shaped by a "fantasmatics," and literature and art are the privileged sites of its formulation, but *not* of its realization. The principal five *fantemas* [fantasy scenarios][33] at work in literary texts are seduction, castration, the family novel, the return to the womb, and the *Urszene* [primal scene]; these scenarios express trans-subjective structures that the subject adopts in order to tell his story.[34]

What is the function of fantasy in Saer? For Saer presenting an Œdipal fantasy is a way of reducing it to the rank of spectacle, given that it is a well-established fact in literary culture that any determination of the Œdipus complex is already a construction.[35] Saer's writing constantly frustrates the mythical interpretation of psychoanalysis precisely because it is the writer who transforms himself into a mythical figure:

> las *victorias regias* que flotaban cerca de las orillas... evocaban un cordón umbilical... les hicieron pensar a Pichón a causa de esa flor un poco separada del círculo verde pero un poco dependiente de él, igual que un planeta y su satélite en esas *diosas arcaicas y solitarias* que, fecundándose a sí mismas parían, por entre sus miembros vigorosos *un dios menor*, blanco, espigado y frágil, *con el que se elevaba en vuelo nupcial antes de abandonarlo a la mesa del sacrificio para hacerlo despedazar y perpetuar de ese modo su propio culto.* (P 69, my emphasis)

> [The water lilies (*victorias regias*) floating near the river banks... brought an umbilical cord to mind... (they) reminded Pichón, because of that flower slightly separated from the green circle yet dependent upon it, like a planet and its satellite, of those *archaic, solitary goddesses* who, fecundating themselves, gave birth between their vigorous limbs to a *minor god*, white, frail, slender and graceful, *with whom they rose in nuptial flight before abandoning him on the*

sacrificial altar to be hacked to pieces and thus perpetuate their own cult.] (I 66–7, my emphasis, translation modified)

This sequence appears to invert the values of the mythical account of Europe's rape by Zeus and introduces an element that belongs not only to the space of the "zone" but also to its mythical universe (*irupé* or *victoria regia*), although without its legendary correlates.[36] This means that one must treat Pichón's idiosyncratic construction as a *vision*. One can read not only a nucleus that resists the narrative assimilation of the Œdipus complex there, but also the cipher of something located *on this side* of the fantasy: it is a question of self-engendering, birth, and sacrifice—producers of a remainder that perpetuates an autonomous and sovereign cult.

Saer's writing incites a conflict that is not won on the side of the Œdipal identifications that the narration produces. As in *Œdipus King*, Morvan is the victim of narrative causality[37] or, if we agree with Tomatis's hypothesis, Morvan's fantasy functions because of the subjective intervention of the reader-writer Lautret ("his best friend").[38] By *formulating* this fantasy and the mechanism of its construction, Pichón's story exposes the sadomasochistic roots of the "society of the spectacle" (the cultural coordinates in which Pichón locates his story) and thus protects itself from the violence that it begets. But he does *not* achieve victory by exhibiting or formulating this fantasy.

If there is a victory in Saer's text, it is achieved by a series of profound and risky descents into the realm of the *affects*. These are legible at the level of the *dispositio* and *lexis*, in the marks they leave in narrative prose. In "La cuestión de la prosa" [The Question of Prose], Saer speaks about changing the function of the language of narration in order to break with the pragmatic colonization of the State and Market. Saer's art of narration remits to the very limits of realist prose that the poets of "alchemie du verbe" (Rimbaud, Mallarmé, and Lautremont, but also Vallejo) also had to confront. The poem's unsayable is the point of resistance of a prose that seeks to subtract itself from the prosaism of the State and Market.

Pichón's story exhibits a two-faced maternal figure: a giver of life *and* death. The old ("closed") feminine sex is contaminated by the corpse and by a series of impure substances (excrement, blood, urine, and semen), but it is the closed sex that the madness of the criminal wants to reopen. Pichón's narration certainly exhibits a fantasy. The methodical pulchritude of the supposed killer, Morvan, contrasts with the chaos of the scene of the crime. Here *scene* should be read in the sense of a significant construction; the criminal stages a scene of intercourse, birth, abortion, and sacrifice in order to violently displace sexual difference and replace it with the violence of sacrifice and the ritual of purification. It also exhibits in an intransitive sense, since the reader does not know if in fact it is Morvan's staging: Pichón's narration is inconclusive regarding the authorship of the crimes, not only because his gloss of the psychiatric report of "Morvan's case" decomposes its true value, but also because Tomatis proposes another interpretation (the murderer was not Morvan but his best friend Lautret who killed for pleasure and set a trap for the detective).

We must therefore show what function the detective story plays in *The Investigation*. The real or imaginary itinerary that Morvan traces and whose motivations he does not know, according to the narrator, are marked by indications and objects: a recurring dream, a fantasy structured in mythological form, a family romance marked by an Œdipal story, a small white piece of paper that points to him as the criminal. From the beginning, Morvan's investigation folds over itself and becomes an investigation *of* Morvan, or a counterinvestigation that does not seek to find the identity of the criminal but to frustrate the search. That is why Tomatis's comments interrupt the detective story's tedious convention according to which the detective takes control and summarizes the fundamental points of the investigation. In Saer the investigation substitutes the story of the crime and that of the investigation for that of the story *of* the story. *The Investigation* is the search for the story ("object-narration"): the true story consists in the display of the story, of the mechanisms that produce it—the formulation of a fantasy *and* the inscription of its unsayable, impossible *hither side*.

The story of Pichón, who is back after a long *separation* and who has returned in order to enact it by definitely doing away with what little remains of the family estate, assumes the separation proper to the symbolic function (which operates under the law of the father, the Œdipal form). It is not by chance that Pichón returns to his place of birth with his own son:

> En un fulgor instantáneo (Pichón) ha entendido por qué, a pesar de su buena voluntad, de sus esfuerzos incluso, desde que llegó de París después de tantos años de ausencia, *su lugar natal* no le ha producido ninguna emoción: porque ahora es al fin un adulto, y ser adulto significa justamente haber llegado a entender que *no es en la tierra natal donde se ha nacido*, sino en un lugar más grande, más neutro, ni amigo ni enemigo, desconocido, al que nadie podrá llamar suyo y que no estimula el afecto sino la extrañeza, un hogar que no es ni espacial ni

geográfico, ni siquiera verbal, sino más bien, y hasta donde estas palabras puedan seguir significando algo, físico, químico, biológico y cósmico, y del que lo invisible y lo visible . . . no es en realidad su patria sino su prisión, abandonada y cerrada ella misma desde el exterior—la oscuridad desmesurada que errabundea, ígnea y gélida a la vez, al abrigo no únicamente de los sentidos, sino también *de la emoción, de la nostalgia y del pensamiento*. (P 78–9, my emphasis)

[In a sudden flash . . . he has understood why, despite his good will, his efforts even since his arrival from Paris after so many years of absence, his birthplace has produced no emotion in him: because he is at last an adult and to be an adult means, precisely, having reached the point of understanding that *it is not in one's native land that one is born*, but in a larger, more neutral place, neither friend nor enemy, unknown, which no one could call his own and which does not stir emotions but strangeness; a home that is neither spatial nor geographical, nor even verbal, but rather, and insofar as those words can continue to mean something, physical, chemical, biological, cosmic, and of which the invisible and the visible . . . is not in reality his homeland but his prison, itself abandoned and locked from the outside—the boundless darkness that wanders, at once glacial and igneous, beyond the reach not only of the senses, *but also of emotion, of nostalgia and of thought*.] (I 76–7, my emphasis)

What better narrative "mode" than the detective story (which is highly formalized, with easily recognized conventions) structured in psychoanalytic key (Œdipus, the first detective) in order to *formulate* it?[39] Even if from the reader's unconscious perspective one could see in the detective story the wish to present a less painful and more pleasing rendition of the *Urszene*,[40] the type of crime that Pichón's story narrates seems to frustrate or perturb that very possibility.

He who separates himself (is separated)[41]—Morvan/Pichón—the son, "touches" the mother, but *The Investigation* is not ruled by the Œdipal triangle given that the subject of fantasy, the writer (who is also the object), transgresses the three positions of the triangle and in this way inscribes a *writing of the affects*.[42] Intermittently, this lasts approximately as long as the story (twelve hours), like the *victoria regia*, "flor de un blanco rojizo que se había abierto en el atardecer, para *relumbrar con un resplandor apagado* durante la noche y volver a cerrarse al alba" ["the white flower with a pink tinge that had opened in the late afternoon, *to gleam with a dim splendor* during the night and close again at dawn . . . "] (P 69/ I 66, my emphasis): a crepuscular flower that condenses Pichón's vision, a sign of an impossible object, a threshold and a limit. This vision introduces a supplemental drive [*Trieb*] of horror and death into the original fantasy [*Urfantasien*] that impedes the images from crystallizing as images of desire or of nightmares, dissipating them in sensation (pain) and rejection (horror)—the *affects*. The scene of scenes is the image of birth, a reverse incest, a shattered identity, horror and beauty, sexuality and the brutal negation of sexuality.

This vision (and its writing of the affects) is ambiguous: if it can be said to have a demarcating function, it is not able to totally separate the subject from what threatens it. The writing of the affects reveals it to be in permanent danger. From the archaic pre-objectal relation, from the immemorial violence with and by which a body separates itself from another in order to be, language conserves the signs of an "archaic disaster": the night in which the contours of the signified thing is lost and in which the affects are at work, what in *The Investigation* is called "*the forces pulling down toward darkness.*" Writing fails to transform this combat with darkness into a fantasy and so the writer can do no more than constantly return to the same mechanism of symbolization. He does this not in order to find in the object he names the nothingness of the void, but rather in the operation itself: the "object-narration" that like the modern poem is without object.

Pichón's story formulates the *impossible* dimension of the fantasy (Œdipal incest as transgression of the limits of the proper), but the basic story (hypodiegetic) goes farther and, by displaying the attempt to symbolize the "origins," inscribes the other side of the paternal prohibition: pleasure and pain. *The Investigation* tells another version of the *Relación de abandonado* [Account of the adventures of a child lost in the world] that like *The Witness* exhibits the frame of the paternal law in order to inscribe its inassimilable remainder.[43] *The Witness* erases the narrator-protagonist's gender and inscribes the "scene of writing" transforming the story into an "auto-fiction" that is played out in the rejection of the symbolic law represented by Father Quesada. The memories of the narrator-protagonist become an abject theater that, playing on the three poles of the Œdipal metanarrative in order to transgress it, touches the roots of the symbolic order and shows this side of the fantasy, the nothing that is "el color justo de nuestra patria" [the true measure of our homeland] (E 155).

As in *The Witness*, the *fascinum* of *The Investigation* is not fantasy. Saer's text allows us to "see what is behind fantasy" (Jacques-Alain Miller): "the *nameless distortion* that teems on the reverse side of what is clear" (I 131, my emphasis) and which is one of the faces the nothing assumes in his narrative universe. That is why the vision (the affects) allows for a crucial operation that concerns the writer's place—the Place: the subtraction of "birth place" from its representation ("the zone"). *The Investigation*, an "object-narration" *without* object, transforms the subject of writing into an object of its fantasy *but* by sacrificing it in order to pass to the other side and *"perpetuate its own cult"* (P 69/ I 67, my emphasis) it finds (itself) *on this side* of fantasy, with the unsayable-impossible *real* to which it gives its own body.

Notes

1. Lévinas locates the possibility of a saying that exceeds the grasp of the said (although not without being betrayed by it) in the amphibology of language. This betrayal and the irreducible echo of the saying encompass the infrastructure of language or ethical relation. In order to expose this infrastructure, Lévinas must accomplish a reduction of the said (propositional utterance), an operation of writing that unleashes the potentialities of poetic language. For a detailed analysis of this operation see my *Intrigues: From Being to the Other*.
2. In *Otherwise than Being, or Beyond Essence*, Lévinas conveys the violence of coherence, its dissimulation of the relation to the other (*intrigue*) in terms of a literary scene taken from Maurice Blanchot's *The Madness of the Day*. This is a scene that presents the "association of philosophy with the State and with medicine." Repression and mediation appear here under the guise of the ophthalmologist and the psychiatrist, the two figures that interrogate "the interlocutor that does not yield to logic" and, therefore, who resists the complete assimilation of the saying to the said, as well as the violent suppression of the saying.
3. Juan José Saer (1937–2005), his first texts appeared in the cultural supplement of the newspaper *El Litoral*, of which he was editor between 1956–1957. During that time Saer took part in several local literary groups and, through his acquaintance with the poet Juan L. Ortíz, collaborated in *Poesía Buenos Aires*, a group of poets that renewed poetic language. Saer also taught film at the Instituto de Cinematografía de Rosario and, before leaving for Europe in 1968 to study film, he published several collections of short stories and novels: *En la zona* (1960), *Responso* (1964), *Palo y hueso* (1965), *La vuelta completa* (1966), *Unidad de lugar* (1967), and *Cicatrices* (1969). Saer's narrative prose, as in *Cicatrices* (1969), *El limonero real* (1974), *La mayor* (1977) and *Nadie Nada Nunca* (1980), can be situated in the context of the narrative avant-garde of the last century. He not only engages it in a productive dialogue, but also solves some of its most pressing technical problems. *El entenado* (1983), a text that dialogues with the *Chronicles of the Indies* and other anthropological accounts, marks a turn in Saer's conception of narrative fiction. *Cicatrices, Nadie Nada Nunca, Glosa* (1986), and *Lo imborrable* (1993) contain elements of the political novel, being set at the time of Peronism, or during the "dirty war" of the 1970s. *La pesquisa* (1995) revisits

some of these issues by combining elements of thriller and the political novel and, for the first time brings together Paris and the "zone," the recurring setting of the area around the Paraná River characteristic of Saer's fictional universe. *El río sin orillas* (1991) revisits the travelogues of nineteenth-century French and British travelers to the River Plate area, as well as the genre known as the essay of national interpretation. It presents a personal account of Argentine culture that, at times, intersects with Saer's own fictional prose and thus must be considered an auto-fiction. Saer also published *La ocasión* (1988), *Las nubes* (1977), novels, and *Lugar* (2000), short-stories. *La grande* (2005), a novel, and *Trabajos* (2006), essays, were posthumously published.

4. See Scarpetta, *L'Âge d'or du roman.*
5. See Juan José Saer, "La novela" in *El concepto de ficción*, 127–131.
6. Severo Sarduy, *Barroco* en *Obra Completa, II*, 1195–1262.
7. See Juan José Saer, "La selva espesa de lo real," 272–276 and "Una literatura sin atributos," 269–270, in *El concepto de ficción*.
8. By the term *anomaly*, I aim to condense developments by Theodor W. Adorno, in particular from *Notas sobre literatura* and *Teoría estética*, as well as from Lyotard, who, corrects Adorno's *pathos*. See Lyotard, *A partir de Marx y Freud* and *La condición postmoderna*; and Blanchot, "La littérature et le droit à la mort" in *La part du feu* and *El diálogo inconcluso*. For a systematic reflection on the status of contemporary literature, Bessiére, *Enigmaticité de la literature* and *Quel statut pour la littérature?*; Marx, *L'adieu à la littérature. Histoire d'une dévalorisation, XVIIIe-XXe siècles*.
9. Saer, *La narración-objeto*. 56.
10. Badiou, *Conditions*. 41.
11. Saer, *La narración-objeto*. 59.
12. Gabriel Riera, "For an 'Ethics of Mystery.' " 61–85.
13. Badiou, *Petit traité d'inesthétique*. 23.
14. Saer, *Las nubes*.
15. In *La narración-objeto*, Saer states:
    although I intentionally introduced some elements of the hard-boiled in several of my stories, approaching the detective genre head-on presented a series of problems because my deepest conviction is that the hard-boiled novel is a dead genre. The "metaphysical detective fiction" that is announced by so many predictable back covers is as much a stale genre as the modernist sonnet . . . I thought that going back to the *origins of the genre* could be an interesting solution not to parody it, but to rather take it as a point of departure and then go my own way. (159–160)

    However, Saer's treatment of the classical detective story ("its conscious and renewing use" [160]) authorizes us to include it in what has been called *anti-detective* fiction (see note 26 below). Morvan, the detective's name, can be easily related to the series of anti-detectives that, although inaugurated by Borges, has homophonic resonances with Beckett's Moran (*Molloy*) and Robbe-Grillet's Morgan. The figure of the detective that Pichón's story constructs combines features from the classical detective à la Dupin with those of the hard-boiled's private investigator. Morvan has the characteristics of the former: a singular way of life, an extreme austerity, loneliness, eccentricity, and superior analytical abilities ("His métier was not so much a job or a duty as a passion. He was the most upright officer . . . and the most punctilious as regards the law" [pp. 26–28]). Lautret condenses all the features of the private investigator: dubious methods that include the use of physical violence, a complete insertion in the realm of action, and the interaction with both the criminal underworld and legal channels. What characterizes Pichón's narration is its focalization on the inner sphere that, as in Simenon's "Maigrets" is what distinguishes the detective from other agents of the law.

16. The existence of a total text of detection is phantasmatic [*fantasmática*]. The idea of a story able to propose a true enigma and the presentation of the rigorous deduction to its solution is structurally contradictory. As both Chandler and Simenon realized, in a detective story the solution to the mystery is not the consequence of rigorous reasoning, but rather the result of the arbitrariness of the represented events (of the *narrative logic* that is problematic in itself). In "Casual Notes on the Mystery Novel," Chandler states: "it is the paradox of the mystery novel that while its structure will seldom if ever stand the close scrutiny of an analytical mind, it is precisely to that type of mind that it makes its greatest appeal."
17. Vallejo's verse is from "En las tiendas griegas" in *Los heraldos negros*.
18. See Ovid's *Metamorphosis*.
19. In River Plate slang "vieja" also means mother.
20. To which we must add the enigma of the narrative voice I mentioned above. The text stages the question of literature's *enigmatic* status by bringing together the signs of the literary transaction and those of everyday communication. The version of *literariness* that the text puts into scene falls upon the side of *conditionality*. For a distinction between constitutive and conditional poetics, see Genette, *Fiction et diction*. 3–5. Saer deals with this regime of *literariness* once again in *Las nubes*, a framed narrative in which Soldi ponders about the status of a manuscript he found in Santa Fé, that he transcribes and sends to Pichón with a letter in which *literariness* becomes the main issue: "We are very interested in your opinion because contrary to what I think, Tomatis affirms that we aren't dealing with an authentic historical document but with a fictional text. But I ask myself, what are the *Annals*, Lavoisier's *Memory on Calcination*, and the Napoleonic Code, the multitudes, the cities, the suns and the universe?" *Las Nubes*. 13.
21. Tzvetan Todorov, "The Typology of Detective Fiction," 42–52.
22. See Champigny, *What Will Have Happened*.
23. See Derrida, *La vérité en peinture*.
24. Saer, *La narración-objeto* also rewrites sequences of *El río sin orillas*, *La mayor* ("A medio borrar") and of early short stories.
25. For a more detailed analysis of Saer's position on the *nouveau roman* and for his use of hyperrealist narrative procedures, see my *Littoral of the Letter: Saer's Art of Narration*.
26. The narrator establishes a chronological connection between Gato's disappearance and Julia's separation, the episode that allows for the discovery of *In*

the Greek Tents: "Following the death of Washington Noriega, some eight years before, at almost the same time (casi en los mismos días) as the disappearance of Gato, Pichón's twin Brother, his daughter Julia . . . separated from her husband and came to Rincón Norte to live in Washington's home" (P 51/ I 47, my emphasis).
27. Pichón's story also begins *in media res* and with a phrase that seems to elide its antecedent: "There, however, in December, night comes on swiftly" (P 9/ I 1).
28. See Sigmund Freud, "Letter to Fliess, October 15, 1897" in *The Complete Letters;* and *The Interpretation of Dreams.* For an interpretation of the "times" of the Œdipus complex, see Lacan, *Les formations de l'inconscient.*
29. Julio Premat affirms that "one can read Saer's whole work as the progressive approach to the formulation of a destructive, sadic sexual drive whose roots are Œdipal . . . Fantasy [*el fantasma*] that *The Investigation* puts into scene can be considered an essential fantasy that structures the whole work and . . . that it is therefore linked to the characteristic autothematism of Saer's writing," see *La dicha de Saturno. Escritura y melancolía en la obra de Juan José Saer.* 112.
30. As in Borges's "Ibn Hakkan-al Bojari, Dead in his Labyrinth," the mystery and its solution are also open to discussion and disagreement.
31. See Sigmund Freud, "Estudios sobre la histeria," in *Obras Completas, III*; "Tres ensayos de teoría sexual," in *Obras Completas, VII*; "El delirio y los sueños en la 'Gradiva' de W. Jensen," in *Obras Completas, IX* and "Se pega a un niño"; Harari, *Fantasma, ¿fin del análisis?;* Jacques-Alain Miller, *Dos estructuras clínicas: síntoma y fantasma;* and Laplanche and Pontalis, "Fantasma originario, fantasmas de los orígenes, origen del fantasma," 103–143; and ed. Chemana, *Diccionario actual de los significantes, conceptos y matemas del psicoanálisis.*
32. In "Kant avec Sade" Lacan speaks of the "logic of fantasy," given that the fundamental fantasy is a type of phrase that in logic is called axiom. Jacques-Alain Miller claims "the *fundamental fantasy* is not an object of interpretation by the analyst, but rather the object of a *construction*. In 'A Child Is Beaten' the fundamental fantasy never appears as such in experience. It is a limit point of analysis that corresponds to the *Urverdrängung,* to what can never come to light in repression (Freud, *Inhibition, Symptom, Anxiety*)" (13). Fantasy is a formation that shields us from the anxiety caused by the Other's desire.
33. Harari employs the term in *Fantasma, ¿fin del análisis?* 8–9.
34. See Lacan, "Kant avec Sade," unpublished.
35. Rabant, *Encyclopedia Universal.* "Œdipe." Paris: PUF, 1986. 403.
36. The story of the lovers Moratí y Pitá, the witch Y Kuñapayé and the deity Tupá. See Equipo NAyA, http://www.cuco.com.ar/.
37. See Chase, "Œdipal Textuality: Reading Freud's Reading of Œdipus," 175–195.
38. It would be possible to establish a homology between the positions of the detective and the criminal in both *The Investigation* and Borges's "Death and the Compass": Morvan is to Lonröt as Lautret is to Red Scharlach. If this is so, Pichón's detective story exhibits the law of the genre, from which it distances

itself for two reasons. First, because it is recounted in terms of conventions closer to the hard-boiled or Simenon's "Maigrets," and second because it shares a series of features (the detective defeated by the criminal; the world, the city or text as labyrinth; the purloined letter; metanarration; *mise en abîme* or object-narration; ambiguity, omnipresence and lack of signification of clues) with so-called *anti-detective* fiction: "stories that evoke an impulse for 'detection' . . . only to violently frustrate it by refusing to solve the crime." See William Spanos, "The Detective and the Boundary," *boundary 2* 1.1 (1972): 147–168, and Ewert, "A Thousand and Other Mysteries."
39. Shoshana Felman reads *Œdipus King* as a proto-detective fiction and argues that "the stroke of genius of the detective form in Sophocles . . . shows us in which sense one must understand Freud's suggestion according to which the structure of Œdipal suspense ressembles psychoanalysis: as in the process of analysis, detective fiction indeed consists in *narrating the displacement of the interpreter's blind spot*; in its being the narration of the interpretation's self-subversion." Felman calls the narrative that is founded in its own self-subversion (a reversal of the reader and detective's consciousness) an "analytic story." *The Investigation* stages an "analytic story," but *only* as *one* of its moments. See Shoshana Felman, "De Sophocle à Japrisot (via Freud), ou pourquoi le policier?" *Littérature* 49 (1983): 40–41.
40. Penderson-Krag in "Detective Stories and the Primal Scene" argues that the distinctive feature of detective fiction is the intense curiosity it arouses by suggesting to the reader the existence of a "secret fault between two people." The author links this feature to the interest we express in the "primal scene" [*Urszene*], and links the crime of the detective fiction to sexual intercourse, the victim to the paternal figure with whom the reader entertained negative feelings (oedipal) in childhood, and the criminal with the parental figure he associated with positive characteristics and that he imagines (unconsciously) to have been involved in a "secret crime."
41. On the fantasy's passive regime [*pasivación*], see Miller, "Dos estructuras clínicas," and Harari, *Fantasma ¿fin del análisis?*
42. "*Traversée du fantasme*" is the expression Lacan uses in order to define the analytical process. It is interesting to note that Harari thinks it is better to translate "*traversée*" by "going through" [*atravesamiento*] and not "crossing" [*travesía*], since the latter suggests the notion of a displacement along a surface (such as the crossing of a river [*travesía fluvial*] and if "we were to accept only the meaning of crossing [*travesía*], we would be suggesting a certain drifting which would not be totally inaccurate if we place it within its just limits. The drifting is situated in the realm of the Symbolic . . . What is truly localizable in the Real is the consequence of the *going through the* fantasy and not the fantasy itself." (16–17). We should keep this distinction in mind since it allows us to differentiate between the writing of the affects, localized in the real, and the fantasy, localized in the symbolic order.
43. For a more detailed analysis of this text, see my *Littoral of the Letter: Saer's Art of Narration*.

Works Cited

Adorno, Theodor W. *Notas sobre literatura*. Barcelona: Ariel, 1962.
Alexandre-Bergues, Pascale. "Hélène," in *Dictionnaire des Mythes Féminins*, ed. Pierre Brunel. Paris: Èditions du Rocher, 2003. 909–915.
Alter, Jean. "L'enquête policier dans le nouveau roman." *Un Nouveau Roman?* ed. J.H. Matthews. Paris: Minard, 1964.
Avelar, Idelber. *The Untimely Present: Postdictatorial Latin American Fiction and the Task of Morning*. Durham: Duke UP, 1999.
Badiou, Alain. *Conditions*. Paris: Èditions du Seuil, 1992.
———. *Court traité d'ontologie transitoire*. Paris: Èditions du Minuit, 1999.
———. "L' âge des poètes," in *La politique des poètes. Pourquoi des poètes en temps de détresse?* ed. Jacques Ranciére. Paris: Albin Michel, 1992. 21–38.
———. "Philosophie et poésie: au point de l'innomable," *Po&sie* 64 (1993): 1–18.
———. *L'éthique. Essai sur la conscience du mal*. Paris: Hatier, 1993.
———. *L'être et l'événement*. Paris: Èditions du Seuil, 1976.
———. *Petit traité d'inesthétique*. Paris: Èditions du Minuit, 1999.
Bessiére, Jean. *Enigmaticité de la literature*. Paris: PUF, 1993.
———. *Quel statut pour la littérature?* Paris: PUF, 2001.
Blanchot, Maurice. *El diálogo inconcluso*. Caracas: Monte Ávila, 1970.
———. *La part du feu*, Paris: Gallimard, 1949.
———. *Le livre à venir*. Paris: Gallimard, 1978.
———. *L'entretien Infini*. Paris: Gallimard, 1969.
———. *L'espace littéraire*. Paris: Gallimard, 1970.
Bonnefoy, Yves. *Mythologies, I*. Chicago: U of Chicago P, 1998.
Borges, Jorge Luis. *Obras Completas*. Vols. I, II, III. Buenos Aires: Emecé, 1974.
———. *Obras Completas*, Vol. 4. Buenos Aires: Emecé, 1996.
Brook, Peters. "Freud's Masterplot: Question of Narrative," in *Literature and Psychoanalysis*, ed. Shoshana Felman. Baltimore: The Johns Hopkins UP, 1982.
Calveriro, Pilar. *Poder y desaparición*. Buenos Aires: Colihue, 2001.
Champigny, Robert. *What Will Have Happened: A Philosophical and Technical Essay on Mystery Stories*. Baltimore: John Hopkins UP, 1980.
Chandler, Raymond. "Casual Notes on the Mystery Novel," in *The Raymond Chandler Papers: Selected Letters and Non-fiction, 1909–1959*, ed. Tom Hiney and Frank MacShane. New York: Atlantic Monthly Press, 2000.
Charney, Hanna. "Oedipal Patterns in the Detective Novel," in *Psychoanalytic Approaches to Literature and Film*, ed. Maurice Charney. Rutherford, NJ: Fairleigh Dickinson UP. 238–248.
———. "Pourquoi le 'Nouveau Roman policier'?" *The French Review* 46.1 (1972): 17–23.
Chase, Cynthia. "Œdipal Textuality: Reading Freud's Reading of Oedipus," in *Decomposing Figures. Rhetorical Readings in the Romantic Tradition*. Baltimore: Johns Hopkins UP, 1981. 175–195.
Chemana, Roland, ed. *Diccionario del psicoanálisis. Diccionario actual de los significantes, conceptos y matemas del psicoanálisis*. Buenos Aires: Amorrortu, 1998.

Chiampi, Irlemar. *Barroco y modernidad*. Mexico: FCE, 2000.
Combés, Dominique. *Poésie et récit. Une rhétorique des genres*. Paris: José Corti, 1989.
Corbatta, Jorgelina. *Juan José Saer, arte poética y práctica literaria*. Buenos Aires: Corregidor, 2005.
Couturier, Maurice. *La figure de l'auteur*. Paris: Éditions du Seuil, 1998.
Debord, Guy. *La société de le spectacle*. Paris: Gallimard, 1972.
de la Campa, Román. *Latin Americanism*. Minneapolis: U of Minnesota P, 1999.
Del Lungo, Andrea. *L'incipit Romanesque*. Paris: Éditions du Seuil, 2003.
———. "Pour une poétique del incipit," *Poétique* 94 (1998): 131–152.
Derrida, Jacques. *La vérité en peinture*. Paris: Champs/Flammarion, 1978.
Dubrovsky, Serge. *La place de la Madeleine, écriture et fantasme chez Proust*. Paris: Mercure de France, 1974.
Dugastes-Portes, Francine. *Le nouveau roman: une césure dans l'histoire du récit*. Paris: Nathan, 2001.
Eisensweig, Uri. *Le récit impossible: forme et sens du roman policier*. Paris: Christian Bourgois, 1986.
Equipo NAyA. *Diccionario de Mitos y Leyendas*. http://www.cuco.com.ar/.
Ewert, J. "A Thousand and Other Mysteries." *New Literay History* 56, 4 (1980): 263–278.
Ezquerro, Milagros, ed. *Rencontre avec Juan José Saer*. Montpellier: CERS, 2002.
Felman, Shoshana. "De Sophocle à Japrisot (via Freud), ou pourquoi le policier?" *Littérature* 49 (1983): 23–42.
Frappier Mazur, Lucienne. *Sade et l'écriture de l'orgie*. Paris: Nathan, 1991.
Freud, Sigmund. *Collected Papers, III–IV*. London: Hogarth Press, 1952–1953.
———. *The Complete Letters of Sigmund Freud to Wilhem Fliess (1887–1904)*, trans. and ed. Jeffrey Moussaieff Masson. Cambridge: Belknap Press, 1985.
———. "El Delirio y los sueños en la 'Gradiva' de W. Jensen" and "El creador literario y el fantasma," in *Obras Completas, IX*. Buenos Aires: Amorrortu.
———. "Estudios sobre la histeria," in *Obras Completas, III*. Buenos Aires: Amorrortu.
———. "Fragmento de análisis de un caso de histeria. Tres ensayos de teoría sexual y otras obras," in *Obras Completas, VII*. Buenos Aires: Amorrortu.
———. *The Interpretation of Dreams*. New York: Norton, 1965.
———. "La interpretación de los sueños," in *Obras Completas, IV–V*. Buenos Aires: Amorrortu.
Fusillo, Massimo. *Naissance du roman*. Paris: Éditions du Seuil, 2002.
Genette, Gérard. *Fiction et diction*. Paris: Èditions du Seuil, 1991.
———. *Figures III*. Paris: Èditions du Seuil, 1972.
———. *Introduction à l'architexte*. Paris: Èditions du Seuil, 1979.
———. *Métalepse*. Paris: Èditions du Seuil, 2004.
———. *Nouveau discours du récit*. Paris: Èditions du Seuil, 1983.
Gibson, Andrew. *Postmodernity, Ethics and the Novel: From Leavis to Lévinas*. London: Routledge, 1999.
Gilman, Claudia. *Entre la pluma y el fusil*. Buenos Aires: Siglo XXI, 2003.
Giordano, Alberto. *La experiencia narrativa. Juan José Saer, Felisberto Hernández, Manuel Puig*. Rosario: Beatriz Viterbo Editora, 1992.
Glaudes, Pierre. "Après coup." *Revue de Sciences Humaines* 50 (1995): 240–260.

Goldberg, Florinda. "*La pesquisa* de Juan José Saer: alambradas de la ficción." *Hispamérica* 76–77 (1997): 89–100.

Gramuglio, María Teresa. "El lugar de Saer," in *Juan José Saer por Juan José Saer*. Buenos Aires: Editorial Celtia, 1986. 261–307.

———. "Juan José Saer: el arte de narrar." *Punto de Vista* 7 (1979): 3–8.

———. "La filosofía en el relato." *Punto de Vista* 20 (1984): 35–36.

Gramuglio, María Teresa, Martín Prieto, Matilde Sánchez, and Beatriz Sarlo. "Literatura, mercado, crítica. Un debate." *Punto de Vista* 66 (2000): 1–9.

Grimal, Pierre. *The Dictionary of Classical Mythology*. London: Blackwell, 1996.

Harari, Roberto. *Fantasma, ¿fin del análisis?* Buenos Aires: Nueva Visión, 1998.

Holquist, Michael. "Whodunit and Other Questions: Metaphysical Detective Stories in Post-War Fiction." *New Literary History* 3 (1971–1972): 135–156.

Kilito, Abdelfattah. *L'auteur et ses doubles*. Paris: Éditions du Seuil, 1984.

Kohan, Martin. "Saer, Walsh: una discusión política en la literatura." *Nuevo texto crítico* VI, 12–13 (1994): 121–130.

Kristeva, Julia. *La révolte intime. Pouvoirs et limites de la psychanalyse II*. Paris: Fayard, 1997.

———. *Pouvoirs de l'horreur. Essai sur l'abjection*. Paris: Èditions du Seuil, 1980.

Lacan, Jacques. *Autres écrits*. Paris: Èditions du Seuil, 2001. 11–22.

———. "Kant avec Sade," in *Écrits*. Paris: Èditions du Seuil, 1968.

———. *Le Séminaire de J. Lacan, Livre IV: La Relation d' Objet*. Paris: Èditions du Seuil, 1995.

———. *Le Séminaire Livre V. Les Formations de l'Inconscient*. Paris: Èditions du Seuil, 1998.

———. *Le Séminaire Livre XVI. Logique du fantasme (1966–67)* (unpublished).

———. *Le Séminaire Livre VII. L'Ethique de la psychanalyse (1959–60)*. Paris: Èditions du Seuil, 1986.

———. *Les formations de l'inconscient*. Paris: Èditions du Seuil, 1998.

Laplanche, Jean, and Jean-Bertrand Pontalis. "Fantasma originario, fantasmas de los orígenes, origen del fantasma," in *El (lo) inconsciente freudiano y el psicoanálisis francés contemporáneo*. Buenos Aires: Nueva Visión, 1969. 103–143.

Larranaga Machalski, Silvia. "Argumentos de Juan José Saer: transgresión de géneros y estetica de lo fragmentario." *America* 18–19, 1 (1997): 281–290.

———. "Juan José Saer: la locura de lo real," in *Locos, excéntricos y marginales en las literaturas hispanoamericanas*, ed. Joaquín Manzi. Poitiers: Centre de Recherches Latino-Americaines-Archivos-C.N.R.S.-Université de Poitiers, 1999. 542–552.

———. "*La pesquisa*: el género policial a la manera de Juan José Saer." *Río de la Plata* 17–18 (1997): 60–77.

Leclaire, Serge. *Démasquer le réel*. Paris: Èditions du Seuil, 1990.

———. *On tue un enfant: un essai sur le narcissisme primaire et la pulsion de mort*. Paris: Èditions du Seuil, 1975.

Létoublon, Françoise. "Europe," in *Dictionnaire des Mythes Féminins*, ed. Pierre Brunel. Paris: Èditions du Rocher, 2003. 698–706.

Lévinas, Emmanuel. *Autrement qu' être: ou, au-delà de l'essence*. Paris: Kluwer Academic, 1978.

———. *Otherwise than Being: Or, Beyond Essence*, trans. Alphonso Lingis. Pittsburgh: Duquesne UP, 1998.
Lyotard, Jean-François. *A partir de Marx y Freud*. Buenos Aires: Everest, 1988.
———. *Dérive à partir de Marx et Freud*. Paris: 10/18, 1973.
———. *La condición postmoderna*. Madrid: Cátedra, 1982.
———. *L' Inhuman: Causeries sur le temps*. Paris: Galilée, 1988.
———. *Lo inhumano (Charlas sobre el tiempo)*. Buenos Aires: Manantial, 1998.
Martín-Barbero, Jesús. *De los medios a las mediaciones. Comunicación, cultura y hegemonía*. 1987. México: Ediciones G. Gili, 1991.
Marx, William. *L'adieu à la littérature. Histoire d'une dévalorisation, XVIIIe–XXe siècles*. Paris: Les Èditions de Minuit, 2006.
Mervalle, Patricia, and Susan E. Sweeny. *Detecting Texts. The Metaphysical Detective Story From Poe To Postmodernism*. Philadelphia: U of Pennsylvania P, 1999.
Miller, Jacques-Alain. *Dos Dimensiones clínicas: síntoma y fantasma*. Buenos Aires: Ediciones Manantial, 1989.
———. *Dos estructuras clínicas: síntoma y fantasma*. Buenos Aires: Ediciones Manantial, 1989.
Miller, J. Hillis. *The Ethics of Reading*. New York: Columbia UP, 1987.
———. *Reading Narrative*. Norman: U of Oklahoma P, 1998.
Moreiras, Alberto. *Tercer Espacio: literatura y duelo en América Latina*. Santiago: Universidad Arcis, 1999.
Ovidio. *Metamorphoses*. Loeb Classical Library, Cambridge: Harvard UP, 1994.
Pederson-Krag, Geraldine. "Detective Stories and the Primal Scene," *Psychoanalytic Quarterly* 18 (1949): 207–214.
Premat, Julio. *La dicha de Saturno. Escritura y melancolía en la obra de Juan José Saer*. Rosario: Beatriz Viterbo, 2003.
Prieto, Martín. "Escrituras de la 'zona,'" in *Historia crítica de la literatura argentina* 10, ed. Noé Jitrik. Buenos Aires: Emecé, 1999. 343–357.
Rabant, Claude. "Œdipe," in *Encyclopedia Universal*. Paris: PUF, 1998. 403.
Riera, Gabriel. "For an 'Ethics of Mystery': Philosophy and the Poem," in *Alain Badiou: Philosophy and Its Conditions*, ed. Gabriel Riera. Albany: SUNY Press, 2005. 61–85.
———. *Littoral of the Letter: Saer's Art of Narration*. Lewisburg/London: Buckell UP, 2006.
———. *Intrigues: From Being to the Other*. Bronx, NY: Fordham UP, 2006.
Rosman, Silvia. *Dislocaciones culturales: nación, sujeto y comunidad en América Latina*. Rosario: Beatriz Viterbo, 2003.
Saer, Juan José. *El concepto de ficción*. Buenos Aires: Ariel, 1997.
———. *El entenado*. Barcelona: Destino, 1988.
———. *El río sin orillas*. Buenos Aires: Alianza Editorial, 1991.
———. *The Investigation*, trans. Helen Lane. London: Serpent's Tail, 1994.
———. *La narración-objeto*. Buenos Aires: Seix Barral, 1999.
———. *La pesquisa*. Buenos Aires: Seix Barral, 1994.
———. *Las nubes*. Buenos Aires: Seix Barral, 1997.
———. *Nadie Nada Nunca*. México: Siglo XXI, 1980.

Saer, Juan José. *Nobody Nothing Never*, trans. Helen Lane. London: Serpent's Tail, 1993.
——. *The Witness*, trans. Margaret Jull Costa. London: Serpent's Tail, 1990.
Sarduy, Severo. "Barroco," in *Obra Completa, II*, Buenos Aires: ALLCA XX/Editorial Sudamericana, 1999.
Sarlo, Beatriz. "La condición mortal." *Punto de Vista* 46 (1993): 28–31.
——. "Narrar la percepción." *Punto de Vista* 10 (1980): 34–37.
Scarpetta, Guy. *L'âge d'or du roman*. Paris: Grasset, 1996.
Scavino, Dardo. "*La pesquisa* de Saer o la deconstrucción de los hechos." Nestor Ponce, Sergio Pastormerlo, Dardo Scavino. *Literatura policial en la Argentina. Waleis, Borges, Saer*. La Plata: Facultad de Humanidades y Ciencias de la Educación, 1997. 45–62.
——. *Saer y los nombres*. Buenos Aires: El cielo por asalto, 2004.
Sirvent, Michel. "Reader-Investigators in the Post-Nouveau Roman." *Romanic Review* 88: 2 (1997): 315–335.
Spanos, William. "The Detective and the Boundary: Some Notes on the Postmodern Literary Imagination." *boundary 2* 1.1 (1972): 147–168.
Todorov, Tzvetan. "The Typology of Detective Fiction," in *The Poetics of Prose*. Ithaca: Cornell UP, 1977. 42–52.
Vallejo, Cesar. *Los heraldos negros*. Buenos Aires: Losada, 1976.
Vernant, Jean-Pierre, and Pierre Vidal Naquet. *Œdipe et ses mythes*. Paris: Complexe, 2001.
Vezzetti, Hugo. *Pasado y presente. Guerra, dictadura y sociedad en la Argentina*. Buenos Aires: Siglo XXI, 2002.

Abbreviations

AE	*Autrement qu' être; ou, Au-delà de l'essence*
E	*El entenado*
NNN	*Nadie Nada Nunca*
NO	*La narración-objeto*
OB	*Otherwise than Being: Or, Beyond Essence*
P	*La pesquisa*
RO	*El río sin orillas*
W	*The Witness*
I	*The Investigation*

7

INFRAPOLITICS AND THE THRILLER: A PROLEGOMENON TO EVERY POSSIBLE FORM OF ANTIMORALIST LITERARY CRITICISM. ON HÉCTOR AGUILAR CAMÍN'S *LA GUERRA DE GALIO* AND *MORIR EN EL GOLFO*

Alberto Moreiras

Moral Politics and Political Morals

If the history of thought is a history of murder, as Max Horkheimer and Theodor Adorno claim in their *Dialectic of Enlightenment* (117), why couldn't the history of murder become a history of thought? We can link the literary treatment of murder, which seeks to unveil it, not just to express it, with the narrative form called "thriller." The thriller constitutes the dominant and perhaps even normative narrative structure of our time. A thriller is, in every case, an ethical aestheticization of politics. It renders the political in a narrative form, and it does so from a primarily ethical stance.

An ethical stance is not a moralistic stance. Immanuel Kant succinctly established the difference between the two in a section of *Perpetual Peace* where he opposes the "moral politician" to the "political moralist." The former is "someone who conceives of the principles of political expediency in such a way that they can co-exist with morality" and the latter, "one who fashions his morality to suit his own advantage as a statesman" (Kant, *Perpetual* 118). For Kant the moralists and the moralizers are those who "resort to despicable tricks, for they are only out to exploit the people (and if possible the whole world) by influencing the current ruling power in such a way as to ensure their own private advantage" (119). The moral politician, like the ethical individual, relates to politics in a nonopportunistic way, in fact, in a way that might force him or her to postpone their own advantage, given not just ethical duty but the simple legality of the situation in which they find themselves: "there can be no half measures here; it is no use devising hybrid solutions such as a pragmatically conditioned right halfway between right and utility. For all politics must bend the knee before right, although politics may hope in return to arrive, however slowly, at a stage of lasting brilliance" (125).

The lasting brilliance of politics depends, of course, on its conformity to right: "A true system of politics cannot therefore take a single step without first paying tribute to morality. And although politics in itself is a difficult art, no art is required to combine it with morality. For as soon as the two come into conflict, morality can cut through the knot which politics cannot untie" (125). Cutting through the knot that moralistic politics cannot untie: that is the critical function of the thriller. Its stance is therefore radically antimoralist, provided we stick to the definition of moralism as opportunistic behavior. To say that the history of murder may equal the history of practical thought is to say that the history of murder is the history of singular actions and reactions to radical evil in any particular political space. The thriller, insofar as it is written, is the aestheticization of such a history, that is, its presentation in symbolic form.

In Martín Luis Guzmán's *La sombra del caudillo*, the only character who survives among General Aguirre's group is Axkaná, the fellow who escapes the mass murder and can therefore tell the story, thus becoming the embodiment of the ethical perspective in the novel. The novel is about politics, but it gives politics an ethical treatment. Axkaná's function is to give the political a tongue, to give letters to the political, which means to articulate politics into a discourse that, by virtue of its very articulation, becomes thoroughly invested with ethics, with an ethical perspective. The novel pursues, within its own context, an ethics of truth, of nondistortion, and it aspires to the radicality of an engagement with things as they are, whatever happens. When one of the characters says that there are no friends in politics, that "friendship does not figure . . . in the field of political relations" (58), he may mean to make an exclusively political statement, he may mean to speak only about politics, but he cannot avoid the ethical connection even if his purpose were precisely to refute that there exist ethics in politics. Because the sentence "there are no friends in politics," in the context of a conversation, is not an ethically neutral statement, it calls ethics into question, just as it calls politics into question.

Simone Weil's writing on the *Iliad* might help explain what is meant here. For Weil, if the *Iliad* "is a miracle," it is because the poem spares us no bitterness in its account of human misery, of the human subjection to uncontrollable force, and yet "its bitterness is the only justifiable bitterness" (33). The expression of bitterness is at the same time a triumph over bitterness. The poetic victory over force is simply its ability to express its own irreducibility to it. Because we have the *Iliad*, Weil says, we can claim not to be reducible to the force that spares no one. This is so for all of literature: literature is structurally "a miracle" to the very extent that it enables us, in view of its faithful representation of the human condition, to take a step back from it. This internal distance from its own object is the literary apparatus itself: what allows literature not to be confused with its object, and what thus preserves both literature and its object intact every time.

It does not matter that *La sombra del caudillo* is a radical presentation of the brute force of the political in Mexican life, or even of politics as brute force in postrevolutionary Mexico. What is essential is that every perspective on the political within the novel, by virtue of its structural articulation within the narrative, is always already beforehand an ethical perspective. This is also true, for instance, of the very curious "novel without fiction" that Héctor Aguilar Camín wrote on the murder of presidential candidate Luis Donaldo Colosio in 1994, entitled *La tragedia de Colosio*, and which is in so many ways, at least in its first part, a literal rewrite of *La sombra del caudillo*. Aguilar Camín only selectively reproduces fragments from the massive, four-volume *Informe de la investigación del homicidio del licenciado Luis Donaldo Colosio*, prepared by the state attorneys investigating the case and published by the Procuraduría General de la República in 2000. But his reproduction is guided both aesthetically, since without aesthetics there would not be a novel, even a "novel without fiction," as the subtitle reads, and ethically, since Aguilar Camín's purpose is to render the enigma of a murder case whose very resolution, if it is true that the crazed Mario Aburto committed the murder entirely on his own, is just as enigmatic as any nonresolution would have been. The very presentation of the murder of a Mexican presidential candidate as a matter of chance, as the crossing of paths between a particular presidential candidate and a particular psychopath, is already an ethical presentation, particularly in the context of the story regarding the succession to President Salinas, the Neozapatista insurrection, and the rivalry between Luis Donaldo Colosio and Licenciado Manuel Camacho.

The thriller therefore is always structurally the embodiment of the formal principle of practical reason. There is a formal and then there is a material principle of practical reason. The material principle says that you must ordain practical behavior in accordance with your aim as an object of the will. If you want to eat a chocolate, you orient your behavior so that you obtain, and then eat, the precious chocolate, even if you must take it from someone else. The formal principle, in Kant's formulation, is to ordain practical behavior in accordance with the principle of freedom: "Act in such a way that you can wish your maxim to become a universal law (irrespective of what the end in view may be" (*Perpetual* 122). No doubt this is dumb impolitical behavior from the point of view of the political moralist. And yet it is the only kind of behavior that opens to freedom, which in the order of the political is genuine republicanism: "genuine republicanism," Kant says, "could be the object only of a moral politician" (122).

From a political perspective, therefore, the affirmation of an ethical stance is the affirmation of the radically democratic republicanism of the last man and of the last woman, including every murder victim: nothing else is needed.

> And the reason for this is that it is precisely the general will as it is given a priori, within a single people or in the mutual relationship of various peoples, which alone determines what is right among men. But this union of the will of all, if only it is put into practice in a consistent way, can also, within the mechanism of nature, be the cause which leads to the intended result and gives effect to the concept of right. (*Perpetual* 123)

The practice of the thriller is an ethical practice of right in literary terms. It abandons a merely technical approach to literature because its inspiration is thoroughly antitechnical: the thriller is not a means to an end, but an affirmation of the end as ethical end. It must proceed to it, of course, in view of a prior transgression against the end, in view of an ethical fault.

Any narrative under the guise of a thriller effectuates a particular chiasmus. A thriller is always a political reaction to the suspension of ethics. A crime against a fellow human being is always a suspension of ethics. A political reaction to a crime is embodied in the novel, in the thriller, as an ethical reaction through the sort of unavoidable structural elements Weil reveals for the *Iliad* (an epic thriller if there is one).

The ethicopolitical structuration of the thriller, we could say, turns the thriller into a special form or a special way of thinking the political: it is an ethical form for thinking the political that is also a political form for thinking the ethical. For this chiasmatic structure I will use the term "infrapolitical." The thriller is the dominant form of infrapolitics in literature. Infrapolitics, or better, the infrapolitical is the theoretical moment of the thriller, that is, the moment when the thriller exposes itself simultaneously as an interruption of the ethical by the political and of the political by the ethical. We will see perhaps to what extent the infrapolitical perspective in the thriller coincides with its most proper literary dimension—and how literature, as a result, emerges, in at least one of its dimensions, as an apparatus of practical reason to be equated neither with ethical nor with political reason: something else, for which Kant says there is a need that is obscurely related with the need for friendship.

Chance and Necessity

At the end of Aguilar Camín's *La guerra de Galio*, the murder of his protagonist, Carlos García Vigil, terminally suspends an important decision. Just before his death, Vigil does not know—or the reader does not know if Vigil knows—whether he would have accepted the offer to return to the newspaper *La república* as general editor or whether he is more interested in continuing his work as a historian, including the writing of a novel about his catastrophic personal experience as a journalist during the 1970s in Mexico; journalist or historian, in a context where the option of journalism suggests fundamentally a political affirmation and that of historiography (or literature) is bound to the priority of an ethical stance. But the alternative is no real alternative, hence the indecision. If the very potential for politics in Mexico is in fact profoundly determined by the country's history, then the ethical option is more fundamentally political than politics itself. If, on the other hand, the move toward journalism is determined by a sufficiently sophisticated degree of historical consciousness and a maturity of experience, then the apparently political option acquires a predominantly ethical aspect. The contraposition of terms that allows for the shifting of politics into ethics and of ethics into politics—and this is crucial to the literary game in the novel—also sets the stage for its metaliterary dimensions, that is, for its intentional lessons on experience and knowledge.

The intersection of ethics and politics in the novel is not an intersection of reciprocally-autonomous spheres. Both seem to be subordinate to a decision of an epistemological nature (a decision regarding the historical consequences of seeking social change through violent means, which of course cuts across both ethics and politics), and such a decision takes place against the backdrop of the collapse of revolutionary illusions that are represented in the novel by the *guerrilla* experiments of 1970s Mexico. The narrator notes of Vigil's labor as historian:

> In his first book he had allowed a certain juvenile sympathy for socially motivated violence to appear between the lines—for *villismo* or for *zapatismo*—alongside an explicit rejection of conservative violence, whether militaristic or reactionary. In his second volume he maintained a sympathy for the confused but profound thirst for justice that charged the people's armed brigades, but his perspective on violence was uniformly pessimistic, drawing no distinctions between ideological camps or ultimately cruel motivations. (*Guerra* 511)

The sum of Vigil's journalistic experience happens between the writing of the two books. He works first for *La república* and later at *La vanguardia*, in both cases under the orders of Octavio Sala. It is also the time of the end of his youth, of the death of his friend Santoyo, killed for his participation in revolutionary armed struggle, and of the death of his true love, Mercedes Biedma.

In early middle age, Vigil must decide how to negotiate the tedious emptiness he suffers. He is murdered before doing so, which also keeps him from reading the book that his antagonist and mentor, "the conservative intellectual, the genius of evil, the fascist" Galio Bermúdez, had promised to write for him (*Guerra* 452). When Galio's book is eventually published we learn that its fundamental idea is that "all of Mexican history could be read as a struggle between modernizing elites and traditionalist societies, like a permanent civilizing coercion that descended from impatient and despotic heights to recalcitrant, immemorial foundations" (547); that it was a book "'against Utopia and against urgency,' against the idea of 'shortcuts and historical epiphanies,' against 'rupturist solutions and also against paralyzing stability'" (509).

Galio's book is, of course, Galio's war, which gives the novel its title. If Galio's book is the referential horizon of the novel's narrative, we must perhaps understand Aguilar Camín's book as politically reformist, committed to the unhurried modernization of the Mexican state, to its gradual democratization, to a fight against historically-grounded violence and injustice that affirms their teleologically-determined defeat in the final maturity of the nation, in some perhaps not-so-distant future. The patently state-centered nature of such a political stance emerges clearly during an early conversation between Vigil and Galio. Galio says:

> Mexico, like Gaul conquered by Caesar, is still a barbarous place that propagates itself in a state of nature beyond the borders of civilization. If history is correctly perceived as always already universal history, as Hegel would have it, our path could not be, nor will it be for quite some time, different from what it has been: the path of necessity. Mexico has to pay its share of violence in order to tame its barbarism and open itself to the realistic possibility of civilization, of history accomplished. This is the war of the history of the world. (198)

These are Galio's words. Is the implied author also speaking through Galio, or does a turn of the screw come to complicate matters and to develop within the novel an alternative vision of the political? It will be useful to turn to the novel that precedes *La guerra de Galio* in Aguilar Camín's production: *Morir en el golfo*.

The novel, published in 1988, recounts events that principally occurred between 1976 and 1980, more or less the period of López Portillo's presidency. All good thrillers tend toward ontological eternity, even though their ostensible topics are always and precisely concerned with nothing other than time and history. The political context of the novel's setting is the beginning of the long terminal crisis of the Partido Revolucionario Institucional (PRI) in the postrevolutionary period, the moments that would result in the 1977–1985 Mexican oil boom (*Morir* 121).[1]

In *Morir en el golfo*, there is love, the narrator's anguished and pathetic love for Anabela Guillaumín, and there is money—the prospect "of an enormous federal investment in Chicontepec's Paleolithic canal zone, whose potential petroleum supply . . . was equivalent to that which the country had possessed in its entire history" (*Morir* 117). Such an influx of federal funds sets the stage for the "imminent completion of Francisco Rojano Gutiérrez's wildest dreams of being right on the crest of the wave, where the money and the power were" (117). Rojano, who is married to Anabela, is vying for the municipal presidency of Chicontepec, the site of the investment. He is also trying, along with Anabela, to acquire land within the municipality, which brings him into conflict with the apparent plans of his protector and/or political rival, the oil boss Lázaro (or Lacho) Pizarro. With this predicament on the horizon, Rojano requests the help of his old friend and capable political journalist, our narrator. Rojano capitalizes on the long-standing friendship and, above all, on his friend's painfully obvious love for his wife, which, as both Rojano and Anabela are well aware, continues to smolder. Rojano and Anabela—or, perhaps, Anabela and Rojano—get the journalist mixed up in an investigation into the assassinations, supposedly committed by Pizarro's hired guns, of *ejidatarios* [collective land owners] who stand in the way of the latter's land grab. The reasons for Pizarro's designs on the land are, in addition, complicated, as they go beyond simple economic calculations: "A working-class popular revolution is underway here," Pizarro tells the journalist, "What we're doing here is a socialist revolution because we are going to take over the factories, the capital, the production ... The petroleum-workers' union defends all of the country's marginalized" (98). The union will not hesitate to reach these objectives by any means necessary: "two lives are worth more than one and three are worth more than two. It's the arithmetic of history and of true equality ... violent deaths are unavoidable because that's the law of history. To transform them into fertile deaths, creative deaths, that's the task that faces us now. Nothing else" (107–108). Pizarro's socialism is a socialism of the will to power, only tactically committed to respect for the law. It coincides historically with what was then referred to as "Oil Maoism." Anabela and Rojano's desire for land is, on the other hand, entirely meretricious.

The coordinates of an infrapolitical thriller are emerging: the narrator's possible ethical stance, difficult to the very extent that he must overcome his "pathological" attachment to Anabela, is set against Pizarro's grand politics, and both of them are set against Rojano and Anabela's greed. There is ethics on the one hand and a desire for power on the other. The narrator acts out of friendship and love, although not necessarily freely, and he must confront, in the midst of radical suspicion, which is also radical doubt, the excesses of those who are prepared to pursue their desire for accumulation at all costs. As an ethical agent, the narrator represents honor. The opposition of honor against corruption lies at the heart of all thrillers. Aguilar Camín structures his novel around a relatively conventional double articulation. In the first moment or register, the narrator, who is a journalist in the place of a detective, seeks fulfillment of the law of the community against those who transgress its principles: Pizarro (i.e., initially, until he notices that Rojano and Anabela are also doing it).

In a second moment, which is always the truly heroic moment of the double articulation, the detective must abandon his first register, pass beyond his fantasy of legalistic fulfillment, and compromise his very being in an act of violence—the ambiguity regarding the act's character as an ethical act, that is, whether the act is an ethical act of violence or an act of ethical violence, must remain—that will alter the coordinates of the possible and reestablish a new possibility of civility.

Why is love always on the side of the character that searches for truth, while money and power are always the enemy's ill-gotten gains? The answer is simple: the structure of the thriller always works to maintain Kantian moral law—including, if necessary, its anticommunitarian moment—as the only possible support of civil community (the social as such is not at stake, as there can be society in a state of nature, but there can be no civil society in a state of nature). But this means that love, in a thriller, is never simply a pathological affect, but always already an ethical allegory of the moral law, as Rafael Bernal's *El complot mongol* fascinatingly established for Mexican literature. Love in the thriller is a narrative representation of the categorical imperative, which commands one to act so that the maxim of conduct can be upheld as a universal rule.[2] The thriller establishes, in a first register, a conflict between ethics and politics in which the implied author can appear to be systematically on the side of ethics. And the resolution of the story consists of the dialectical transformation of ethics into politics, and in the subsequent reduction of what once appeared as political to pathological affect. This is the thriller's substitution of every possible moralism for ethics, and also the thriller's fundamental position that, in Kant's words, "morality will cut through the knot that politics cannot untie" in order to restitute a properly republican politics.

As the allegorical incarnation of the moral law, the detective's position incarnates a transcendental field of pure potentiality. *Potentia*, or *dynamis*, belongs to the transcendental detective long before the concrete detective can make it his or hers. Or, one could say, the detective can only enjoy his pure *potentiality* between cases, and not during the cases themselves.[3] The detective's *dynamis* works against the fallen *energeia* of the agents or patients whom he must investigate. In *Morir en el golfo*, none other than Pizarro recognizes this fact when he describes our narrator as "a *wa'ya*, as they say in totonaca, a hawk, a vulture: one who, while seeking food, is always planning to soar again" (133). The actualization of the detective's pure potentiality, always reluctant and uncommitted, can only be explained by love. For the detective, the possibility of action—an exceptional possibility, as the possibility of resolving a case or of attaining thought always is—has nothing to do with war. War—the war between Lacho and Rojano or Anabela, for example—can only produce commitment, and thus ideology. The detective withdraws from war as he engages it—engagement and withdrawal are the same gesture—because war is, in the best of cases, an interruption of *dynamis*. Polemical action is a distraction and a descent into *energeia*. Literary truth in the thriller thus coincides with literary truth in general as it works to constitute a politics of nonpower, a moral politics against every moralism, against every pathology of power or of money, against every merely personal advantage. But *Morir en el golfo* also complicates its structural oppositions.

The political horizon against which the narrative unfolds is clearly utopian in at least one way. The approaching oil boom was, in 1977, "the promise of collective euphoria based on a potential utopia, a Mexico without the same old brutal and excruciating flaws, sovereign and wealthy, desirable; another country, noble and generous, as we always believed and wanted it to be; the great country equal to our nationalism and our ill-fated love for it" (122–23). Although he remains skeptical, shaken by the evidence of corruption that practically defined the political class under López Portillo, and although he is suspicious of his friends' motives, the narrator does not hesitate to support Anabela and Rojano's war against Lacho Pizarro's rising provocations. Anabela requests it after another day of lovemaking: "the war has begun. Anything you can do to help us counts. Each and every columnist or paper that tracks your information, every political opportunity, every conversation, every step that supports Pizarro's defeat is of fundamental importance" (153). The narrator publishes an article that describes incriminating acts that, according to Rojano and Anabela's story, seriously compromise Pizarro. But the narrator's contact in the Ministry of Interior, who is in charge of the Mexican political police, shows the narrator how his friends have been manipulating him by presenting evidence that Rojano and Anabela had tampered with the photographs used to make their case. Events unfold at a dizzying pace. The narrator breaks off his adulterous relationship with Anabela, puts up with Pizarro's righteous anger, and decides to forget everything out of spite. A few weeks later, however, Rojano is murdered, lynched by the enraged inhabitants of his town. His body appears with a shot to the temple, a style of execution that, according to what Rojano had told the narrator, is Pizarro's calling card. The journalist, shaken and moved to action once again, returns to his "paper war" (174). His articles so effectively incriminate the petroleum union, and thus PEMEX (the giant state-run Mexican oil corporation) indirectly, that the president's office intervenes. Negotiations are made to appease Pizarro, and Anabela and her children move in with the narrator, abandoning the countryside of Veracruz and the land she and Rojano had purchased in better times. Peace seems to have arrived, the past is past, and the narrator settles into a pleasant domestic routine, which is only to be abruptly interrupted by the news that Anabela plans to have Pizarro killed, and that, in fact, she has already ordered his murder.

The assassination attempt fails, but Pizarro, who is gravely wounded, will not live much longer. Anabela and the children must leave Mexico. The narrator, now alone, stubbornly adheres to a merciless work regimen, shutting himself off: "Never before those days did I feel so immersed in the simple tasks of investigating and communicating. Never so neutral, so detached from my writing's personal and political implications, so dispossessed of secondary purposes, so objective and dispassionate, at absolute peace with myself" (265). The narrator has returned to his *dynamis*, his moral ataraxia, and he faithfully fulfills his nonpathological destiny. But his ethical peace crumbles after one of his columns exposes information prejudicial to Pizarro's oil Maoism. The latter summons the narrator, via the chief of the political police, suggesting that if the narrator does not attend the meeting Anabela and her children might be endangered. The narrator, obliged to come forward, discovers that Pizarro is in fact about to die, but not because of what turns out to be the nonexistent hit job Anabela had supposedly paid for, but rather as a result of a more prosaic pancreatic cancer. Pizarro's death fills Anabela with joy.

The second articulation of Aguilar Camín's novel becomes clear at this point. By virtue of the first articulation, the narrator would not have wanted anything but to help his friends defeat a corrupt *caudillo*, or despotic regional leader, who had no problem turning to crime as a way of realizing his own political ambitions. But things have changed, for the narrator has become aware, in spite of himself, of the infinitely complex situation that is entrapping him in a game of mirrors. Pizarro is not innocent, but there are no innocents. The narrator's efforts appear, in retrospect, to have been distorted by an erroneous moral impetus, based on ignorance. His ethics are exposed as a particularly pathological form of politics. His actions have been disastrous. There are now two alternative versions of reality, the one Anabela prefers to endorse, and the one the narrator knows via the chief of the political police in his Bucareli Street building. Of them,

> Bucareli's version of a long series of coincidences, misunderstandings, and a minor delinquent's mythomania seemed to be more in the realm of the real, closer to the true dramatic imperfection of things, its always slack and true texture. It conceded some facts, centrally among them Rojano's execution in Chicontepec. But the rest faded away in the crucible of motivated fabrications, lies, false conclusions, spectacular coincidences, and the natural course of events. Anabela's version described, on the contrary, a strict geometry of combat, a battle of clean and radical lines, whose coincidences were effects clearly caused by the contestants' will; any element of chance merely disguised the decisions and their results, the terminal point of an arithmetic whose essence could not be summed up by anything better than Pizarro's own motto: *He who knows how to add knows how to divide*. (303)

The problem is not that the narrator cannot choose, but rather that the will to choose gets lost in the face of the choice itself. Anabela chooses, and her act leads to the tragic necessity that the narrator renounce her. The truth of that which the detective ascertains is excessive with respect to the truth—the truth exceeds itself by casting aside an uncontainable reality with respect to which any construction of subjectivity is false or illusory. The detective "traverses his fantasy," and he loses not only his object of desire but, more profoundly, also his pathological will itself: he can no longer desire, and, with his pathology, he loses his capacity to follow any kind of moral law.[4] He is paralyzed. He has lost his honor, and everything else with it. What remains for him? Or rather, what remains for the thriller, for the reader who is alert to the literary truth that might or might not emerge there?

Through the deconstruction of the ethical stance by the political stance and vice versa, *Morir en el golfo* carries out a process of infrapolitical affirmation. The infrapolitical is the political interruption of ethical sovereignty and simultaneously the ethical interruption of all political sovereignty. Oil Maoism cannot sustain itself in the infrapolitical dimension, but neither can Rojano's nor Anabela's hateful greed, nor the anguished moral conscience of the detective, whose actions always end up being as premature as they are late. The narrator always acts too late or too soon, and there is no glory in his untimeliness, only ridicule. For us, however, the infrapolitical remainder persists as the double possibility of thought: against politics, against ethics, but not outside of ethics, not outside of politics.

The same infrapolitical remainder constitutes the horizon of the construction of knowledge in *La guerra de Galio*. There are numerous structural parallels in the novelistic composition between *La guerra de Galio* and *Morir en el golfo*. First, the protagonist, who in *Morir en el golfo* is also the narrator, is essentially an intellectual who writes and who locates through writing the unstable center of his own social being. Second, both protagonists are painfully marked by affect: love and friendship not only strike intimate and catastrophic chords within them but, in a certain sense, also constitute them through an emotional homelessness with respect to which writing serves as refuge and salvation, or compensation. Writing is always for them a way out of the aporias of their affect. Third, in both cases, affect and writing intercede for an ethicopolitical option against the corruption and violence of power. Fourth, the impossibility of attaining a clear conscience, the impossibility of thinking that positive options are immediately transparent and unchallengeable, the impossibility of believing that it is enough to be against the corruption and violence of power in order to work effectively against them—these impossibilities are the very object of the narrative. Democratic voluntarism ends in ridicule in *Morir en el golfo*, and it ends in the worst kind of corruption in *La guerra de Galio*—the corruption of Octavio Sala, who is consumed by resentment and the desire for revenge. It is as if Aguilar Camín were warning us that there is nothing necessarily good about good intentions—that something else is needed, and that, without it, we are beyond lost, in the very hell of willful stupidity.

Both novels theorize a crucial moment of decision, beyond any program for action. It is the moment that in each case sutures the relationship between ethics and politics. But the decision never completes itself textually—even if nothing but decisions take place within the text. In the earlier novel, as we have seen, the narrator is unable to decide between the conflicting versions of reality presented by Bucareli's version of the facts and by Anabela's version of the facts. In the later novel, Vigil, the protagonist, is murdered, under circumstances never clarified, before the decision is made evident in its practical effects (the reader never knows if the protagonist decides before dying, because the narrative strategy in *La guerra de Galio* is elaborated through an interposed, nonomniscient narrator). But it is precisely the fact that the decisions are never textually complete that reveals how both novels are structurally invested in the very act of making a decision.

The later novel's narrator, who is Vigil's former professor, refers on two occasions to the "insoluble practical problem" that he used to enjoy discussing with Vigil. The second reference appears in the narrator's direct transcription of Vigil's journals, in which Vigil describes his last conversation with his professor:

> He told me: "I have dedicated my whole life to constructing those obscurities, as you know. Because only in the darkness can light exist." I reproached him for his maieutic facileness, telling him that where there is light, no light is needed, because nothing needs to be illuminated. He accepted my impertinence and returned affectionately to the insoluble logical problem that he had detected and with which he knew how to hypnotize his students, generation after generation. "Is it possible to avoid a car accident?" I remembered the argument and told him: "Impossible. If it could be avoided, by definition it would not be a car accident. It would be a voluntary act. An effect of someone's will who, capable of avoiding his misfortune, does not avoid it." "Not bad," said the professor: "What is the practical conclusion of this exercise?" "Live however you want," I said. "What must happen will happen." (*Guerra* 535)

A decision, then, only implicates the decision itself, in a context in which there are no possible guarantees that its result can affect a possible gain, and in which there are no possible guarantees that in any case it could be correctly oriented. "Where there is light, no light is needed." If there is a decision, there is no light.

Everything has to do, then, with how to choose your decision, with the intimate dynamics of the idea to "live how you want"; take any decision you want that does not change destiny but that, precisely because it cannot change it, affirms it or subtracts it. Gilles Deleuze, in *Nietzsche and Philosophy*, refers to Nietzsche and Mallarmé's radically opposed conceptions of the act of decision. For Nietzsche, according to Deleuze, "the dice which are thrown once are the affirmation of *chance*, the combination which they form on falling is the affirmation of *necessity*. Necessity is affirmed of chance in exactly the sense that being is affirmed of becoming and unity is affirmed of multiplicity" (26). For Nietzsche, "the second moment of the game [the roll of the dice on the table] is also the two moments together or the player who equals the whole" (27). To affirm the law of becoming, to affirm necessity in chance, is therefore an act of affirmation of the totality and a commitment to the decision, a "live however you want" that is at the same time, and impossible to dissociate from, a "love how you live": *amor fati*. Mallarmé's understanding of the decision, according to Deleuze, is alternate and even opposite, for Mallarmé "always understood necessity as the abolition of chance" (33). Deleuze continues:

> Mallarmé's poem belongs to the old metaphysical thought of a duality of worlds; chance is like existence which must be denied, necessity like the character of the pure idea or eternal essence ... It matters little whether depreciation of life or exaltation of the intelligible prevails in Mallarmé. From a Nietzschean perspective these two aspects are inseparable and constitute 'nihilism' itself, that is to say, the way in which life is accused, judged, and condemned. (33)

Nietzsche's operation is opposed to Mallarmé's operation. *La guerra de Galio* offers a version of the mutual opposition of these two operations precisely through the confrontation between Galio and Vigil. Galio occupies the place of Mallarmé, and Vigil the other position. Galio's state-centered and teleological perspective, based upon, as he himself tells Vigil, the Hegelian idea of world history or *Weltgeschichte*, is a perspective based upon the well-known duality opposing barbarism to civilization. In the Hegelian historical teleology, the East, Greece, Rome, and the "Germanic" world (the latter representing the totality of modern Europe) are orders of experience oriented toward the final subsumption of history into the state apparatus that constitutes its culmination and utopian promise. From this point of view, as Ranajit Guha has insisted, the historicity of the world does not coincide with but remains as what is negated by Hegelian *Weltgeschichte*, because the latter accepts for its constitution only the teleological elements that lead to the formation of a state apparatus understood as the end or the goal of history.[5] The book that Galio publishes after Vigil's death is titled *The Enlightened Coercion*, and it grounds itself precisely in the insistence upon the gradual development of a state-centered system in Mexico. Galio explains to Vigil the tragic "vulnerable hypothesis" that sums up his life's work:

> There is only one instrument capable of completing the civilizing task that we need, capable of ending our own war against the barbarism of our past ... This instrument is what we imperfectly call the State and what our forefathers called simply Federation. The federation's cold steel, its centralizing, civilizing bayonets, like Caesar's, spill blood today in Guerrero, blood both innocent and young that will prevent further bloodshed ... I regret each one of the deaths that our barbarity accrues in Guerrero. But in the midst of the howls and the fire, I can

see a possible form of the country, opening a path toward itself, finding its territorial identity, its political nucleus, its potential civilization. In a word: deciding its history. (199)

Galio's legitimation of state-supported violence is, therefore, the necessary logical consequence of the will to abolish chance. State violence is necessary because undertaking the task of abolishing chance is necessary.[6] Against teleological necessity, however, against Hegelian *Weltgeschichte*, chance incarnates the full and open historicity of the world. Through its open historicity, Vigil's book, Vigil's future work, presents the unfulfilled promise of a way of condemning violence as "uniformly dark," regardless of where it may find cover. For Vigil the decision—the decision to dedicate himself to journalism or to history, to ethics or to politics—is not primarily a decision between those two terms or in favor of either of those modes of action. It is above all a decision against violence, against the paradigm embodied by Galio, who is the unconditional defender of a "dictatorship of the sabers," in Juan Donoso Cortés's formulation, that would be preemptive of the decomposition of the world into anarchy and disorder.[7] It is therefore a decision in favor of absolute historicity against the fetish of state violence and against the fetish of antistate violence; against teleology, in whose justifying logic there is always seated an abolition and not an affirmation of chance.

In the novel, Galio is the reactionary subject of pathological affect in the Kantian sense, while Santiago and Carlos Santoyo, Paloma, and the rest of the *guerrilleros* are also pathological subjects of a will to power that is antistate but not therefore any less teleological or less based in Hegelian *Weltgeschichte*. The liquidation of the guerrilla adventure in Guerrero, as a violent and martial adventure that perpetuates violence and thus also the legitimation of state violence, extends into the open pathologization of Octavio Sala's character, a subject defined by resentment and bad faith, who is defeated, more than by his expulsion from *La república*, by his own ghosts, which reveals how, in the end, the game of truth and journalistic transparency that Sala played was an equivocal game of tricks, because it was the pathological-political instrumentalization of an ostensible factual truth that will be sacrificed the minute it becomes expedient.

Thus Galio's war is not a war restricted to the Mexican political class, but rather the war of all those who, in the novel, give themselves over to the fight for power on the basis of their own desires. Just like Anabela in *Morir en el golfo*, Sala and the *guerrilleros*, despite the tragic disparity of force, maintain in *La guerra de Galio* the pretense of "a strict geometry of struggle, a battle of clean and radical lines whose coincidences were effects brought about unquestionably by the will of the combatants; chance was there a disguise of decisions and results." But the political decisions and results, the abolition of chance, are always products of darkness: "Real politics always occurs in the shadows. It is by nature vampiric, secret... The politicians of the open societies you're talking about simply dedicate a bit more time to protecting themselves from the light, in order to be able to act like one acts in politics: in the cellars, in the shadows" (*Guerra* 151). Real politics, the narrator is telling us, is always the expression of the moralism of power—but, of course, the very fact that such things can be said, following Weil's lesson, introduces the very necessity of another kind of real politics: fundamentally antimoralist, republican, ethical.[8]

Where there is light no light is needed. Vigil's (in)decision, or infrapolitical trajectory, equal to that of the narrator in *Morir en el golfo*, presupposes something other than an open denunciation of politics that would condemn its necessary reliance on cellars, traps, and betrayals, on violence and concealment. This trajectory equally presupposes something other than a well-meaning and thumb-sucking form of ethics. The infrapolitical trajectory in Vigil, and in the narrator of *Morir en el golfo*, affirms the necessity of an infinite interruption of the ethical by the political and of the political by the ethical, and thus the acceptance or affirmation of chance as necessity. Within absolute historicity—the realm of chance—neither the political nor the ethical is closed. Both open themselves to a mutual deconstruction whose slippage can also be understood as the obligation to an infinite democratization of the state—a republicanism of the last man and of the last woman, since such is the other side of the teleological abduction of the state by civilizing and despotic elites. This is the decision Vigil must make, either in historiography or in journalism: a decision perhaps more literary than philosophical, but in any case a transcendental or theoretical decision, like every decision. As to the narrator of *Morir en el golfo*, his decision was always already made: he understands, after the fact, that he no longer has to choose. He had in effect chosen, and it was the game of dice that led him to confront consequences not of his making.

In *Morir en el golfo* and *La guerra de Galio*, Héctor Aguilar Camín presents two superb political novels whose defining characteristic is a radically disenchanted vision of the political and an equally disenchanted but fiercely stubborn embrace of the ethical stance. Their "impoliticality," to borrow an expression from Roberto Esposito, has very little or nothing to do with fashionable pieties, be they reactionary or progressive. That literature, in these two texts by Aguilar Camín, finds itself at the service of politics means that literature, in this case, reclaims its undeniable privilege as a means of thinking about democracy, which is also, or above all, a means of imagining the possibility of a decision outside calculative reason. Decision guarantees nothing—the roll of the dice in Mallarmé's *Igitur* does not resolve, as we have seen, anything more than a Hegelian abolition of chance, within which are concentrated all of the horrors and all of the truths of domination. That is precisely Galio's dubious wager, his "vulnerable hypothesis." But there is another kind of decision, the nonmilitant and infrapolitical decision upon which depends any possibility of access to the antiutopian realm of absolute historicity. It holds up against any abduction of history—by the powerful, by the treacherous, by the subjects that pathologize upon occupying moral law and who thus become worthy of the hardly romantic accusation of Kantian radical evil. This is literature against civilizing elites—something uncommon, moreover, in a tradition that continues to oscillate between the two tendencies of *Sarmientismo*; a tradition that, given the opposition between civilization and barbarism, cannot but redefine it, hardly daring to suspend it.

Antimoralist Exposure

The infrapolitical dimension of the thriller, or even the thriller as infrapolitical dimension, gives us a possible way to think about the literary outside national allegory, or outside the national-identitarian ideologies that have plagued Mexican and Latin American literary reflection for more than a century.[9] It also gives us a possible form to think about the ethicopolitical, and thus to understand the possibility of a properly democratic literature, a literature thoroughly invested by and in ethical universalism. That is no doubt what Paco Ignacio Taibo and Subcomandante Marcos tried to do in the novel published as a serial in *La Jornada* and entitled *Muertos incómodos (falta lo que falta)*. It is a bad novel, but it is also a novel that has a democratic intentionality, that thinks of itself as democratic literature, and literature for democracy.[10] And, of course, between *La sombra del caudillo* and *Muertos incómodos*, we have all the crime fiction written in Mexico after the Revolution. It is possible to read through that history of Mexican crime fiction—and who will say that not every piece of fiction is always already crime fiction? Roberto Bolaño opens his Mexican novel *Amuleto* with a statement that is no doubt intended as a possible shibboleth for all literature:

> This will be a terror story [or: a history of terror, *historia de terror*]. It will be a police story, a *serie noir* or a terror series narration. But it won't look like it. It won't look like it because it will be me telling it. I am the one who speaks and that is why it will not look like it. But at bottom it is the story [the history] of an atrocious crime. (4)

—an interesting history of ethicopolitical reflection in Mexico that has little to do with the communitarian or at least apparently communitarian thought of the nation.

In the very long section of *2666* devoted to the murders of Ciudad Juárez, Bolaño says: "Nobody pays attention to those murders, but they hide the secret of the world" (439). In the murders of Ciudad Juárez, the secret of the world hides and lies concealed. An obligation to investigate them—the never fulfilled obligation to pay attention to those murders—is an obligation of knowledge. Literature cannot claim the disciplinary monopoly of that investigation. But literature thinks of those murders—the murders of Ciudad Juárez or any other murder—in order to unconceal the secret of the world. That investigation, in literature, has a literary character—sociology does not have a literary character, and anthropology looks for anthropological facts, but literature looks for literature, although the goal of literature is perhaps not literary. To recognize, to unconceal, to show the secret of the world, if that is the essence of the literary, is an extraliterary essence. The relation between literature and murder seems to posit that the essence of the literary is not itself literary, that the literary apparatus deploys its potentiality at the service of something other than itself. That something other—the secret of the world—determines the structure of the literary apparatus.

We could then speak of a radical heteronomy of the literary apparatus: the essence of the literary apparatus is transliterary. Literature cannot determine its own conditions of enunciation. Literature is therefore not properly, but rather improperly, literary. And in that radical impropriety, literature displays its historical presence, and its historical and political efficacy, or effectivity. If the effectivity of the literary depends on its capacity to unconceal the secret of the world, that is, if the effectivity of the literary follows heteronomous and transliterary conditions, where hides the final order of determination?

In the name of what or with respect to what is literature effective? Is the secret of the world of a theological, ontological, historical, political, or ethical nature? At what level and in what order do we find a possible autonomy of knowledge? Of what order of activity could we say that its essence is thoroughly contained by and in itself?

When Bolaño says in 2666 that in the investigation of the crimes of Ciudad Juárez nothing other than the unconcealment of the world's secrets is at stake, the necessary question is the question about the epistemic nature of that secret. If the secret is not literary (although it may be sought by the literary), is it a historicopolitical secret? Is it an ethical secret? Is Bolaño promising without promising an ethical revelation? If literature's secret is in itself transliterary, if that can be accepted from the thought that literature, when looking for the secret (which literature always does), is looking for something other than itself, and if from that point of departure we must question the transhistorical, transpolitical, transontological nature of literary revelation, would it be a surprise to discover that we might not be able to affirm that such a revelation is also transethical? The revelation of what revelation destroys, in Maurice Blanchot's sentence on literature (Blanchot 47), could end up having a thoroughly ethical nature.[11]

But it would not be an ethics of the good life. Infrapolitical ethics comes with a bite, and it is not enough to say that it serves to condemn every possible moralism. Infrapolitical ethics must also encounter and critique the moralistic residue in contemporary philosophical positions whose appeal to weak definitions of the ethical seem to empower them to occupy some kind of self-assigned high ground. I will briefly reference two of them: Giorgio Agamben's endorsement of an apparently Deleuzian ethics of the blessed life, and Peter Hallward's endorsement of an apparently Badiouan ethics without others. To the extent that infrapolitical ethics are always necessarily the supplement to a radical republicanism of the last man and of the last woman, to the extent that they might constitute something like a subalternist ethics, they reject the notion of an ethics without others as well as every possible notion of an ethics of mere life. I will try to show how both notions conceal a misguided moralism of ontotheological origin—regardless of their good intentions, or precisely because of them.

Agamben's essay "Absolute Immanence" constitutes a rather uncritical endorsement of the later Deleuze's determination of the "plane of immanence" as something resembling what another philosophical tradition would have called the name for the Being of beings. The Deleuzian plane of immanence is equated by Agamben to a new thought of life that establishes, he says, "a legacy that clearly concerns the coming philosophy" (220). Agamben establishes a first divide in modern philosophy that would concern immanence and transcendence. On the side of immanence, he would place Spinoza and Nietzsche and, after a certain detour through Heidegger's antisubjectivism, Foucault and Deleuze. On the side of transcendence, he would place Kant, Heidegger, Levinas, and Derrida. If Heidegger succeeds in pointing us in the direction of "the new postconscious and postsubjective, impersonal and non-individual transcendental field" (225), then after Heidegger immanence becomes, Agamben says quoting Deleuze, "the vertigo of philosophy" (226). Levinas and Derrida would suffer from ear trouble, and they can't handle the vertigo. They would have proven unable to hang on to what is for Agamben the most difficult and extreme thought, namely, the thought of the plane of immanence as the movement of the infinite (228). Levinas and Derrida would have fallen victims to a "necessary illusion" that would consist of "think[ing] transcendence within the immanent" (227), and precisely by opening their philosophies to a thought of the other that they register as the limit of every possible immanence. For Levinas and Derrida the other is the transcendent. But not for Deleuze.

Spinoza is invoked as the predecessor, given his thought of the *conatus* as the universal persevering of every being in its own being. Through the Spinozan conatus Agamben can gloss Deleuze as the thinker of "a life," that is, the transcendental field of every concrete life, which is nothing but the immanence of desire to itself, the desiring of one's own desire. In *conatus*, desire and Being coincide "without residue" (236). The program for a philosophy of the future must hold on to the new potentiality without action of the plane of immanence in order to reach "complete power, complete beatitude," which are not the consequences of a life, but rather the very content of a life itself: "A life is the immanence of immanence, absolute immanence: it is complete power, complete beatitude" (Deleuze, "Immanence," 386). The ethical program for such a philosophy would be to uphold the priority of "a life" over against any concrete life, through the discernment of "the matrix of desubjectification itself in every principle that allows for the attribution of a subjectivity" (238); in order to avoid the danger that beatitude, power, and desire become transcendental illusions, that is, in order to avoid the danger that the upholder of desubjectification becomes resubjectified through its own principle of action, "we will have to see [and, one figures, eliminate] the element that marks subjection to biopower in the very paradigm of possible beatitude" (238). This is then a program for an ethics of the good immanent life, an ethics of power increase at the service of the desubjectified, impersonal "contemplator without knowledge," free "of all cognition and all intentionality" (239). Whether one likes the rhetoric or not, it is still obvious that the Nietzschean moralism of the strong is active here, even if this time through the affirmation of a certain necessary practice that, to the extent that it demands consistency with the transcendental field of immanence, turns toward asceticism in its disavowed attempt to fill the otherwise impossible gap of desire. No politics are possible under this conceptualization other than a politics of the increase of power, where the very encounter with the power of the other as ethicopolitical encounter can only be understood as an encounter with the power of bad biopolitical power—which needs to be resisted, and somehow overcome.

The very notion of an ethicopolitical encounter is rejected from the start by Hallward's positing of an "ethics without others" in Badiou. Badiou's statement, quoted by Hallward, is certainly unequivocal: "the whole ethical predication based upon recognition of the other should be purely and simply abandoned" (29–30). Badiou's ethics is not an ethics of life, but rather an ethics of truth, which therefore exercises itself in a fidelity to events of truth that are indeed constitutive of the subject as such. Politically, the ethical condition of a truth is that it be valid for all and based upon the principle of universal equality. His is therefore a republicanism of the last man/woman, and there is no possible infrapolitical objection to the ongoing critique of every particularity, or to the indifference to every difference from the point of view of the affirmation of political universalism. Where is, then, the moralistic residue? In the very fact that the rejection of recognition—the stubborn refusal to negotiate the political encounter with beings for whom the event of truth might be differentially interpreted, or for whom there has been no political truth-event, and thus no political constitution of subjectivity—runs the risk of turning Badiouan political practice into always already Jacobinist, and way too impersonal. Yes, "philosophy has never been possible without accepting the possibility of an anonymous statement" (27), but political life in the name of anonymous statements could be dangerously close to unhinged moralism, since there is always a subject of those anonymous statements, namely, the subject of truth. And knowledge of truth is power over the ones that do not have it, or that refuse to have it. Hallward mercilessly criticizes, in Badiou's name but also in his own name, the ridiculousness of those who think "that ethics should be organized around the will of the other," perhaps refusing to understand that the ethical "passivity" endorsed by Levinas and Derrida, for instance, is far from being a renunciation of responsibility, an acceptance of compromise, or an embrace of "antiphilosophy" in Badiou's sense that passivity is nothing but the recognition that the demand for universal equality is empty if it is not accompanied by the transcendental priority of the rights of others over my own rights. If I affirm my own truth to be universal and valid for all and refuse to let my neighbor disagree for his own good, the fundamental problem is not intolerance: it is rather the fact that I become structurally incapable of engaging in the ethical adjudication of any possible ethicopolitical conflict, whatever the lasting brilliance of the politics at stake. The truth of politics is the last refuge of a moralism that will not listen to the untruth of the other.

Crime fiction—that is, the thriller—would in any case be the kind of literature that would enable us to reach that conclusion. We say that any murder conceals or hides a secret. Crime literature seeks to unveil that secret. Such a secret, the secret inscribed in the Ciudad Juárez murders, for instance, conceals the secret of the world. So crime literature looks at the world from an ethical perspective. The attempt to unconceal the secret of the world is an ethical endeavor, because no murder is primarily a theological, an historical, a political, or a literary murder (although there may be literary murders, as in Taibo and Marcos's novel). Rather, every murder is primarily an ethical breach, an ethical fault. Otherwise it would not be murder. Every murder is a relation to the other, and it is essentially a relation to the other. There is no murder, and there can be no murder, if the "ethical predication based upon recognition of the other [is] purely and simply abandoned." There will only be political adjudications of murder. Murder radically suspends the ethical imperative of the radical priority of the other, and it is therefore a negative relation to the other. But the inversion, the negation of a relation, does not destroy the relation.

The relation between literature and murder shows thus, in a privileged and remarkable way, the heteronomy, the impropriety of the literary. In particular, it shows the ethical impropriety of the literary, as literature must yield its autonomy to the pressure of ethics. In that relation, ethics disappropriates the literary, whereas literature does not, and cannot, disappropriate the ethical, which is structurally embedded in the form of language. The murders of Ciudad Juárez, not Bolaño's novel on the murders of Ciudad Juárez, hide the secret of the world. Literature looks for it, if it is at all true that something or someone looks for it, rather than that no one pays attention to any murder.

If literature seeks an ethical secret, then the ethical relation to the other dominates literature and imposes its law.

It is possible to imagine a comprehensive literary history that would deal with the relations between literature, politics, and crime. Literature is an epistemic apparatus whose radical heteronomy manifests itself fundamentally as ethical impropriety, or even as ethicopolitical impropriety. This is not because literature is improperly ethical, rather it is because literature is disappropriated by ethics even as it follows the law of ethics. Literature's impropriety is not just ethical, it is also ethicopolitical. If the murders are fundamentally an ethical relation, albeit denied or suspended, the need to investigate literarily, as much as the need to investigate historically, or even fiscally, or by the police, the very presence of murder in a given community or in the social is a need of a political order.

Murder is a suspended ethical relation, but the investigation of murder is always an ethicopolitical relation to murder. Literature, in the concrete case of crime literature, or of the thriller, when it makes of any murder, or of any crime, its focus of investigation, becomes a political apparatus that seeks to give response to an ethical suspension. Murder is ethical, insofar as it is primarily a negation or suspension of the ethical. But the need to investigate murder, the need to understand it, and the need to articulate that comprehension in language is no longer primarily an ethical obligation. It seeks to intervene in ethics, to restitute ethics, to correct, even if symbolically, an interruption or a suspension of ethics. But it is already improperly ethical, because the attempt itself, the need and the expression of the need to investigate, to understand, can only be determined out of its own distance from the ethical. That distance from the ethical is already of a political nature. Even if the very need for a literary investigation of murder finds at its very point of departure the ethical law of the radical priority of the other, if that is its heteronomy or secret law, the ethical imperative determines the literary need only improperly. The literary need is primarily, even if not exclusively, the need for a political response to the suspension of ethics and enters an ethicopolitical relation with the suspension of ethics, not just an ethical relation. This is the other side of infrapolitics, the other side of literature's heteronomy. Because literature is language and the language of a community, its ethical impropriety expresses itself necessarily in a political dimension.

That is, the literary need, as a response to the suspension of ethics, is marked by ethics, but it is also marked by the political mediation of its own apparatus, unavoidably. From the point of view of the literary apparatus itself, it is conceivable that the relation be seen as a literary mediation. But, from an ethical perspective, the literary mediation is always already political. So, from an ethical perspective, a literary reaction to a crime, or to crime, constitutes a political response to the suspension of ethics. But it is a political response that is thoroughly conditioned by the ethical relation. It is therefore an ethicopolitical response, and improper at that, on both sides. It is infrapolitical.

We have the paradox that the infrapolitical impropriety of the literary apparatus, as an ethicopolitical response to the suspension of ethics, may be literary property or literary propriety itself. Could it be that crime literature is the condition of possibility of all literature? Could it be that the thriller is the dominant narrative form not just of our time, but in fact of all time? What interests me in particular is the regional question of the relation between literature and crime, and its relation with the ethical secret of the world. Literary history, or literary criticism, could investigate the historical conditions of articulation of literature's ethicopolitical impropriety. Mexican literary history could be reinterpreted from the point of view of the study of the ethicopolitical reactions to the suspension of the ethical in Mexican life. What is at stake is the study of an improper ethics, of an improper politics, marked by literary articulation. What is at stake is the history of Mexican literary ethics as an ethicopolitical history of the suspension of ethics. This brings us to a technical problem.

Is the suspension of ethics in itself historical? Or is the suspension of ethics the limit of history and its condition of possibility, the always already past event of history that determines every possible history and every possible historical temporality? If there is a history of literature, is there also a history of denarrativization? If there is a history of ethics, can there be a history of the suspension of ethics? Or are denarrativization and the suspension of ethics theoreticopractical moments equivalent to the conceptual moment of the subaltern in Gayatri Spivak's phrase "the absolute limit of the place where history is narrativized as logic" (Spivak 17)? Perhaps the study of the improper relation between literature and crime in Mexico is nothing other than the study of the concept of the subaltern in Mexican literary production.[12]

The ethical impropriety of crime fiction, the radical heteronomy of the literary in general and of murder literature in particular, configures a structure at the very heart of the Mexican literary apparatus that disarticulates every attempt to present Mexican literature as national allegory, or as an identitarian enterprise. Impropriety is paradoxically or aporetically literature's most proper tradition. The improper literary tradition, if it is a tradition, that says that literature can never think of murders (remember Bolaño: "nobody pays attention to those murders"), but rather that literature is thought out by the murders, that tradition that restitutes a sinister heteronomy at the heart of the literary, that tradition that denies the thorough textualization of the literary, the Romanticization of the literary apparatus, that tradition that says that literature is thoroughly ruled by an outside-the-text, and that this outside-the-text is of an ethical nature and is only given a response through the ethicopolitical relation we call literature, that is also the tradition, if it is a tradition, that says that, in terms of national allegories, transculturations, identities, or any other form of attempting to configure a thinking of the nation, literature always falls short or goes too far; that it is always too literary, and thus not literary enough. Murder literature, any thriller, as part of the ethicopolitical apparatus devoted to a response to the suspension of the ethical cannot find in the national horizon any secret of the world but rather shows that the secret is always beyond the national, and that it is inaccessible to the national; that the national, and any of its present-day variations, such as the local, the global, the regional, is in fact the structure that covers over, that conceals and betrays the unthinkability of the secret. Every national/communitarian proposal in literature is a part of the ideological structure of compensation for the suspension of the ethical, for crime as such, and cannot constitute a political response to the suspension of the ethical. It is a political response, but it is not a commensurate political response. It is rather the negation and the suspension of a proper political response. The assumption of absolute historicity, as we saw, implies an affirmation of chance, a rejection of teleological necessity, and an embrace of the infrapolitical stance. Everything else is moralism.

If the elaboration of a nationalist structure in literature, or of any of its variations, is an antipolitical gesture, by virtue of being always too literary, hence not literary enough, then literary nationalism collaborates in the suspension of ethics and is therefore implicated in the crime that nobody pays attention to, but that nevertheless conceals the secret of the world. Literary nationalism is, in Mexico, and everywhere else, a heteronomous structure of concealment of the suspension of ethics, that is, concealment of the suspension of the radical priority of the other, and hence a concealment of the process of subalternization and sacrifice.

Against nationalism, and against any of its identitarian variations, one can only affirm democracy. Literature's impropriety, literature's ethical heteronomy, is the democratic mark at the heart of the literary endeavor—for a republicanism of the last man and the last woman. There is no crime fiction without ethical universalism and there is no reflection on the suspension of the ethical without a democratization of the political. In 1958, the Spanish philosopher María Zambrano, writing in Italy after having spent a few years in Mexico, said that a democratic politics was the tendential movement toward the abandonment of the sacrificial structuration of history (Zambrano 42). Crime fiction—that is, the reflexive intersection of literature and crime, heteronomically marked by the political need to interrupt the suspension of the ethical and by the ethical need to interrupt the suspension of the political—is democratic literature and seeks the abandonment of the sacrificial structuration of history. Crime literature configures an improper ethicopolitical or infrapolitical projection.

Infrapolitics is in sum the ethical charge of the literary apparatus, and the cipher of its heteronomy. In literary infrapolitics—in the not properly political but improperly ethical and improperly political—we find the link between literature and democracy, understood as the movement toward the end of the sacrificial structuration of history. Think about the literary responses needed to respond to the Ciudad Juárez's murders.

"In Mexico, *si no le madruga usted a su contrario, su contrario le madruga a usted*" (Guzmán, *Sombra* 203); "Mexican politics can only conjugate one verb: *madrugar*" (220). *Madrugar* means to wake up early in the morning, but by making the verb transitive the sentences become untranslatable. It is by now popular to say that politics in Mexico means "*madrugarle al otro*," a hard-to-translate expression that conveys the sense that politics is the art of one-upping the enemy. That would be true for Mexican politics and for any other politics. What is slightly shocking about the sentence is the cynicism involved in substituting the notion of the other by the notion of the enemy. Is every "other" an enemy? Is that what its companion sentence, "there are no friends in politics," might mean? The combination of *madrugarle al otro* as a definition of the political act and the affirmation that, in politics, there are no friends is obviously deadly for any kind of antimoralism. Indeed, the statement that the political act is the act of advantageously dealing with every other as an enemy, although widespread enough in practical terms, is the epitome of moralism, as it involves a consideration of the politician as someone who lives in permanent suspension of the ethical law, which would not apply to him or her. But the unintended consequence of such a definition is the corollary that every politician, insofar as he or she is a moralist politician, is the enemy of the human race, that is, of every last man and of every last woman. This is indeed the case. What would be the infrapolitical response?

The autonomy of the political is based on the existential threat that every enemy poses. Indeed, the enemy, in politics, can only be he or she who threatens your existence. Confronted with the existential threat, the ethical law is suspended, and the political becomes an autonomous realm of action: you are permitted preemptively to destroy he or she who, given the chance, would destroy you. The autonomy of ethics, whose ultimate goal politically speaking is the consolidation of a civil constitution in the republicanism of the last man and of the last woman, is therefore an autonomy that relates to the behavior to be observed regarding the friend, or at least the nonenemy. When there is no existential threat, there is no enemy. If the field of the political is to be understood as the field of division between friends and enemies, in Carl Schmitt's definition, then it is essential to understand that only the unjust enemy is to be fought (as Kant says, abysmally enough, "A just enemy would be one that I would be doing wrong by resisting; but then he would also not be my enemy" [Kant, *Metaphysics* 119]).[13] Everybody else is a friend.

What is, then, friendship? Kant devotes four important pages in his *Metaphysics of Morals* to a discussion of the concept of friendship, upon which he elaborates under the heading "Conclusions of the Elements of Ethics." He quotes Aristotle in the first of these pages: "My dear friends, there is no such thing as a friend" (215). As the paradoxes of this position have already been explored by Jacques Derrida in *The Politics of Friendship* (a book that can indeed be understood as a commentary on the Kantian pages I am referring to), I will not dwell on them, it would suffice to say that the sentence from Guzmán's book, "friendship does not figure . . . in the field of political relations," proffered during a conversation between friends, is a direct echo. Friendship is for Kant a duty, "no ordinary duty but an honorable one" (215). However, Kant recognizes, friendship is difficult. In its perfection, it would be "the union of two persons through equal mutual love and respect" (215). But there are many obstacles in the way of maintaining such perfect equilibrium of equality, and, Kant concludes, this form of perfect friendship "is an ideal of one's wishes, which knows no bounds in its rational concept but which must always be very limited in experience" (217).

Aesthetic friendship, therefore, friendship based on feeling or affect, Kant says, can only act as regulative idea. Moral friendship, that is, the limited form of friendship that consists of "complete confidence of two persons in revealing their secret judgments and feelings to each other, as far as such disclosures are consistent with mutual respect" (216), is, however, not just an ideal but "(like black swans) actually exists here and there in its perfection" (217). According to Kant, the notion of moral friendship serves as a model for political activity: "A friend of human beings as such (i.e., of the whole race) is one who takes an affective interest in the well-being of all human beings (rejoices with them) and will never disturb it without heartfelt regret" (217). The friend of human beings is a moral friend. Be a friend of your friends—perhaps nothing else is meant by the notion of a republicanism of the last human. No thriller has ever said anything else.

There is, however, an enigmatic sentence in Kant's pages, and I will conclude with it: "The human being is a being meant for society (though he is also an unsociable one), and in cultivating the social state he feels strongly the need to *reveal* himself to others (even with no ulterior purpose)" (216). The *need* for antimoralist revelation, for a self-exposure without calculation—it is not yet ethical, and it certainly has nothing to do with politics. It is something else and points to a realm of practical reason that can hardly be captured by the division of the latter into ethics and politics. Is it a rhetorical need? It conditions all rhetoric. It is perhaps from the incalculable abyss of this need that there can be something like an infrapolitical position, which is in itself neither properly ethical nor properly political, but which nevertheless abhors moralist betrayal. Is this not, finally, the ultimate reason for the existence of the thriller, for the need for the thriller? And is it not, finally, the only reason why there should be literature?

To José Luis Villacañas, thriller writer

Notes

*The second section of this essay subsumes a previously published article entitled "Ethics and Politics in Héctor Aguilar Camín's *Morir en el golfo* and *La guerra de Galio*" (*South Central Review* 21.3 (2004): 70–84). John Verbick and Ryan Long did the original translation of those pages from Spanish. I have simply revised it in the process of expansion of my argument.

1. Ryan Long sustains that the novelistic paradigm of the 1970s and 1980s in Mexico remains unavoidably marked by the events of Tlatelolco in 1968. In agreement with him, it is perhaps only illusory to consider *lópezportillismo* autonomously, but in any case the decline of hegemony of the PRI in the wake of the Tlatelolco massacre and the Mexican oil boom directly impact *Morir en el golfo*. References to the Tlatelolco events will be much more obvious in *La guerra de Galio*.
2. For Kant's discussions of the categorical imperative, see principally *Foundations of the Metaphysics of Morals* and *Critique of Practical Reason*. Alenka Zupančič has explored the productive nature of the aporias that emerge from the Kantian position in regard to analyzing the cultural logic of postmodernity. See Zupančič, *Ethics of the Real*.
3. The relationship between *potential* and decision is of course essential. See Giorgio Agamben, who writes "This 'I can' does not mean anything—yet it marks what it is, for each of us, perhaps the hardest and bitterest experience possible: the experience of potentiality" ("On Potentiality" 178); and "To be capable of good and evil is not simply to be capable of doing this or that good or bad action . . . Radical evil is not this or that bad deed but the potentiality for darkness. And yet this potentiality is also the potentiality for light" (181). See also Ernesto Laclau on the grounding of ethics in the binary withdrawal/engagement, a grounding that moves away from the Aristotelian understanding of the notion of *potentia* ["Ethics"].
4. The notion of "traversing the fantasy" is essential to Lacanianism, where it has an unabashedly positive signification. See for instance Slavoj Žižek, "what this means is that in order to liberate oneself from the grip of existing social reality, one should first renounce the transgressive fantasmatic supplement that attaches to it" (*Fragile Absolute* 149).
5. Guha demonstrates how the Hegelian concept of *Weltgeschichte* (whose proper translation would be world-history), in order to define its conceptual specificity, must base itself upon a Eurocentric notion of history that erases any possibility of recuperating the history of the world. Through his character Galio Bermúdez, Aguilar Camín takes to their limits certain consequences of this Hegelian concept.
6. A reference to Jorge Luis Borges's "La lotería en Babilonia" is necessary here, since Borges's story is the story of a systematic abolition of chance as undertaken by a "shadowy corporation"—the State.
7. "One must choose between a dictatorship that comes from below and a dictatorship that comes from above. I choose the one from above because it comes from the most clean and serene regions. Finally, one must choose between a dictatorship of the dagger and a dictatorship of the saber. I choose the dictatorship of the saber" (131–132). This is also Galio's option, against whose backdrop the novel presents the need for Carlos García Vigil to make a decision.
8. Which does not mean, of course, that it is easy to tell them apart. See Fenves, *Late Kant*, Chapter 4, for a good discussion of the difficulties surrounding the adjudications of radical evil and moral law to the motivations for any given political or personal action.
9. We seem to be far indeed from the moment in 1986 when Fredric Jameson affirmed, from the fact that "a certain nationalism is fundamental in the third

world" (65), that "all third-world texts are necessarily, I want to argue, allegorical, and in a very specific way: they are to be read as what I will call national allegories, even when, or perhaps I should say, particularly when their forms develop out of predominantly western machineries of representation, such as the novel" (69). Notice the mandate to the critic: texts *must be read* as national allegories. I don't think it is much in our interest to do so nowadays, which of course creates a potentially significant problem for the tradition of criticism in Latin America, which has hardly ever ventured beyond identitarian and allegorico-national frameworks.
10. See Derrida, "Passions," for comments on the structural connections between literature and democracy.
11. See Fynsk for an ethical explication of Blanchot's essay "Literature and the Right to Death." Fynsk thematizes the strange power of literature to endure in negation in ways that I think are closely connected to the basic position Weil detected in the *Iliad*. "The question [of literature], we may presume, has to do with the abstract character of the negation to which literature commits itself, possibly even the delirious character of this engagement when it is undertaken without reserve, but equally with something that escapes its murderous power: something that haunts its movement of negation and becomes an obsession" (Fynsk 229). This something that escapes any murder and every murder, and which haunts the literary, is what I am calling "infrapolitical"—although it might be something else as well.
12. The initial moment of this paper was a conversation with John Kraniauskas on the importance of the intersection of literature, crime, and politics in Mexico for any commensurate understanding of the representation of subaltern struggles in that country. Of course this essay has benefitted from many more conversations with John on thrillers in general, and Mexican literature in particular.
13. Cf. Schmitt, *Concept*, for the classical definition of the field of the political as the field of division between friends and enemies, and also for his discussion of the autonomy of the political in the existential determination of the enemy as he/she who threatens your survival.

Works Cited

Agamben, Giorgio. "Absolute Immanence." *Potentialities. Collected Essays in Philosophy*, ed. and trans. Daniel Heller-Roazen. Stanford: Stanford UP, 1999. 220–239.
———. "On Potentiality." *Potentialities*. 177–184.
Aguilar Camín, Héctor. *La guerra de Galio*, 2nd edition. Madrid: Alfaguara, 1994.
———. *Morir en el Golfo*. Barcelona: Circe, 1988.
———. "La tragedia de Colosio. Novela sin ficción." Unpublished manuscript.
Blanchot, Maurice. "Literature and the Right to Death." *The Gaze of Orpheus*, ed. P. Adams Sitney, trans. Lydia Davis. Barrytown: Station Hill, 1981.

Bolaño, Roberto. *2666*. Barcelona: Anagrama, 2004.
———. *Amuleto*. Barcelona: Anagrama, 1999.
Borges, Jorge Luis. "La lotería en Babilonia," in *Prosa completa*, Vol. 1. Barcelona: Bruguera, 1980. 441–447.
Deleuze, Gilles. "Immanence: A Life . . . ," in *Two Regimes of Madness. Texts and Interviews 1975–1995*, ed. David Lapoujade Ames Hodges and trans. Mike Taormina. New York: Semiotext(e), 2006.
Deleuze, Gilles. *Nietzsche and Philosophy*, trans. Hugh Tomlinson. New York: Columbia UP, 2002.
Derrida, Jacques. "Passions. 'An Oblique Suffering,' " in *On the Name*, ed. Thomas du Toit and trans. David Wood. Stanford: Stanford UP, 1995. 3–31.
———. *Politics of Friendship*, trans. George Collins. New York: Verso, 1997.
Donoso Cortés, Juan. "Discurso pronunciado en el Congreso el 4 de enero de 1849 [sobre los sucesos de Roma]," in *Obras*, Vol. 2, ed. Manuel Donoso Cortés and dir. Juan Manuel Ortí y Lara. Madrid: San Francisco de Sales, 1904. 109–132.
Esposito, Roberto. *Categorie dell'Impolitico*. Bolonia: Il Mulino, 1988.
Fenves, Peter. *Late Kant. Towards Another Law of the Earth*. New York: Routledge, 2003.
Fynsk, Christopher. *Language and Relation. . . . that there is language*. Stanford: Stanford UP, 1996.
Guha, Ranajit. *History at the Limit of World-History*. New York: Columbia UP, 2002.
Guzmán, Martín Luis. *La sombra del caudillo*. Mexico: Porrúa, 2001.
Hallward, Peter. "Ethics Without Others. A Reply to Critchley on Badiou's Ethics." *Radical Philosophy* 102 (2000): 27–30.
Horkheimer, Max, and Theodor Adorno. *Dialectic of Enlightenment*, trans. John Cumming. New York: Continuum, 1989.
Jameson, Fredric. "Third-World Literature in the Age of Multinational Capitalism." *Social Text* 15 (Fall 1986): 65–88.
Kant, Immanuel. *The Metaphysics of Morals*, ed. and trans. Mary Gregor. Cambridge: Cambridge UP, 2006.
———. *Perpetual Peace. A Philosophical Sketch*, in *Political Writings*, ed. Hans Reiss and trans. H.B. Nisbet. Cambridge: Cambridge UP, 2004. 93–130.
———. *Practical Philosophy*. [Includes a translation of *Grundlegung zur Metaphysik der Sitten* y *Kritik der praktischen Vernunft*.], trans. Mary J. Gregor. Cambridge: Cambridge UP, 1996.
Laclau, Ernesto. "Ethics, Normativity, and the Heteronomy of Law." Unpublished manuscript.
Long, Ryan. "Mourning the Future of the Past: The State, 1968, and the Mexican Novel." PhD Dissertation. Duke U, 2002.
Marcos, Subcomandante, and Paco Ignacio Taibo II. *Muertos incómodos (Falta lo que falta)*. Barcelona: Destino, 2005.
Schmitt, Carl. *The Concept of the Political*, trans. George Schwab. Chicago: U of Chicago P, 1996.

Spivak, Gayatri Chakravorty. "Subaltern Studies: Deconstructing Historiography," in *Selected Subaltern Studies*, ed. Ranajit Guha and Gayatri Spivak. New York: Oxford UP, 1988. 3–32.

Weil, Simone. "The Iliad, or the Poem of Force," in Weil, Simone and Rachel Bespaloff. *War and the Iliad*, trans. Mary McCarthy. New York: New York Review Books, 2005. 1–37.

Zambrano, María. *Persona y democracia. La historia sacrificial.* Barcelona: Anthropos, 1988.

Žižek, Slavoj. *The Fragile Absolute—or, Why is the Christian Legacy Worth Fighting For?* London: Verso, 2002.

Zupančič, Alenka. *Ethics of the Real. Kant, Lacan.* New York: Verso, 2000.

Part IV

THE EXPERIENCE OF READING

8

ETHICAL ASYMMETRIES:
LEARNING TO LOVE A LOSS

Doris Sommer

A few years ago, I wrote a sober "Advertencia/Warning" to preface *Proceed with Caution, When Engaged by Minority Writing in the Americas* (1999). That book offered provisional names and examples of bilingual and other tropes that maneuver in the asymmetries that classical rhetoric doesn't consider, because the classics count on cultural continuity between orator and public. The new tropes call attention to the culturally coded unevenness of information and power, especially when minority artists play to mixed audiences. Moves can hold out a chance for authorial intimacy with the reader and then hold back. "Slaps and embraces" Toni Morrison called the syncopated rhythm of minority performances, calibrated to whet desire and then to leave a lover unsatisfied. Why should a reader presume to get satisfaction or to achieve reciprocity when the decks of power are unevenly stacked? Unevenness is the point in minority writing that refuses to pander to power. Should we miss the point, trying harder to level the playing field by leveling the opposition? That would be to cultivate misrecognition, not improved reading habits.

So far, there's been little engagement with my "rhetoric of particularism," though the Spanish version, *Abrazos y rechazos: cómo leer en clave menor* (FCE, 2006), seems to be a welcome relief to Latin American readers who know that fields are not level and that the weaker players develop tricks for getting ahead of stronger ones.[1] Possibly, the general point about certain books that put some people off was off-putting to First World readers who do presume that they should gain full access and intimacy as they respond to texts that beckon for attention. The point is thorny, an irritating extension of lessons that put the reader at the center of criticism, a standard approach from the 1960s probably until today. More familiar versions of reader-response criticism make the reader into the coauthor who knows at least as much as the partner who wrote the text. Exemplary of the standard lessons that imagine a level field, or dance floor, is Georges Poulet's ideal of reciprocity between the reader's desire and that of the book:

> Books are objects. On a table, on shelves, in store windows, they wait for someone to come and deliver them from their materiality, from their immobility. When I see them on display, I look at them as I would at animals for sale, kept in little cages, and so obviously hoping for a buyer. For—there is no doubting it—animals do know that their fate depends on a human intervention . . . Isn't the same true of books? . . . They wait. Are they aware that an act of man might suddenly transform their existence? They appear to be lit up with that hope. Read me, they seem to say. I find it hard to resist their appeal (56).[2]

Once this reader-prince commands a performance and then succumbs to his own sensitivity, the rest of the essay follows a rhythm of reciprocal possession. The first move is to purchase a partner, and to feel chosen by that book; the next is to appreciate its "offering, opening itself . . . It asks nothing better than to exist outside itself, or to let you exist in it. In short, the extraordinary fact in the case of a book is the falling away of the barriers between you and it. You are inside it; it is inside you" (57).

While *Proceed with Caution* tried in earnest and mostly in vain to argue with English-language readers against this penchant for penetration, citing serious creative writers who perform asymmetry by claiming inassimilable elements of minority cultures, *Abrazos y rechazos*, as I said, seemed like a natural for Latin Americans who do not presume to be the center of irresistible attentions. Since seriousness about asymmetry left my Anglo colleagues cold, and sometimes offended when they were making every effort to understand minority writers, my next book, *Bilingual Aesthetics: A New Sentimental Education*, would try to make a similar point, by turning it into a pleasurable joke about self-serving symmetries. "Ask her if she has TB," the doctor orders in a joke I borrowed from Roberto G. Fernández. "He says if you have a television." The competing diagnoses for the difficulty of getting a green card soon climax in a hilarious and doubly-pertinent conclusion: "This is

America," says the translator, who missed the technical point but certainly got the general message. Here, the Cuban translator is ridiculous, of course, but so is the Miami doctor who has no ear for Spanish in a city where he can hardly avoid hearing it. He, as much as she, therefore curtails the cure in the microstory "Wrong Channel."[3]

Bilingual Aesthetics takes a lesson in strategy from Sigmund Freud. He published his little joke book, *Wit and its Relation to the Unconscious* (1905), barely five years after the major tome *The Interpretation of Dreams* (1900). That book disappointed readers and their readings disappointed Freud, as he explains in a pause between telling jokes that work like dreams, but more enjoyably. While dreams are private and sometimes unspeakable, jokes are public and pleasurable events. The heavy book left readers confused or skeptical, if not upset; the light one was sure to entertain and maybe win them over to consider even painful themes.

"Irritate the State" is one painful theme that can turn into mature pleasure and that I would like to review in this chapter. What does an irritating foreignness do for the public good? In fact, the gains for host countries should be counted more broadly than the narrowly economic calculations, because difficulty in communication can be a goad to procedural neutrality. It is strangeness, after all, that makes perception difficult and thereby requires the careful consideration that democracy depends on. Strangeness is also the name that Victor Shklovsky gave to the aesthetic effect of renewing what had seemed familiar and thereby refreshing our attention to and our love for the world. Cultural habits and preconceptions can mire due process, so that when procedure confronts unfamiliar cultural assumptions it may be obliged to offer cautious and conscious explanation. Law is not synonymous with a particular "natural" language. It is rather a lingua franca to coordinate particular cultures into a constitutional state. If the state were monolingual, if communication were habitual and easy, a natural language with its unexamined associations might pass for the law. To keep "natural" and constitutional languages distinct and in dialogue means that democratic subjects belong to at least two cultures: that of a particular nation or culture and that of a general state. Double consciousness, then, is not only the bane of minority subjects, as W.E.B. DuBois had complained at the turn of the last century, it is also the normal and flexible if somewhat neurotic condition of late modern life. Anything less seems intolerant of a normally complex subject as well as politically dangerous.

Acquired Taste

The advice to take aesthetic pleasure and political advantage from discomfort, contradiction, and neurosis is probably easier to understand than to assimilate. A related, maybe equally counterintuitive, distance between a simple message and the anticipation of a difficult reception describes the challenge of Emmanuel Levinas's writing. I mention him briefly here, not to presume that a short reference can do any justice to his profound work, but only to register two stunning lessons that I take from Levinas as guidelines for a bilingual aesthetics that can irritate the state and keep it alert. One lesson is the ethical value of *training over explaining* (probably inherited from medieval theology,[4] and maybe—*pace* the ironic company—also from Wittgenstein for whom explanation seemed counterproductive, an obsession for philosophers, because it is training that constitutes useful language lessons.[5])

For Levinas, contemplating the Other teaches that *asymmetry* is the normal design of relationships. Levinas's ethics begins and keeps returning to the unequal shape of the association of the lowly self, hostage to the exalted, sacred, Other. The ethical subject is born by literally subjecting self to Other. Beginning with an ontology of the self, he warned, dooms philosophy to see the rest of the world in function of the originary "I." Ontology is "egolatry." This is not a hard concept to understand. But it is so fundamentally alien and unfriendly to Western subject-centered habits of thought and feeling that each new formulation of Levinas's derivative and lowly subjecthood reads like a revelation. Adding one formulation to another was his way to retrain anticipation and sensibility. I am convinced that Levinas elaborated a recursive style that fills long books not so much to explain the rather simple lesson, but to keep readers busy and fixed on the unfamiliar and unflattering point until resistance wears down and anticipations of respectful asymmetry replace the centered self with doubt and, above all, duty toward the Other.

Extended sessions with Levinas can indeed alter a reader's instincts about ethical behavior, upsetting secular self-reliance with a sense of awe smuggled in from metaphysics. Awful responsibility to infinite difference summarizes both the drama and the impasse of his thought. No wonder Levinas has been criticized for an idealism that keeps ethics clear of politics, because nonnegotiable responsibility keeps the incommensurable Other cordoned off from the obedient self. How to "use" Levinas is a dilemma for disciples; for some it has been a reason to desist from the effort. But the training to anticipate asymmetrical relationships without the ambition to level them is too precious to simply forfeit. Perhaps the training can lead to artistic and political ways out of the impasse between self and Other, whether or not Levinas would have approved. He did admit, nevertheless, that the demands of justice (involving more than one Other) interfere with abstract ethics and break the enchantment of absolute otherness.

Ironically, the way out of impasses is paved by awe itself. The tremor it provokes can pry open detours around the paralysis that awe imposes in a first moment. We humans don't sustain the impact for long; instead we look away and survive. And surviving even quotidian shocks and unpleasantness produces a mature pleasure that aesthetic theory since Kant calls the sublime. The point I am making is that competent reading locates a constitutive lack in our understanding; it engages with more, not less, refinement than theorists generally access because they tend to mistake foreignness as interference, something to be overcome rather than as a sign of sacred otherness. Emmanuel Kant is an ally for multiculturalism, despite some conservative claims on him. While some teachers object to cultural particularism because current practices of ethnic essentialism can dismiss aesthetics as extraneous or elitist, the aesthetic attractions of foreign, even fearsome, cultural differences should claim our attention as literary and cultural critics. The disturbing sublime offers more intense effects than easily lovable beauty. The sublime elicits respect, not love; and it offers a thrill of survival that comes close to catharsis. Few of us can avoid fear today in a world where neighbors are often strangers. Can strangeness itself, then, become our nonviolent commonality? Perhaps, but it will take the refinement of a new sentimental education that anticipates the sublime and works through its stages of fear, survival, and the profound pleasure of accessing resilient reason. We will have to prepare reason to process the pain of incomprehension into the joy of contemplating a complicated world.

To reflect on the pain of losing control is to gain an intellectual perspective on one's limitations; that is, a maturity that enhances and finally flatters the once fearful subject. As a result, the gratifying result of confronting awful difference becomes (to follow Roland Barthes's neurotic inspiration) an incentive to endure the pain. A certain taste for the risk and a tolerance for personal demotion allow the sublime to work its unsettling effects. In other words, if we can submit to the shock of otherness (in the face that stares down Levinas's reader, in Muslim scarves, in foreign accents), the impact can explode our fragile confidence in understanding and open a path for reflection. Our lack of understanding triggers reason to rescue us; and reason teaches us that we are limited, that the world is complex beyond our understanding, worthy of respect while we reasonable survivors are worthy of admiration. The taste for risk and the tolerance for irritation are—as I said—easy principles to appreciate but hard feelings to acquire. That is why a new sentimental education should be on our collective agenda. To put it urgently, the predisposition for democracy cannot depend on existing stages of our faculties for reason and judgment. These faculties are innate but underdeveloped. They depend on education.

Training programs are arduous but this need not dissuade seasoned teachers. After all, teaching is a socializing activity, whether this is intentional or not. And teachers might take conscious responsibility to promote a new sentimental education. We can count on distinguished mentors. Among the precursors of an education in artful embraces of asymmetry are Friedrich Schiller, Vicktor Shklovsky, Sigmund Freud, Walter Benjamin, and Roland Barthes. They lead in the general direction of aesthetics, through rough or gnarled detours around speechlessness (whether its cause is unremarkable familiarity or unspeakable passions). All of them know the byroads to politics. Political masters of the detour and unconventional maneuver are surely available as well. I will mention the examples of Antonio Gramsci and a couple of his best readers as an invitation for you to recall others.

Paso Doble

"Scientific" Marxism would have advised Gramsci to wait for an appropriate historical conjuncture in Southern Italy. The forces that should have lined up in a neat ordered hierarchy, from economics at the top to culture at the epiphenomenal bottom, were underdeveloped. But with Gramsci's peripheral vision from Southern Italy (suggesting other southern and subaltern perspectives), if the forces of history didn't add up right, workers would have to force change by other means. The apparently reasonable advice to be patient didn't paralyze Gramsci; it showed that historical determinants needed some roughing up in order to energize the logic of struggle. Gramsci detoured from the unbeatable odds of capitalist domination with a *jogo de cintura* as Brazilians call the sidestep soccer move. (Puerto Ricans call it *jaibería* for the crablike maneuver to outdo an enemy by avoiding confrontation). The move was from the waist, not forward nor backward, but sideways from existing structures, veering away from both the logic of capital and from the "scientific" Marxism that planned capital's demise.

Gramsci's gesture made mischief with historical fatality. He saw that the unity of an emergent class would depend on ideology, not on any allegedly material determinants of economic destiny. So he bypassed those unpromising determinants to intervene at the level of "superstructure," practically inverting its presumed dependence on the "base."[6] Gramsci promoted cultural and political work as a way out of economistic deadlocks. The push of economic constraints and the pull of a useable culture describe a dynamic interdependent two-step (between conjunctures and science). For a literary critic, the double movement may evoke the "dialectical allegory" between desire and disaster that Benjamin described as history—and the alternation, also the rhythm of "slaps and embraces," between particular (conjuncture) and universal (science) that Toni Morrison describes as the unsettling quality of peripheral or minority art. The inside-outside movement toggles in the asymmetries between "legitimate" and risky positions to improvise the new and improved step of Gramsci's emancipatory politics.

Whereas Hegel and Marx drew the line between elements that could participate in society and those unredeemable elements that could not, Gramsci moves between inside and outside to disturb the distinction and to stretch the limits of society. With one "scientific" step he marks the exclusions of "the rabble" or *lumpen* who represented pure exteriority for philosophy. With the other "cultural" step he translates competing interests into a hegemonic ideology that facilitates alliances between the rabble, the peasants, and the capitalists.[7] Adding the real irritating and disturbing difference of the outliers to the chain of equivalences among insiders means that Gramsci recasts the logic of political participation. He took his cue from the unorthodox excluded demands, lest they rankle and fester instead of fueling a united effort.

Containing those exorbitant demands by bringing them in was a step toward a sturdy and flexible theory of hegemony, which I translate here as asymmetrical codependence: the ruling class depends on other classes that agree to be ruled, and the other classes extract benefits in exchange.[8] The inclusive maneuver roughened and refreshed the logic of equivalences to activate social asymmetries into a war of position. Uneven and codependent class interests of hegemony disturb the "science" of Marxism and turn it into an artful practice of risky coordination, something like juggling sticks on fire.

Gramsci's salve or glue for antagonistic classes that were stuck with one another was a shared culture, "the expressive form of the common general interests of a society; a conception present in the young

Marx."[9] But today, what are we to make of this hegemonic management that speaks for the common "people-nation," as if the concepts of state and nation were not coming unglued? Today, outlying sectors of society show not only class but also cultural differences from the hegemonic center, so that including them stretches the boundaries of permissible participants beyond the ideal of a single "people." Any new hegemonic project will have to woo its allies by preferring the asymmetrical *interruptus* of communication over outdated fantasies of cultural continuity. Should we lament the loss of easy equivalences? No, because the problem for communication is a salutary irritant to politically debilitating habituation. The syncopated rhythm between contact and estrangement among social groups refreshes the distinction between culturally particular nations and the administrative space of a state where nations can engage each other.

Gramsci's single ending of the word "emancipation" shows the single direction of his war of positions, or "passive revolution," to win power for the working class.[10] His sidestep to culture relaxed the class requirements for warriors but left the ideal outcome intact.[11] Outcomes, however, can be more than one, Ernesto Laclau glosses after Gramsci. Laclau rehabilitates "emancipation" by pluralizing Gramsci's move and multiplying the results that follow from unhinging science from Marxism: "By playing within the system of logical incompatibilities; . . . by looking at the effects which follow from the subversion of each of its two incompatible sides by the other," struggle can 'drift away' from any single operation."[12]

There is room to wiggle and to juggle. Fantasies of absolute freedom (Levinas dreaded the egolatry of that desire) as the purpose of politics breaks up into particular *Emancipation(s)* for Laclau. Between the singular and the plural grammar is a political difference that Deleuze and Guattari also marked. It distinguishes between a determination to draw the right line of politics and a penchant for making maps with many spots for trouble-shooting. For some activists and intellectuals, the goal is no longer the dusk of capitalism before the dawn of stable egalitarian utopias, but many smaller, often local, targets of reform. For others, losing a coherent Marxian goal means losing one's way, even if the post–cold war world makes radicalism rhyme with religious extremism. Apparently, monotheism migrates easily from single-minded religious devotion to single-minded sacrificial ideology.[13] Utopian dreams of final solutions, perfect and airless, cannot tolerate the dangerous supplements of dissent and politics. Fear final utopia and pursue politics (a variation on the Sages' "fear evil and pursue the good") is my simple distillation of Laclau's eloquent *Emancipations*. Utopia can be absolutist and inflexible, beyond conflict and therefore intolerant of politics. That is why democracy (which thrives on politics, i.e., antagonisms) cannot afford to be utopian in the monological sense.

Democracy depends on difference, as I have been saying, and needs the healthy asymmetrical side-effects of homegrown diversity and of foreign immigration. Immigration, regional, ethnic, and gender rights, all upset the airless compact between nation and state, while stretching liberal practices toward a greater realization of liberalism's own promises. Universalism itself depends on difference, to follow Laclau's provocative formulation shared by some critical legal scholars. The universal has survived classical philosophy's dismissal of particularity as deviation, the medieval collapse of universality into Christ, and it has outlived a European Enlightenment that conflated the universal (subject, class, culture) with particular (French) incarnations.

Today's universalism is a paradox for the past, because it turns out to be the space for particularist demands. They unmoor universalism from any fixed cultural content and keep it open to an "always receding horizon."[14] The corollary paradox of democracy, Laclau admits without embarrassment, is that it requires unity but depends on diversity. Tension and ambiguity are structural elements for democracy, which neither Habermas's ideal of rational communication nor Lyotard's lament over conflicts between discursive regimes care to underline.[15] The point of politics is to win ground and rights from centers of power, not to eliminate the power that provokes irritation and struggle. This is perhaps the closest that political philosophy comes to appreciating antagonism as democracy's normal condition, very close to Judith Butler's psychoanalytic twist that makes personal subjecthood depend on opposition.[16]

Struggles for particular freedoms don't presume to destroy the state; they need it as an antagonist in a contest for concessions. Without locating a lack, there are no struggles and no victories. The object is to win ground in hegemonic arrangements; and those arrangements are open to adjustments because hegemony depends on popular consent. The program of "passive revolution" irritates the state in ways that stimulate concessions of progressively-increasing rights and resources. Of course, this reformist dynamic is disappointing to many critics of capital who prefer systemic responses to an unfair system. But the unquestionable virtue of this pluralized approach is the recognition of multiple agendas and voices, whereas the single thrust of most utopian movements would subordinate or cancel particular concerns. The knack of stepping aside from power in order to win some ground is being honed in various ways; any project for a new hegemony will need to acknowledge this range of talent.

I Don't Dance

Political theory has been slow to pursue the advantages of asymmetry. Bonnie Honig's exploration is an exception that highlights the general reluctance to address cultural unevenness as an enabling condition of liberal democracy. She defends foreigners, not only as legitimate beneficiaries of the host state, but also as salutary irritants to entrenched practices. Tellingly, Honig takes a detour through creative literature, the Story of Ruth, and gothic novels, because the discipline of political theory would mire her speculation in anxieties about foreigners. They are a problem for most theorists, a strain or an interruption of national arrangements. When theory is not being defensive about immigration, it responds with compensatory designs to make obligatory room for difference, often spelling out rights and responsibilities for citizens who no longer speak the same native language.[17] Conventional political thought continues to conflate the concepts of nation and state and considers monolingualism the natural, if not ideal, condition for communication. Bilingualism is either unnecessary complexity, or an unfortunate lack of coherence. At most, standard political thought acknowledges that in some countries the one-people-one-language ideal can break down regionally, where local language groups demand autonomy for the same "nationalist" goal of coherent cultural identity that the country in question favors at the state level. Some theorists favor regional autonomy and others worry about the disintegrating effect on the country. In either case, the assumption is that people choose between language identities rather than live with both. Why assume this either/or choice? Most people have never lived like that. And it's a good thing.

Although studies in international relations are beginning to suggest that demands by immigrants enhance liberal politics,[18] except for Honig's work, we don't often ask how immigration at home stimulates our own liberal respect for difference.[19] Two stimuli seem obvious nevertheless: One potential advantage is the bilingual's unsettling sense of human arrangements. For a foreigner who thinks in more than one language, arrangements are obviously constructed and precarious. The tentative and fissured be-longings of many bilinguals demand caution and respectful distance from others whom we cannot presume to understand easily.[20] That is why formal modes of address that cast interlocutors as distant third persons are more democratizing than the utopian dream of grammatical symmetry imagines.[21] Another possible advantage of the migrant's feeling of fitting badly is precisely that *Unheimlichkeit* is unhappy and restless. (Johann von Herder's defense of the *volk* had diagnosed bilingualism as indigestion.[22]) The benefit of being at a loss and cautiously anticipating unpredictable differences is that one experiences existing arrangements with a margin of disidentification and, possibly, with the frustration that generates action.

These stimuli to democracy urge those of us who interpret and teach about the arts to catch up to multicultural creativity. The lag among humanists is alarming, even if social scientists remain skeptical about what we do. What humanists *do* is teach taste, judgment, sensibility, that is, a predisposition for one kind of politics or another. "Habits of the heart" is what Tocqueville called the disposition for democracy, even if he grounded them in Christian sentiment.[23] Tocqueville should be nudged to more neutral ground, says William Connolly, because religious sentiment and politics feed on one another, and the comment about Christianity could invoke a range of sacred traditions.[24] By locating belief at a "visceral register," Connolly's reading of Tocqueville brings religion close to the aesthetic perceptions that humanist train their students to develop. This proximity between belief and aesthetics steers politics clear of some sticky interfaith competitions and puts the training of democratic dispositions on shared ground.

Hearts and minds remain undervalued organs for democracy, according to recent reports on civil society.[25] Therefore, teaching those enabling habits at this late stage of democratic developments can renew an opportunity (and an obligation) for alliances between politics and literature, among other arts. Laclau's proposals for plural emancipations and for a universalism that hosts particular demands needs pedagogues who can teach a taste for irritation; and literary studies can take this opportunity to count its own practices of interpretation among the urgent contributions that democracy needs now. This will mean learning and teaching to love the lack (of understanding, symmetry, mastery) as a constitutive element of literature.

Alter-Nations

The necessary training will be to think and feel on one's feet, both of them, as does Gramsci. With one leg in a shared political culture and another in particular religious or linguistic cultures, we move in syncopated rhythms that fall out of step with holy wars. Doubleness or tripleness or more is the sane answer to single-minded zeal. For Christ's sake, we might take Jesus at his word when he admitted two poles of obligation: one belonging to Caesar and the other to God ("zu Got und zu lad" is the Yiddish version). This doesn't assume that monotheism relieves the faithful from secular duties, or that it leaves a suicidal void if faith lapses.[26] The world is not the kingdom of heaven. But this devout lesson in doubleness is lost on ardent believers and patriots who insist on either this or that. In the Catholic tradition of Latin America, Jesús Martín-Barbero notes, religion and radical politics are often Janus faces for monotheism. A pity, he says, in a continent where the church developed a splendid taste for baroque twists and turns that cannot fill in the mystery of faith.[27]

Just off the continent, Puerto Ricans typically brush off both the Spanish-only and English-only ideologues of monolingual coherence with "Hablamos los dos" [We speak both]. From their cultural margin, folded into flexible wedge into both the mainland offensive and the defensiveness of a *patria chica*, Puerto Ricans, like many other bilinguals, play a counterpoint between the inclusive political state that speaks English and the particular cultural nation that speaks Spanish. Nineteenth-century liberalism had collapsed that difference, dreaming of an ideal coherence between a constitutional administrative structure and sentimental cultural ties. The disastrous result of confusing general law with particular feelings is sometimes called fascism. More sensible citizens of the work in progress called democracy assume the normal asymmetry of double consciousness between public and private duties and desires.[28]

W.E.B. DuBois had complained about that burden in the case of African Americans, divided against themselves, because the minority and the majority consciousnesses clashed too violently for anyone who wasn't white. To him, dissonance, irritation, and bicultural blues were unfair and unappealing. But today, double consciousness and bilingual binds no longer seem soluble nor do they require solutions. The split soul might look, if we focused right, like an intense experience of the general split structure of language and of living as human beings. Jacques Lacan helped to make this split a standard feature of human sciences. In fact, the unhappy minority consciousness that DuBois complained about could be a vanguard for our best cultural defense of humane practices, because doubleness and dissonance won't allow the meanness of one thought or one striving after an outdated alchemical gold-standard of cultural value.

Can we develop our taste for dissonance instead of feeling forced to chose and lose between identity politics and abstract universalism?[29] By now, in late modernity, it's time for this new taste for discord so we can enjoy counterpoint, because simpler sounds cannot be democratic By definition, bilingualism cultivates both particular identity and universal law. It is no communitarian bastion of a single tradition that might resist learning the common code, as some alarmists imagine. On the contrary, immigrant parents notoriously favor the lingua franca over their own heritage language for children who would otherwise forfeit many of the opportunities that encouraged migration in the first place.[30] Can we adjust to the overloads of language, music, and sense of humor, in ways that let cultural differences sound good for democracy? Dissonance, after all, distinguishes between the state as an inclusive construction and the particular national traditions that might irritate the state just enough to keep it flexible.

It is a challenge that we might seize like an opportunity. We cannot, frankly, afford to ignore differences among us—neither ethically if we take seriously our commitment to democratic pluralism nor pragmatically, given the inevitability of global migrations, of worldwide transportation, and the thickening networks of intercultural commerce. Cultural differences are internal too, now that the word "identity" sounds like an oxymoron for describing the multiple be-longings that pull individuals in different directions.[31] Defense from fanaticism will need to include pleasure in one's exorbitant self. It needs a change of heart. The kind of suicidal single-mindedness that inspires jihads (and corresponding crusades) makes terror wax, not wane.

Continued threats of terrorism are bound to raise more demands for revenge. If the ardor of militants on one side and the escalating responses of avengers on the other side are difficult to diffuse, some of us should step back and consider how to mitigate future dangers of terrorist networks. The networks apparently attract new recruits and count on broad sympathies of people who object to the United States for both good and bad reasons. One unfortunately good reason for hating the United States is its habit of cultivating a self-defeating variety of democracy that sometimes plants tyranny abroad and then feeds on it. Whether or not less-damaging policies would win sympathy and support is a matter of conjecture. However, a finer taste for democratic culture in the United States would certainly shore up the alternative to intolerance at home. Democracy is a cultural taste to a degree that some may be reluctant to acknowledge; it is taste for constitutional culture that makes minority subjects, who also belong to particular nations, at least bicultural. And biculturalism is also the characteristic of peace loving "alternative modernities."[32] Affirming both the language of local traditions and that of universal rights defends developing countries from fixing on a single goal, for instance, the efficient monocultural extremism that produces terror. Democracy as an alternative to terror depends on a preference for experimental hits and misses as it coordinates a modern state with traditional nations. Like the lingua franca that a democracy speaks in multicultural environments, democratic culture takes on meaning from its *convivencia* with particular "natural" languages. It will sing the bilingual blues, because losses of meaning are unavoidable effects of *alternancia* [code-switching] in countries where no one masters all the codes. Maybe that is not a pleasing option for everyone. But learning to love the losses of coherence will prepare hearts for a mind to be democratic.

Notes

1. Josefina Ludmer. "Tretas del débil."
2. Georges Poulet. "Criticism and the Experience of Interiority." 56–72; reprinted in *Reader-Response Criticism: From Formalism to Post-Structuralism*, ed. Jane Tomkins. Baltimore: The Johns Hopkins UP, 1980. 41–49.
3. Roberto G. Fernández. "Wrong Channel." *Micro Fiction: An Anthology of Really Short Stories*, ed. Jerome Stern. New York: Norton, 1996.
4. See William E. Connolly's "Refashioning the Secular" on Talal Adad's exploration of the medieval Christian perspective on intersubjectivity, shared by Nietzsche (157–192).
5. Ludwig Wittgenstein, *Philosophical Investigations*, See §6c on the necessity for more than ostensive teaching. Training is needed as well.
6. "What was previously secondary and subordinate, or even incidental, is now taken to be primary—becomes the nucleus of a new ideological and theoretical complex." Gramsci, *Quaderni dal Carcere*. Quoted from Laclau and Mouffe, *Hegemony and Socialist Strategy*. 68.
7. See Laclau and Mouffe. 65–71.
8. See also the "political, intellectual and moral leadership over allied groups." Gramsci, *Selections from the Prison Notebooks*, 161.
9. Mouffe, "Introduction," in *Gramsci & Marxist Theory*. 10.
10. Gramsci, *Prison Notebooks*. 114.
11. Laclau and Mouffe. 69–70.

12. Laclau, *Emancipation(s)*. 2, 8.
13. Jesús Martín-Barbero, "Desencantos de la socialidad y reencantamientos de la identidad." 9.
14. Ernesto Laclau, "Universalism, Particularism and the Question of Identity." 93–108. 107. Judith Butler cautiously agrees that universality can be a site of translation. See Benhabib et al., *Feminist Contentions*: "The universal is always culturally articulated, and that the complex process of learning how to read that claim is not something any of us can do outside of the difficult process of cultural translation."
15. Lyotard, *The Differend: Phrases in Dispute*.
16. Butler, *The Psychic Life of Power*.
17. For a review of this issue, see Benhabib, *The Claims of Culture*.
18. See Albert, Jacobson, and Lapid, *Identities, Borders, Orders*.
19. From Hobbes on, liberalism understands that conflicting interests and values demand the institutions of government. One way to pose the dynamic is to appreciate and even promote conflicts (economics calls it competition) as stimuli to insure the vitality of those institutions. This is the twist Reiker puts on his defense of *Liberalism Against Populism*.
20. Dahl, *On Democracy*.
21. Scott, *Domination and the Arts of Resistance*, 31:
    In the past, the polite and familiar forms of the second person pronoun (*vous* and *tu* in French, respectively) were used asymmetrically in a semantic of power. The dominant class used *tu* when addressing commoners, servants, peasants and received back the more polite, dignified *vous* . . . Inasmuch as there was a determined effort by the revolutionaries in France immediately after 1789 to ban the use of *vous*, we can take it for granted that this semantic of power was not a matter of popular indifference. To this day, at socialist and communist gatherings, Europeans who are strangers will use the familiar form with one another to express equality and comradeship. In ordinary usage *vous* is now used *reciprocally* to express not status, but lack of close acquaintance.
    There is no hint in Scott that the third person can continue to show respect, even affectionately, while it marks asymmetry. Even when it is used reciprocally, it can perform the necessary distancing that safeguards against intimate overlapping and the danger of *fungibility*.
22. See my *Bilingual Aesthetics*, Chapter 2 "Aesthetics is a Joke."
23. Tocqueville's *Democracy in America* (1835) is one of the inspirations for Jean Bethke Elshtain's defense of religious institutions in "Civil Society, Religion, and the Formation of Citizens." On page 267, "According to Tocqueville, democracy requires laws, constitutions, and authoritative institutions. But it also depends on what he called 'habits of the heart' forged within the framework such institutions provided."
24. Connolly, "Refashioning the Secular." 163.
25. *Alternative Conceptions of Civil Society*, ed. Chambers and Kymlicka. See especially Chapter 4, Anne Phillips, "Does Feminism Need a Conception of

Civil Society?" 71–89 and Chapter 5, Simone Chambers, "A Critical Theory of Civil Society," 90–110.
26. I refer here to Steiner's version of Western history, through Pascal, Kierkegaard, Dostoyevsky, for whom skepticism corrodes all value once faith fails (*In Bluebeard's Castle*, quoted in Martín-Barbero, "Desencantos de la socialidad y reencantamientos de la identidad." 5).
27. Martín-Barbero, "Desencantos de la socialidad y reencantamientos de la identidad." 6.
28. Part of Puerto Rico's nonaggressive heroism is the refusal to give up Spanish, despite half a century of "English-only" restrictions in education and politics. And on the mainland, Latinos continue to speak both. "One in four New Yorkers is Latino, and most speak both English and Spanish." Curiously, as if the either/or language logic of U.S. assimilation cancelled the news she reports, the title of Navarro's article is, "Redefining 'Latino,' " 30.
29. Identity affirmation is, of course, not only a tactic for the poor and excluded, but also a reaction to them by nativists, not only in the United States. Martín-Barbero mentions "the intolerance present in Argentina and Chile that works to exclude Bolivian or Paraguayan migrant laborers through their own working sectors of the population." ["la intolerancia con la que en Argentina o Chile son excluidos, por los propios sectores obreros, los migrantes provenientes de Bolivia o Paraguay." 10.] See also Grimson, *Relatos de la diferencia y la igualdad*. Russell Hardin gives this useful formulation of democratic life as belonging to more than one community: "Unless a community is merely one of many to which I belong, none of which makes very great demands on my life, there cannot be genuine communities in the modern world." *One for All*. 25.
30. Immigrants and internal migrants also watch TV and listen to radio in particular circuits that can strain against the national networks (Quechua radio plays in Lima; Aymara in Bolivia). Martín-Barbero reports some worries about the loss of collective values in segmented audiences that no longer amount to a public that can take to the streets or even meet at the movies (3). But he hears heartening responses to the fragmentation from feminists who admit their fissured subjectivity, between the identity politics of gender, and general goals of emancipation. A politics of recognition also sounds promising to him, but I am not sure why, since it hopes to heal the fissures by closing the ranks of community.
31. See Hall for his widely cited formulation. "Cultural Identity and Diaspora," and *Identity: Community, Culture, Difference*, ed. Rutherford.
32. On this concept, see *Alternative Modernities*, ed. Dilip Parameshwar Gaonkar.

Works Cited

Albert, David, Mathias Jacobson, and Josef Lapid. *Identities, Borders, Orders: Rethinking International Relations Theory*. Minneapolis: U of Minnesota P, 2001.
Benhabib, Seyla. *The Claims of Culture*. Princeton: Princeton UP, 2002.
Benhabib, Seyla, Judith Butler, Drucilla Cornell, and Nancy Fraser. *Feminist Contentions: A Philosophical Exchange*, intro. Linda Nicholson. New York: Routledge, 1995.

Butler, Judith. *The Psychic Life of Power: Theories in Subjection*. Stanford: Stanford UP, 1997.

Chambers, Simone, and Will Kymlicka, *Alternative Conceptions of Civil Society*. Princeton: Princeton UP, 2002.

Connolly, William E. "Refashioning the Secular," in *What's Left of Theory?: New Work on the Politics of Literary Theory*, ed. Judith Butler, John Guillory, and Kendall Thomas. New York: Routledge, 2000.

Dahl, Robert. *On Democracy*. New Haven: Yale UP, 1998.

Elshtain, Jean Bethke. "Civil Society, Religion, and the Formation of Citizens," in *Making Good Citizens: Education and Civil Society*, ed. Ravitch and Viteritti. New Haven: Yale UP, 2001. 263–278.

Fernández, Roberto G. "Wrong Channel," in *Micro Fiction: An Anthology of Really Short Stories*, ed. Jerome Stern. New York: Norton, 1996.

Freud, Sigmund. *Der Witz und seine Beziehung zum Unbewussten [Wit and its Relation to the Unconscious]*. Vienna: F. Deuticke, 1905.

———. *Die Traumdeutung* [The Interpretation of Dreams]. Vienna: F. Deuticke, 1900.

Gaonkar, Dilip Parameshwar, ed. *Alternative Modernities*. Duke UP, 2001.

Gramsci, Antonio. *Quaderni dal Carcere* Vol. 2, ed. V. Gerratana. Turin: Einaudi, 1975. 1058.

———. *Selections from the Prison Notebooks*, ed. and trans. Q. Hoare and G. Nowell Smith. London: Lawrence & Wishart, 1973.

Grimson, A. *Relatos de la diferencia y la igualdad: Los bolivianos en Buenos*. Buenos Aires: Eudeba, 1999.

Hall, Stuart. "Cultural Identity and Diaspora," in *Identity: Community, Culture, Difference*, ed. Jonathan Rutherford. London: Lawrence & Wishart, 1990.

Hardin, Russell. *One for All: The Logic of Group Conflict*. Princeton: Princeton UP, 1995.

Laclau, Ernesto. *Emancipation(s)*. London: Verso, 1996.

———. "Universalism, Particularism and the Question of Identity," in *The Identity In Question*, ed. John Rajchman. New York: Routledge, 1995.

Laclau, Ernesto, and Chantal Mouffe. *Hegemony and Socialist Strategy: Towards a Radical Democratic Politics*. London: Verso, 2001 [1985].

Ludmer, Josefina. "Tretas del débil," in *La sartén por el mango, encuentro de escritores latinoamericanos*, ed. Patricia E. González and Eliana Ortega. Río Piedras, P.R.: El Huracán, 1984.

Lyotard, Jean François. *The Differend: Phrases in Dispute*, trans. Georges Van Den Abbeele. Minneapolis: U of Minnesota P, 1998.

Martín-Barbero, Jesús. "Desencantos de la socialidad y reencantamientos de la identidad." Paper presented at the New York University, New York. 3 Oct. 2001.

Mouffe, Chantal. "Introduction," in *Gramsci & Marxist Theory*, ed. Chantal Mouffe. London: Routledge & Kegan Paul, 1979.

Navarro, Mireya. "Redefining 'Latino,' This Time in English." *New York Times*, August 8, 2003, "New York Report," 30.

Poulet, Georges. "Criticism and the Experience of Interiority," in *The Structuralist Controversy: The Language of Criticism and the Science of Man*, ed. Richard A. Macksey and Eugenio Donato. Baltimore: The Johns Hopkins UP, 1972.

Reiker, William. *Liberalism Against Populism.* San Francisco: W.H. Freeman, 1982.

Rutherford, Jonathan, ed. *Identity: Community, Culture, Difference.* London: Lawrence & Wishart, 1990.

Scott, James C. *Domination and the Arts of Resistance: Hidden Transcripts.* New Haven: Yale UP, 1992.

Sommer, Doris. *Abrazos y rechazos: cómo leer en clave menor.* Mexico: FCE, 2006.

———. *Bilingual Aesthetics: A New Sentimental Education.* Durham: Duke UP, 2004.

———. *Proceed with Caution, When Engaged by Minority Writing in the Americas.* Cambridge: Harvard UP, 2004.

Steiner, George. *In Bluebeard's Castle: Some Notes Towards the Redefinition of Culture.* New Haven: Yale UP, 1971.

Tocqueville, Alexis de. *Democracy in America*, trans. Henry Reeve. London: Saunders and Otley, 1835.

Wittgenstein, Ludwig. *Philosophical Investigations*, trans. G.E.M. Anscombe. New York: Macmillan Publishing Co., 1953, 1968.

9

READING FOR THE PEOPLE AND GETTING THERE FIRST

Francine Masiello

It is 5 a.m. and the airport van scoops me up from my Berkeley doorstep. Listless, I prepare for yet one more transcontinental trip, papers in order, flash drive tucked in, tomatoes from my garden for those *porteño* friends long stuck in the gloom of winter. I am exhausted by the prospect of travel even as I leave my house. Nonetheless, the sociology of criticism kicks in, a motor without a mind, while the van meanders through the local streets toward the freeway and then the airport. I see one, two, eight homeless men pushing shopping carts in these predawn hours. Beating the municipal garbage collectors by an easy stretch, they forage for that scrap of glass or cardboard that will claim some redemptive value. I have scarcely paid them heed over time, but today they claim my attention. After all, I'm en route to Buenos Aires to see the *cartoneros* [garbage pickers]. Slumped on the bus, I can't help asking about the irony of my tourist-like gesture. Clearly, I have my own *cartoneros*, my homeless neighbors at home. What allows me to think that the Argentine condition will solicit something different? I also remind myself that if I'm in a quandary, my middle-class Argentine colleagues haven't managed this problem much better.

Almost to echo Hardt and Negri, who eagerly predicted the fall of neoliberalism through the efforts of the multitude, intellectuals took the social actors of 2001 as the favorite topic of a new literature and art. *Cartoneros, piqueteros* [picketers], women in occupied factories, figures of the postwork world who migrate from country to city—they all became fertile ground for film, literature, and essay. Yet this celebration took a strange course of events. Under the editorial oversight of Eloísa Cartonero (in reality, Fernanda Laguna), *cartoneros* were hired to staple avant-garde fiction and verse between sheets of recycled cardboard; in tangent, the art magazine *Ramona*, an invention of Roberto Jacoby, announced on the Web that if you bought a book from this particular series, one of the *cartoneros* would deliver the purchase to your door.

Shake hands with the *cartonero*. Get the chance to sit next to a homeless man. Present your book in a *librería*, cash in on the cultural capital that the homeless man provides, invite him to share the spotlight with you as your friends read texts in your honor; come celebrate yourself and the poor man as well. *Cartoneros* as the subjects of heroic couplets, of romances and melodramas, even avant-garde writing; E-bay will sell you a scrap of metal harvested by the Argentine poor. And if in the zest of the Chiapas events, supporters of the Zapatistas sang, "we're all Marcos," in Buenos Aires, the cry went forth "we're all *cartoneros*." Taken to an extreme, *Página 12* (September 10, 2005) reported on *cartoneros*-fashion, a publicity stunt launched by an ad agency that wanted to claim some attention. So if cell phones can be sold to prostitutes, why not exploit this *cartonero* niche as well? But along with this, we as middle-class folk might also want to dress like *cartoneros*, the ad men tell us. For-us-by-us, FUBU up here; *marca rioplatense* over there. Let's get down with the *cartoneros* and cheer for the unemployed. "The *cartonero* attracts interest as an image because he carries a proposal for work," a public relations executive claims. This may draw us toward the banalization of poverty (to rework Hannah Arendt's classic phrase), or toward what others have called our insatiable "hunger for relevance" (Altieri 1).

Edgardo Cosarinksy's recent film, *Ronda nocturna* [Night Beat], a pathetic ode to neoliberal Argentina and a paean to the nightlife of homosexual desire, stakes a claim to originality by bringing us into the visual scene the episodes that I have just described. In the opening scene of this film, *cartoneros* of the early night advance with their wagons and carts along the curbs of Alto Palermo; they traverse the paths of anxious shoppers flagging cabs to carry them home. The final scenes show *cartoneros* pushing their carts into dawn. These figures seem to announce a new subject in the making, silent yet meant to be seen. In fact, the publicity that anticipated the film drew attention to this social image; radical and explosive, they claimed, the "real" Buenos Aires at last. Through staging, improvisation, imposture, the *cartoneros* are meant to be seen in the moment. Their image, *only* their image, strikes at the heart of a problem in literature that links ethics to representation.¹

Shortly after the crisis of December 2001, I was astonished by the trafficking of faith, the trust in miracles that enabled Argentines to plant seeds of hope in the soil of local culture following the economic collapse; today, with the passing of time, I find a need to rethink that proposal. If today, on the one hand, our relation to *image* traps us in cynical reason, on the other, we openly acknowledge a starched lack of feeling, a numbness that enfolds us and that we try to resist. To overcome this, we turn to popular subjects to trigger our social fulfillment and to open the space of art and literature for a material reading of reading. Torn between the suspicion and indulgence that these topics provoke, I want to trace the dual paths that test the limits of experience and ethics.

The People

From the time of Herder, when the "people" were defined as a necessary entry to reach the soul of a nation, writers globally have taken popular subjects within their field of vision.² Often they manufacture difference to enable the workings of a text, and use *lo popular* to engage the cogs of literature and spin the machine into motion. Subaltern narrative identity of this kind raises many issues in the fields of aesthetics and ethics, language shifts and structure, not to mention the function of cultural difference that is played out for middle-class readers. Surely, the conflict between civilization and barbarism underlies this story as it also announces something new from the cusp of contention and salutes modernity rising. In this respect, the *pueblo* appeals to our fascination for the underside of what we know, it reaches out to a zone beyond our usual purview. It is also highly visual: since Columbus's famous staging of Native Americans for view in Sevilla through the televised sequence of New Orleans floods, the spectacle of *otherness* begs to be seen. It works from contractions and elongations of space, it functions off distance and proximity and, in all cases, it confirms the center's unending power. Present time, space, and distance become the elements we need to engage the popular theater expression.³

Hermann Herlinghaus astutely observed in *La modernidad heterogénea* [Heterogeneous modernity] that popular culture (when represented) functions to install lines of demarcation in texts. It legitimates modernity by contrast and distinction and, of course, allows relational concepts to determine all truth in meaning. We might add that if, in some instances, *lo popular* announces a move toward a rural or peasant past, a nostalgia for agrarian wholeness, in others, *lo popular* draws a tight association with the city and the urban proletariat that has been displaced from the working classes: two versions of a single anxiety about modernization on the edge, two stories about peripheral traditions in the service of cultural critique. Yet today both narratives surrender to our current attraction toward hybridity and mixture. Purity is out; polyphony is in. Unintelligibility in terms of Western reason becomes the new draw; this, in sum, is today's seduction of *lo popular*.

We might ask about the political dimensions of this unfolding. In other words, if *lo popular* has consequences for democracy, and if, by reading about the *cartoneros*, we as middle-class readers turn our heads toward insurgency and change, then what? *Lo popular*, in this respect, would be a call to mythical violence, a kind of nostalgia, bound with hope for revolution and for a future with something new. Alternatively, *lo popular* can become some kind of fetish, isolated from real possibilities of action to become a symbol of something other than itself. Raised from the past, *lo popular* in this respect is also devoid of future. Curiously, these inclinations circulate together, both designed to uproot a familiar chronology and history, to become saturated instead in nostalgia or uncertain prospects for the future. In this context, *lo popular* floats upon present time, where it clearly stages a performance of body and voice.

I am reminded here of Kafka's story, "A Hunger Artist," in which the crowd goes to the carnival to see a man who practices and performs the art of starvation. Boundary lines are quickly set up as the man occupies the space of his cage and the audience looks from afar. It is a spectacle, however, that soon runs its course. After years, the manager decides that a hunger artist is a losing proposition and replaces him with a panther. The crowd, newly enthusiastic, rushes to observe the cat as he devours meat in his cage. Kafka makes us see not only the opportunism of the crowd, but also the force of consumer desire and the cunning managers who wish to control it. There are many readings that Kafka offers, among them the way in which the hunger artist defends his purposeful starvation, thus giving a new twist to the concept of agency—agency through nonaction—while also denying us the chance to make any ethical intervention, but for now I am more interested in Kafka's focus on our short-lived fascination with the lives of others. Here, we learn that everything is discardable and subject to erasure. Are we, then, all the impresarios of the hunger artist? Are we willing to let him die as part of a consumerist ploy? And how is the experience of his diminished body registered in the bodies of his observers?

These questions emerge from the dividing line that separates the crowd from the cage. In that distance, a public theatricality emerges, one in which our sympathies are supplanted by a prurient interest. In lieu of direct engagement, a quite perverted vision becomes the basis for entertainment. But this brings up one more detail: if otherness is a question of distance, it also depends on our passions.

On Passion

Much has been made of the passions in recent discussions of ethics and reading. It of course arouses suspicion. Borrowing from classical rhetoric, Terry Eagleton refers to the "ideological convenience" of using emotions as a basis of moral consensus.[4] From another corner, Stanley Fish denounces the affective fallacy as the bad taste of private feelings made public,[5] while Emily Apter challenges the "imperium of affect" as part of a new antiessentialist furor.[6] Having had it with histories of identity production, we now turn to raw emotion, she claims, an easy point where one can quickly connect with the other without studying the past. You perform, I feel, like the hunger artist and his public, like the scenes of New Orleans on television that we watched with eager interest. "Feeling for the other," cloaked in discussions of passion, is felicitously multicultural though it usually goes without analysis. The basis of a circumstantial politics, the politics and aesthetics of affect are like a kind of solidarity through mimicry, a "theory lite" approach to virtual subjects without too much stake in the future (Apter 20).

The discussion of the affects and passion is not exhausted by these observations. Rather, we are left with lingering questions about the ways in which the affects come into play as an encounter with alterity. And insofar as literature is at stake, we might take this encounter as the basis for the very materiality of a text. In other words, if in the broad debate about alterity in political spaces, the affects are considered central to the recognition of a distant other, it may also be time to think of the ways in which pulsations of feeling cross the surface of a literary text and side-swipe conventional circuits of signification, breaking through false comfort and illusions of engagement, in order to produce alternative readings. Not inspired by visual events alone, which would reinforce the gaze as power, the affects are set off by sounds, a touch, a taste imagined, or perhaps a brush with movement. They carry a lingering residue in the mind and body of the beholder.[7] This is a total surrender of the body to the experience of reading. You might say that this is our way to be ravished by the text, as Barthes once upon a time proposed.

This is more than a return to empathy of the kind proposed by Azar Nafisi or, before her, Martha Nussbaum. Rather, I would like to think of this as a return to a material reading of an experience that is fundamentally untranslatable, that empty sign that we cannot read directly or render intelligible within ourselves. Often, that otherness in the text is reached through a round-about manner. This is not the window pane effect—I see the *cartoneros* at a distance—but a ricochet course through language and voice that shifts the way we think and feel. Affect, passion, and emotion, then, as ways to break up modes of reason and to cause a halt in logic, to produce discomfort. Engendered by a constellation of ongoing sensory cues, the affects force us to latch onto meaning in a different way. This engagement is a link between ourselves and the literal immediacy of a text that will undergo transformation and cause us to linger. I want to see if we can reach the point where the affects have "staying power." For this, we need to find the transition from mind to body and back again.

Affective intentions are not just mental states, advises Charles Altieri (7). Indeed, though the affects were originally shaped by beliefs, now they float alone, as if to link a particular otherness in relation to a universal. They prompt a return to thinking. Art causes people to be awakened physically, then to be moved, later to stimulate consciousness of certain kinds of perception. To understand this, it requires first that we expand a conceptual language to accommodate these intensities. Altieri here helps us out:

> The presentation of emotions for an audience invites the audience to respond to the situation as it is expressed rather than as it is described. We [I think Altieri refers to the audience] want to give the speaker the knowledge he lacks... for we recognize his pathos... We are sufficiently moved that we have to construct our own attitudes, and we want to be able to endorse them by thinking of how they might give us access to his underlying situation. (96)

This is more than literature working with doxa. Rather, it is about registering the effects of art and literature by looking at matters of form. The lessons only come later and never in prepackaged mode.

Here, of course, we come face-to-face with the question of how we might account for experience today. Rei Terada asks if we can talk about experience in this age of waning affect. She claims that emotion, intensity, affects, and sensation, paradoxically enough, fill in for the death of the postmodern subject (4). As if to challenge Apter's proposal, to which I referred in earlier pages, Terada takes examples of sensation as proof of our own erasure, our own undoing of self; this, she claims, is especially seen in those emotions that we express in the moment of encounter with the other (*pace* Levinas). Passion, in this manner, drives subjectivity to its own cancellation (5). So you could say that affective intensity is a moment of nonsubjectivity within the very center of the subject. A blind spot in reason. Of course, in order to reach that pathos, you need to confront representation, and I wish to add here, the representation of *lo popular* certainly helps. Extreme otherness, someone different from us, serves as a kind of awakening against our theoretical deadness. It's not that we're fed up with theory (that seems to be Emily Apter's point), but that theory no longer serves us. As compensation, the popular presence is a way to figure experience and form precisely at a moment when our access to experience is lost.

I want to argue that the rediscovery of *lo popular* in Argentine culture is part of a larger agenda to renew a sense of feeling. Again, this is more than *doxa* in the usual sense. It is not that literary texts are set out there to redress social inequality *tout court*. Nor do readers and critics deliberately seek the direct political effects of art, to enter imaginatively into the lives of others or to steer us in judgment, as Martha Nussbaum claims (3–4). Rather, the encounter with *lo popular* invigorates our passions. This may be instrumental if seen only on the surface of things, through the window pane of images that shows us a quick glimpse at the urban poor. But in literary texts, the engagement sometimes opens to unexpected paths of knowledge; unsupervised, unstructured, left on its own, the text produces a material relationship with the reader.

Kant's third critique guides us in that direction helping us to make sense of emotion without confusing it with political acts. En route, in movement, in transition, or Derrida's law of curvature that leads to a *perhaps*. In all of this, a signifying force field surrounds *lo popular*, connecting elements that are not initially given as relational.[8] Without deliberation, a crucial movement emerges, inciting first a blankness of passion and then a state of transition toward some future plan for action. Entwined in the poetics of text and not merely in the image, otherness becomes a constellational moment from which consciousness begins to flow.

Recently, in a course on poetry, my students brought me closer to this understanding when together we looked at Darío and Yeats, from a past historical moment, and then at Diana Bellessi, a contemporary Argentine poet who has taken up the theme of the poor following the events of 2001. Now much has been said about Darío's revolution in verse. The change in prosody and metrics, the modernization of Spanish, a strategy that coincided with the overarching modernity so desired by the liberal state, has been amply traced in Darío's work over the years. But I wanted to remember how he lets otherness into his texts, reminding readers of the emerging *cosmópolis* in which he lived. Darío thus teaches us from the accent and voice of the poem, that Latin America is not singular, nor its populations homogeneous and one. Take *Prosas Profanas* (1896), for instance, published in Buenos Aires. The phonetics of *porteño* Spanish, with its lush fricative [zh] for *ll* and *y*, fully fill the air, separating it from speech in Managua. These sounds take a place in Darío's verse to remind us of popular speech in formation. Take, for instance, the following lines from "Yo persigo una forma":

> Y no hallo sino la palabra que huye,
> la iniciación melódica que de la flauta fluye
> y la barca del sueño que en el espacio boga;
> y bajo la ventana de mi Bella-Durmiente,
> el sollozo continuo del chorro de la fuente
> y el cuello del gran cisne blanco que me interroga.[9]

Two things to be noted: if the poem seeks a perfection of form, a desire for perfect unity, when read aloud in Buenos Aires, it is shot through with local voice and inflection. The universality that should transcend the local is in fact tied down by local rhythms, bounded in an untranslatable mode that affirms a struggle for local identity and voice. Upon bringing the porteño [*ll*] that emerged in Buenos Aires at that time to the center of the poem (*hallo, huye, fluye, sollozo, cuello, bello*), Darío reminds us that universals cannot be separated from local expression. How strange, moreover, that a *porteñismo*—*chorro*—flows through these tercets. Of course, it refers to a stream of water in his poem, but in the Buenos Aires slang of the time, it also means a low life and thief, a neologism in 1890 (when the dictionaries were still ambivalent about *choro* or *chorro*). Darío's poetry is full of these double inflections that aspire to a world of universals while they wink at local linguistic forms. Here, the voice of Argentine Spanish propels modernity with an accent.

Years ago, Noé Jitrik, writing about *modernista* poetry, emphasized the importance of accentuation, of stress, to change the *modernista* machine. This was Darío's way of entering the international market. Modernity carried an accent, stress was the basis of a new poetic order. But, I need to add, *our* contemporary connection to the poem is also found in points of stress; it is the place where we are one with verse, beyond the force of image. Indexing what is modern through this sound collision, Darío brings local voices to a world of new universals. This mixture, then, is in fact constitutive of the new identities that Darío needs for his project to work. And, as listeners, we feel it in our bodies.

A few years later, Yeats wrote his famous poem "Easter 1916" about the Dublin uprising against English colonial rule. I want to refer briefly to the poem's refrain, "I but lived where motley is worn: All changed, changed utterly: A terrible beauty is born." If this is clearly acknowledged as Yeats's lament for the failure of rebellion, it is also his way to recognize the failure of speech, the point at which language stammers. In other sections of the poem, he refers to "polite meaningless words," in itself an infelicitous phrase difficult to hear, and later, "a voice that grew shrill," as a "song" and names are "murmured." Through it all, he repeats that things are changed *utterly*. Speech has the power to lift the hard stone of intransigence (the poem is full of reference to stones) and alert us to something new. Listening to it, we have to reformulate familiar rhythm; we are placed on alert to receive a new voice in Irish culture. It is shrill and abrupt, uttered and stuttered, pushed outward to new form (remember that the word *utter* is from *utera* and *out*). It is what is engendered from the stone, outside access of the lyric voice. But utter, stutter, halting speech nonetheless grabs the listener of the poem. We are left as perplexed as Yeats, waiting for something new. And here is a curious paradox about the ethics of reading: for if Yeats, the conservative, was suspicious of popular rebellion, his poem leads readers in the opposite course, forcing us to stumble over the difficult sounds to think that the movement of stone is worthwhile. Here, our reading clearly touches something outside of authorial intention.

Let us take one more example. Diana Bellessi gives an update on this work with materialized speech in *La rebelión del instante* (2005), a book of poems about the 2001 crisis and poverty in Argentina. In one text, "Notas del presente" [Notes on the Present], sound serves to mark our distance from the poor:

> ¿Y eso ahí? Oh no es nada, sólo
> desconsolación sobre el oro
> del musgo otoñal, bermellón
> y oro la luz del sol bañando
> todo y después, un gris de plomo
> al atardecer, perfecto ahí
> como la pena, y tan quieto
> que parece eterno posado
> en el paisaje igual a ella
> en mi propio corazón;

> [And that over there? Oh no, it's nothing, only
> disconsolation about the gold
> of autumn moss, vermillion
> and gold sunlight drenching
> it all and, later, a lead grey
> dusk, perfect there
> like pain and so still
> that it seems eternally posed
> in the landscape as she is
> in my very heart]

If the string of open [o]s opens the poem in Spanish ("oh no, sólo desconsolación sobre el oro"), over there ("ahí"), and later ("después") signal shifts of force in the poem: what follows is a space of lament in which the soft [a] prevails ("igual a ella"), softly reminding us of what is gone, what has been truncated by events in the present. Bellessi continues,

> cediendo
> a su desnudez las ramas altas
> abril se va, todo se va
> al infierno tanto como esta
> belleza; alzo unos piñones
> que me abrigan de sólo verlos,
> acento de marrón del río,
> frescos y abiertos ofrecen
> aún sus semillas, si mayo
> las acoge quizás me quiera
> también a mí; estoy aquí
> en esta orilla y puedo llorar
> al fin, la furia se deshace

como un pañuelo de seda
en la brisa del anochecer
¿Qué es, ahí? Oh no, no es nada,
sólo desconsolación, tensa
y perfecta como un reloj
acróbata bailando el tiempo
regurgitándolo en pasado;
púrpura el cielo, y misterioso,
tal vez sólo por eso, lloro

[tall branches yielding
to her nakedness
April goes, everything goes
to hell like this beauty;
I pick up some pine nuts
which give me warmth by their simple presence
brown trace from the river
fresh and open they offer
even their seeds, if May
receives them perhaps May will love me too. I'm here
on this shore and I can cry
at last, the fury undone
like a silk cloth in the
evening breeze
What's that, over there? Oh no, it's nothing only
disconsolation, tense
and perfect like a clock
time a dancing acrobat
regurgitating itself in past tense;
purple sky and mysterious,
perhaps only for that, I cry]

The softness of the [a] surrenders to a change, but with a vulgarity unexpected in lyric. Suddenly, *al infierno* alters our system of reading; it is a radical interruption in the present moment of the poem. At the end, Bellessi returns us, full circle, to the [o] with which she opened her text, time regurgitating pastness, in perpetuity, sadness without end. The poem hinges on distance and nearness, on a tension between here and there, on a past that is soft and feminine, and on a disconsolate ongoing present tied to harshness. *Hell* links it all. This unfolds like the rose of Borges's famous poem, which is all about writing, and I am not sure that Bellessi does not mean to do the same. But there is more. Here, she brings us closer to mass poverty, by only indirectly calling its name, "no es nada" [it's nothing]—the negation that represses as it reveals, nature and poverty joined in eternal extension. It touches us through a sound system that directly puts us in present time. It is ultimately the power of breathing that brings us close to the experience of lament. But it is also about hearing, seeing, and feeling viscerally the rhythms of transition between one world and another. Like the Buddhists who believe that we share molecules of air between us, that breathing is thus a communal exchange of bodies, here the rhythm and pause of breathing is a way to reach each other. The sensorium brings us back to an ethics of engagement.

Ricardo Piglia suggests that *lo popular* is an effect of reading. It haunts the corners of the text and unsettles the affirmation of our reading "I." This also responds to the thirst for authentic experience so desired by middle-class culture. The enigma and the monster, says Piglia, are always beyond interpretation, elusive in the hands of the reader, a secret that we wish to reach behind the other's mask (85). This version of *lo popular* is like a phantom, a spectral desire that we carry. It is also the principal tool of the writer, a detective in disguise, who seeks to locate the secrets that the multitude nestled within the book of fiction, within the fiction of state. With it, he drags in his public to witness what is hidden in the crowd. Certainly this works in fiction: hence, César Aira's *Villa*, in which Maxi goes to the edge of the ghetto but fears passing its portals; or Juan Martini's *Puerto Apache*, which ends in unresolved difference, fear, and distrust of the other; or Gloria Pampillo's *Pegamento*, an odyssey through otherness in the city; or Marcelo Cohen's obsession with Faussy, the *panadero* or baker. In each case, distance—the space between the observer and the others—is clearly marked and needed. Fiction keeps the boundaries up and puts us in the realm of fetish, with lines of oppositional thinking that are only crossed through crime and violence. Poetry, I believe, has the chance of collapsing these lines or, at least, taking us in a different direction. Poetry as a form of capture that works deliberately through the effects of sound. I want to propose a theory of reading that links a reading body to an ethical semiosis—a somatic reading that takes in breath and form, a way to find a point of contact between our bodies and that of the poem so that voice, rhythm, stress, and ear are totally involved.[10] An expression that is not inert, but active, wholly contradictory, and even of an alterable kind. Of course, this means we are always rewriting, always shifting places within our assigned position as readers.

Let us say, then, that the experience of reading is one of constant renewal, a rewriting through which we bring our bodies to the literary page, making of reading a sensorial engagement, touching new registers of the real. It then opens our senses to association and to the work of ethics. Here the spectral trope of *lo popular* becomes our first discursive entry for registering this change, a stand-in for the intersubjective work that we want and need. But then there are other ways of registering that allow us to be more open. By showing ourselves to be available, *disponibles y abiertos*, we can also ride the gap between *erlebnis* and *erfahrung*.

Susan Stewart opens her remarkable book *Poetry and the Fate of the Senses* (2002) by considering the material ways in which poetry works as a "force against effacement" (2), a way to establish individuals in a wider social existence. The particular charge of poetry is to draw the figure of the other. Language, and in particular, *poiesis*, propels us toward this intersubjective knowledge. *Poiesis* is based on the figuration of the senses, a way to engage the other through contact, sight, and sound, a way to link my particular responses to the specific responses of others, a way to compensate darkness. It is a material engagement with the imagination to create a human figure in anticipation of a listener or reader. In the process, both writer and receiver touch each other and are then transformed. Art claims its ethical stake through its work of the senses. It is the way to cross the internal bar of each subject, surpassing reason for pulsation.

There are things, then, that we know with our bodies—rhythms, sound, melody, the solidity of sculptured mass, the trace of meaning—the space or distance that goes beyond the force of reason. A friend reminds me that you come to know the materiality of the wind by feeling resistance that our bodies put against it. Similarly, the pulsations of sound and form within and against the text lead us to the touch, the unstated. The somatic experience as we encounter the leaps and fissures and stumbling blocks in the text leads us to see what's askew. From here, we can begin a larger inquiry about an ethics of difference leading to action.

In this respect, poetry is a space for the creation of intersubjectivity, where the senses are awakened and made intelligible to others. We situate ourselves in the particular that is en route to the universal. More important, as we learn to listen to others, we learn to hear ourselves. The senses, as I have tried to show, lead to this ethical awareness. By stimulating sense impressions and then availing them to others, the literary text rescues the concept of experience in the world. This is not a project in which all roads lead back to Rome—to me—but one through which the ricochet of meanings takes us back to an ethical regard for others.

Now, of course, no one would claim that this tension between form and sense is specific to literature alone but, indeed, in the literary space we can study the consequence of representation and, with it, the kinds of social investment that might catch spark in a communal space. Bringing us to the cusp of darkness and knowledge, all literature—poetry, in particular—refocuses experience of the self in relationship to another. And indeed it forces us to seek the sound and voice that lies behind the mask. Inés Azar recalls our Latinate lessons as she tells us that *per-sona* has as its root the Italian *per-sonare* [to sound]. Personhood is for that connection through utterance and voice and its representation is there for the taking, especially in literary art. Behind the mask, we hear sounds and voices, we try to imagine a life. In the process, we leap over that wall of silence that masks our own voice as well.

Conclusion

Let me return to *lo popular* in Argentina. I have no doubt that the *cartoneros*, the *piqueteros*, the women of the occupied factories are central proof of local resistance to neoliberal market policies, to the forces of globalization. Although it may be a contemporary update of that old nationalist feeling, for now, let us leave it alone. More importantly, *lo popular*, as I hope I have been arguing here, is a way to locate ourselves in the split between experience and knowledge, enabling us to touch the material forms that link each other through representation. The reverse of Murdock's decision to take a vow of silence, the new interest in *lo popular* is to show that we are all engaged and to prove, while we are at the crossroads of choice, that we still have options. But without a bodily semiosis as the basis for ethical choice, it is doubtful that this engagement will touch us deeply or allow us to anchor experience in an encounter with the material real.

I was not surprised when Mabel Bellucci, an Argentine social activist trained in sociology and gender studies, denounced the flock of tourists who came to see the *cartoneros*, the *asambleistas* [assembly representatives] of 2001, and the displaced factory workers; what impressed me more was the way in which Bellucci held *lo popular* close to home, as if <u>our</u> *cartoneros*, <u>her</u> *cartoneros*, were not available to the world outside.[11] Perhaps all this discussion is not only about the resurgence of *lo popular*, but also about the celebrity of getting there first, being the first to notice something strange in language or social action, the first to announce our joined experience of dislocation and frustrated desire. We really can't absent ourselves from this public display since, as academics, we are all public readers. This is in fact our job. Perhaps the way to fix this is in the space of private readings where the gain and profit of the text is only for quiet reflection. Far from abjuring responsibility to change or claiming a sense of despair, the return to the material stumbling blocks exposed through close reading make us stop and wonder. Perhaps it's time to cite Beckett, "I can't go on, I will go on." Reading, in its ethical dimension, will catch us privately in this snare.

Notes

1. Sergio Chefjec reminds us of a strange occurrence during the filming of "Ronda nocturna": once Cosarinsky chose select *cartoneros* as subjects for his film, they went home, dressed in their best attire, and returned to the set, prepared for their cinematic debuts. Cosarinsky was notably disturbed about this volta face since, after all, the *cartoneros* had clearly subverted the pitiful representations which he had sought to capture on film.
2. See Martin Jay, *Songs of Experience* and Pascale Casanova, *The World Republic of Letters* on Herder and the "uses" of the people.
3. Once again, Marx's famous sentence from the eighteenth *Brumaire* lurks in the air: "They cannot represent themselves, they must be represented." However, because of mobility and the constantly changing aspects of popular engagement, and the difficulty of fixing the positions of subaltern subjects, those lines of demarcations that we hope to place in evidence are variously occluded from view. With it, the exhortation to represent often ends in failure.
4. Cited in Terada, *Feeling in Theory.* 4.
5. Cited in Tompkins. "Criticism and Feeling." 172.
6. Apter, *Continental Drift.* 18.
7. This brings us back to the Russian formalists and Shklovsky in particular when he wrote, "Art exists that one may recover the sensation of life; it exists to make one feel things, to make the stony stony. The purpose of art is to impart the sensation of things as they are perceived and not as they are known" (12).
8. For a brilliant debate about this, see Robert Kaufman, "Lyric's Expression."
9. Although Kemp's translation of this poem fails to capture the points that I wish to convey, I offer it nonetheless as partial aid to reader: "And I only find the word that runs away, / the melodious introduction that flows from the flute, / the ship of dreams that rows through all space, / and, under the window of my sleeping beauty, / the endless sigh from the waters of the fountain / and the neck of the great white swan, that questions me" (1988: 60).
10. I want to override our attachment to the gaze, which suggests power, domination, and control, in order to open to the other senses that are capable of producing somatic responses. Here, I may sound old-fashioned, perhaps echoing Dilthey, who warned of the dangers of "ocular" mode and of all spectatorial relationships to experience. On this conversation, see Martin Jay (1993).
11. Cited in an interview with María Moreno, "Mabel Bellucci, activista, feminista."

Works Cited

Altieri, Charles. *The Particulars of Rapture. The Aesthetics of the Affects.* Ithaca: Cornell UP, 2003.
Apter, Emily. *Continental Drift. From National Characters to Virtual Subjects.* Chicago: U of Chicago P, 1999.
Azar, Inés. "Garcilaso y el misterio de la voz." Lecture delivered at an Internacional Symposium on Garcilaso de la Vega. Harvard U (September 2004).
Barthes, Roland. *The Rustle of Language*, trans. Richard Howard. New York: Hill and Wang, 1986.
Beckett, Samuel. *The Unnamable.* New York: Grove Press, 1958.
Bellessi, Diana. *La rebelión del instante.* Buenos Aires: Adriana Hidalgo, 2005.
Casanova, Pascale. *The World Republic of Letters.* Cambridge: Harvard UP, 2002.
Darío, Rubén. *Selected Poems of Rubén Darío*, trans. Lysander Kemp. Prologue by Octavio Paz. Austin: U of Texas P, 1988.
Herlinghaus, Hermann. *Modernidad heterogénea. Descentramientos hermenéuticos desde la comunicación en América Latina.* Caracas: Centro de Investigaciones Post-Doctorales, 2000.
Jay, Martin. *Downcast Eyes. The Denigration of Vision in Twentieth-Century French Thought.* Berkeley: U of California P, 1993.
———. *Songs of Experience.* Berkeley: U of California P, 2005.
Jitrik, Noé. *Las contradicciones del modernismo. Productividad poética y situación sociológica.* Mexico: El colegio de México, 1978.
Kafka, Franz. "The Hunger Artist," in *The Metamorphosis and Other Stories*, trans. Donna Freed. New York: Barnes and Noble, 2003. 135–45.
Kaufman, Robert. "Lyric's Expression: Musicality, Conceptuality, Critical Agency." *Cultural Critique*, 60 (Spring 2005): 197–216.
Moreno, María. "Mabel Bellucci, activista, feminista: la visión de una asambleísta." *Página 12* (Buenos Aires, April 29, 2002).
Nafisi, Azar. *Reading Lolita in Tehran. A Memoir in Books.* New York: Random House, 2003.
Nussbaum, Martha. *Poetic Justice. The Literary Imagination and Public Life.* Boston: Beacon Press, 1995.
Piglia, Ricardo. *El último lector.* Buenos Aires: Alfaguara, 2005.
Shklovsky, Viktor. "Art as Technique" (1917), in *Russian Formalist Criticism: Four Essays*, ed. Lemon and Reis. Lincoln U of Nebraska P, 1965.
Stewart, Susan. *Poetry and the Fate of the Senses.* Chicago: U of Chicago P, 2002.
Terada, Rei. *Feeling in Theory.* Cambridge: Harvard UP, 2001.
Tompkins, Jane. "Criticism and Feeling." *College English* 39.2 (1977): 169–77.
Yeats, William Butler, "Easter 1916." http://www.online-literature.com/yeats/779/

List of Contributors

IDELBER AVELAR is Professor of Spanish and Portuguese at Tulane University. He is the author of *The Letter of Violence: Essays on Narrative, Ethics, and Politics* (2004) and *The Untimely Present: Postdictatorial Latin American Fiction and the Task of Mourning* (1999), recipient of the MLA Kovacs award. He has published numerous essays on Latin American literature and Brazilian popular music in journals in Europe and the Americas. He is at work in two book manuscripts: *Genealogy of Latin Americanism: An Essay on the Disciplinary Uses of Identity* and *Timing the Nation: Rhythm, Race, and Nationhood in Brazilian Popular Music (1970–2000)*. He also writes on culture, politics, and soccer on the blog O Biscoito Fino e a Massa (http://idelberavelar.com).

GABRIELA BASTERRA is Associate Professor of Comparative Literature and Spanish and Portuguese at New York University, and Director of Program at the Collège International de Philosophie, Paris. She is the author of *Seductions of Fate: Tragic Subjectivity, Ethics, Politics* (2004).

BRUNO BOSTEELS is Associate Professor in the Department of Romance Studies at Cornell University. He is the author of *Badiou and Politics*, forthcoming from Duke University Press, as well as of dozens of articles on Latin American literature, culture, and politics, and on European philosophy and political theory. Currently he is preparing a book called *After Borges: Literature and Antiphilosophy*. He also serves as general editor of *Diacritics*.

SERGIO CHEJFEC is the author of numerous works of fiction, including *Lenta biografía* (1990), *El aire* (1992), *El llamado de la especie* (1997), *Boca de lobo* (2000), and *Los incompletos* (2004), as well as essays and literary criticism (*El punto vacilante*, 2005).

ESTHER GABARA is Assistant Professor in the Departments of Romance Studies and Art, Art History & Visual Studies at Duke University. Her work examines the relationship between literature and visual culture in twentieth-century Latin America. Her book *Errant Modernism: The Ethos of Photography in Mexico and Brazil* is forthcoming from Duke University Press. She has published articles in *CR: The New Centennial Review*, the *Journal of Comparative and General Literature*, and the *Journal of Latin American Cultural Studies*, as well as in the edited collections *Photography and Writing in Latin America: Double Exposures* (2006) and *A Historiografia Literária e as Técnicas de Escrita. Do Manuscrito ao Hipertexto* (2004).

ERIN GRAFF ZIVIN is Assistant Professor of Hispanic Languages and Literatures at the University of Pittsburgh. Her research and teaching focus upon representations of "Jewishness" in Latin American and Peninsular literature and the intersection between ethical philosophy and literary theory. She has published articles in *MLN*, the *Journal of Spanish Cultural Studies*, *Variaciones Borges*, *Chasqui; revista de literatura latinoamericana*, and *Modern Jewish Studies*. Her book *The Wandering Signifier: Rhetoric of "Jewishness" in the Latin American Imaginary* is forthcoming from Duke University Press.

FRANCINE MASIELLO is Sidney and Margaret Ancker Distinguished Professor in the Humanities and a member and former chair of the Departments of Comparative Literature and Spanish and Portuguese at the University of California, Berkeley. She works on topics related to Spanish American literature of the nineteenth and twentieth centuries, gender theory, and comparative North/South cultures. Her books include *Lenguaje e ideologia: las escuelas argentinas de vanguardia* (1986); *Between Civilization and Barbarism: Women, Nation, and Literary Culture in Modern Argentina* (1992), winner of the Modern Language Association award for best book on a Latin American topic and subsequently revised and translated into Spanish (1997); and *La mujer y el espacio público* (1994). Her book, *The Art of Transition: Latin American Culture and Neoliberal Crisis* (2001; Spanish translation, Buenos Aires: Editorial Norma, 2001) was cowinner of the MLA Kovacs prize and received Honorable Mention for the Bryce Wood Award of LASA. She has also published an English language edition of Juana Manuela Gorriti, *Dreams and Realities* (2003) and three edited volumes. Forthcoming is her book, coedited with Daniel Balderston, on Manuel Puig's *Kiss of the Spider Woman* for the Modern Language Association.

List of Contributors

ALBERTO MOREIRAS is Professor of Romance Studies and Literature at Duke University and Sixth Century Professor of Modern Thought and Hispanic Studies at the University of Aberdeen, Scotland. He is the author of *Interpretación y diferencia* (1991), *Tercer espacio: Literatura y duelo en América Latina* (1999), *The Exhaustion of Difference. The Politics of Latin American Cultural Studies* (2001), and *Línea de sombra. El no sujeto de lo político* (2006). He is coeditor of the *Journal of Spanish Cultural Studies*.

GABRIEL RIERA is Assistant Professor in the Department of Romance Studies at the University of Illinois, Chicago. His books include *Littoral of the Letter: Saer's Art of Narration* (2006); *Intrigues: From Being to the Other* (2006); and *Alain Badiou: Philosophy and its Conditions* (2005). He is the author of numerous articles published in *MLN, Revista Iberoamericana, qui parle?, Romance Studies, Variaciones Borges, Revista de Crítica Literaria Latinoamericana, Angelaki*, and in several edited essay collections.

DORIS SOMMER is Ira and Jewell Williams Professor of Romance Languages and Literatures at Harvard University, where she also directs the Cultural Agents Initiative (http://culturalagents.org). Among her books are *Cultural Agency in the Americas* (2006), *Bilingual Aesthetics: A New Sentimental Education* (2004), *Proceed with Caution, When Engaged by Minority Writing in the Americas* (1999; in Spanish: *Abrazos y rechazos: Cómo leer en clave menor*, 2006) and *Foundational Fictions: The National Romances of Latin America* (1991; in Spanish *Ficciones fundacionales: La novela nacional en América Latina*, 2005); and *One Master for Another: Populism as Patriarchal Rhetoric in Dominican Novels* (1984).

INDEX

abrazos y rechazos, 183, 184
"Absolute Immanence" (Agamben), 166
Aburto, Mario, 149
academics, 4, 108, 113, 191, 214; blogs and 45, 48, 50, 59; Habermas and, 51–54; mass culture and, 63, 69. *See also* intellectuals
Adorno, Theodor, 15, 67, 71–72, 147
aesthetics, 4–7, 121, 185–88, 193; mass media and, 63–66, 68–70; mediation and, 72–73; modernism and, 85, 90–91, 96, 99; otherness and, 20, 108–109, 203, 205; politics and, 1, 2, 105, 113, 149, 175. *See also* art
affective fallacy, 205
affects, 5, 117, 205–206; *The Investigation* and, 123–25, 128, 133, 135–37. *See also* emotions; passions
affirmation, 36, 118, 198; otherness and, 168, 172–73, 212; politics and, 150–51, 158, 162–63
African Americans, 194
Afro-Brazilian music, 70
Afro-Latin, 96
Agamben, Giorgio, 166, 167, 176; "Absolute Immanence", 166
agency, 3, 204; self and, 26–27, 29, 31, 33, 39
Aguilar Camín, Héctor, 149, 151–54, 157, 159, 163–64, 175; *La guerra de Galio*, 151; *Morir en el golfo* (Aguilar Camín), 153, 156, 158–59, 162–63, 175–76
Aguilar Platas, Blanca, 87
Aira, Cesar, 212
"*alchemie du verbe*", 120, 133
alienation, 21, 28, 37
alteration, 28, 37
alterity, 2, 6, 13, 15–17, 116, 205; self and, 30–31, 36–37
Althusser, Louis, 27, 39
Altieri, Charles, 202, 206
American Indians, 13, 73
Amuleto (Bolaño), 165
Anabela Guillaumín (*Morir en el golfo*), 153–54, 156–57, 158–59, 162
anarchism, 72
Anderson, Benedict, 77, 98
anomaly, 118
anonymity, 52, 57, 111, 112
antiquity, 3
Apando, El (Revueltas), 110–12
Apocalittici e integrati (Eco), 54
"Après coup" (Glaudes), 130
Apter, Emily, 205, 207
Arendt, Hannah, 202
Argentina, 5, 7, 112, 116–17, 198, 201–202; modernism and, 64, 96, 99; otherness and, 18, 20, 207–209, 214; 2001 economic crisis and, 7, 203, 208

Aristotle, 174
art, 21, 118, 206, 213, 215; *See also* aesthetics
asambleístas (assembly representatives), 214
asymmetry, 6, 184, 186, 188, 192, 194. *See also* Levinas, Emmanuel
Aurrecoechea, Juan Manuel, 89
autoheteronomy, 35, 36; *See also* heteronomy
automatism, 29
autonomy, 66, 133, 174; Levinas and, 25–29, 31, 33–37. *See also* heteronomy
avant-garde, 4–5, 110, 112, 202; Mexico and, 64–68, 84, 86, 89; modernism and, 70, 89–90, 96
Avelar, Idelbar, 4–5, 12–14, 21
Axkaná (*La sombra del caudillo*), 148
Azar, Inés, 214

Badiou, Alain, 1, 14–18, 21, 40, 166, 168–69; self and, 26–27, 29, 31–32, 37, 39; *Ethics: An Essay on the Understanding of Evil*, 14, 15
barbarism, 116, 153, 161, 164, 203
Baroque, 5, 117
Barthes, Roland, 187, 188, 206
Bartra, Armando, 89
Basterra, Gabriela, 3, 4, 40
Bay of Pigs crisis, 18, 19
Beasley-Murray, Jon, 46, 60
Becker, Gary, 49
Beckett, Samuel, 215
Bellessi, Diana, 208–11; "Notas del presente", 209; *La rebelión del instante*, 209
Bellucci, Mabel, 214
Benjamin, Walter, 71, 72, 188, 189
Bernal, Rafael, 155
Bérubé, Michael, 49

biculturalism, 196
Bilingual Aesthetics: A New Sentimental Education (Sommer), 184, 185
bilingualism, 6, 183, 186, 192–96
bitterness, 149
Blanchot, Maurice, 12, 30, 166
"Bloggers Need Not Apply" (*Chronicle of Higher Education*), 50
blogosphere, 4, 47–48, 55–56, 59
blogs, 4, 45–48, 54, 57–61; Habermas and, 56–60; politics and, 48–50. *See also* Internet
Bodet, Jaime Torres, 68
Bolaño, Roberto, 169, 172; *2666*, 165–166
Boletín Mensual Carta Blanca (journal), 68
Boom in Latin American Literature, 5, 110, 112–13, 117
Booth, Wayne, 12
Borges, Jorge Luis, 96; "Death and the Compass", 140; "The Ethnographer", 13; magazines and, 100; rose image and, 211; "The Superstitious Ethics of the Reader", 11
Bosteels, Bruno, 3
bourgeoisie, 18–19, 86, 90
Brazil, 4, 47–48, 77–80, 84–85, 188; Mexico and, 64–68; modernism and, 70, 73–75, 82, 89, 96, 99
break, ethics of the, 3, 25–26, 28–29, 32, 34, 36–38
breathing, 212. *See also* poetry; sound
Brecht, Bertold, 20
Buddhism, 212
Buenos Aires, Argentina, 64, 143, 145, 201–202, 208
Butler, Judith, 197

Camacho, Licienciado Manuel, 150
Camus, Albert, 106

"Can the Subaltern Speak?" (Spivak), 20
"Canto da Raça" (Ricardo), 81
Capanema, Gustavo, 82
Cardoso, Fernando Henrique, 47
Carlos García Vigil (*La guerra de Galio*), 151–53, 159–63, 176
Carranza, Venustiano, 87, 88
Carta Blanca beer, 69
Cartonera, Eloisa: See *cartoneros*; Fernanda Laguna
cartoneros (garbage pickers), 7, 201–204, 206, 214–15
Castro, Fidel, 18–19, 90
"Casual Notes on the Mystery Novel" (Chandler), 139
Catholicism, 90, 194
Cavalcanti, Emiliano di, 84
censorship, 48, 57
Chandler, Raymond, 139
"Chaos of the Public Sphere, The" (Habermas), 52
Chaplin, Charlie, 74
Chejfec, Sergio, 5, 6
Chiapas, Mexico, 98, 202
Chile, 13, 96, 107, 198
China, 47
Christ, Jesus, 191, 194
Christianity, 193, 196
Chronicle of Higher Education (magazine), 50, 61
Cigarra (magazine), 67, 83, 96
citizenship, 1, 54–58, 60
Ciudad Juárez, 165, 166, 169, 173
civilization, 152–53, 161–64, 203
class, 46, 60, 86–87; democracy and, 197; middle-class and, 83, 90, 96, 201–204, 212; politics and, 66, 154, 156, 162, 189–91; Vlaminck and, 97
coffee, 77, 80, 85
Cohen, Marcelo, 212
Cole, Juan, 47
Colombia, 107
Colosio, Luis Donaldo, 149, 150
Columbus, Christopher, 203
Complot mongol, El (Bernal), 155
Connolly, William, 193
constitution, 46, 66, 69, 131, 174, 193; otherness and, 54–55, 168, 187, 209; subjectivity and, 26–27, 33, 37. See also subjectivity
Constitution of 1917 (Mexico), 86
Contemporáneos, 64, 67, 87, 91, 96
Correio Brasiliense (newspaper), 48
Cortázar, Julio, 109
Cosarinksy, Edgardo, 202, 215
counterrevolutionaries, 18, 19. See also revolution
Creole, 107
crime, 140, 164–65, 212; politics and, 6, 21, 150, 157, 169–73; Saer and, 128, 133–35. See also detective genre; infrapolitics; murder; thrillers
criminology, 73
Critchley, Simon, 13, 14, 15; *Ethics of Deconstruction*, 14
Crow, Thomas, 67, 68
Cuba, 18, 185
Cuesta, Jorge, 68
"cuestión de la prosa, La" (Saer), 133
Cueto, Germán, 91
cultura de masas: See mass culture
cultura popular: See popular culture
cultural studies, 1, 2, 13, 69
culture wars, 59
curvature, 207
Cyberdemocratie (Lévy), 55, 60

Daily Kos (http://www.dailykos.com), 47
Danças Dramáticas (Andrade), 82
Darío, Ruben, 120, 208, 209; "Yo persigo una forma", 208
de Man, Paul, 12
Dean, Howard, 48

de Andrade, Mario, 64–67, 73–77, 80–84, 90, 96; *Hallucinated City*, 85; "Manifesto Pau Brasil", 74; modernism and, 98; *O Turista Aprendiz*, 82; "Pelo jornal somos omnipresentes", 70; "Toada", 75
de Andrade, Oswald, 74
death, 57, 89, 119–21, 157, 161, 207; Aguilar Camín and, 151–54, *The Investigation* and, 121, 128, 133, 136; public sphere and, 52; self and, 27–29, 39. *See also* murder
"Death and the Compass" (Borges), 140
deconstruction, 6, 18, 56, 158, 163
Del arte silencioso (newspaper), 90
Deleuze, Gilles, 160–61, 166–67, 190; *Nietszche and Philosophy*, 160
democracy, 1, 4, 26, 33, 45, 47, 55–58, 60, 88, 150, 159, 164, 173, 185, 188, 191–95, 196, 197, 204. *See also* politics
Democratic Party, 47, 48
dependency theory, 21
Derrida, Jacques, 12–15, 32, 56–57, 59, 167, 169, 207; *The Politics of Friendship*, 174; *Spectres de Marx*, 57; "Violence and Metaphysics", 30
desire, 71, 91, 183–84, 214; ethics of, 14; fidelity and, 25; otherness and, 154, 167–68, 189–90, 202, 208, 212; politics and, 2, 106, 158–59, 162, 194; reading and, 204; Saer and, 119, 121, 123–25, 130–32, 136; self and, 26, 29–30. *See also* love; sexuality
Desnoes, Edmundo, 18, 19
destiny, 120, 157, 160, 189; self and, 27–29, 33, 39

detective genre, 126–29, 138–40, 154–56, 158, 212; Œdipal theory and, 141; Saer and, 117–18, 121–25, 134–35. *See also* crime; murder; thrillers
development, 14; underdevelopment and, 19, 21
Dialectic of Enlightenment (Horkheimer and Adorno), 147
Diário Nacional (newspaper), 80
difference, 25
Dilthey, Wilhelm, 215
dissemination, 45, 56
The Division of Literature: Or the University in Deconstruction (Kamuf), 51
Dogville (film), 20
Donoso Cortés, Juan, 162
Dublin uprising (1916), 209
DuBois, W.E.B., 185, 194
Dussel, Enrique, 3, 16–18, 21–22; *Etica de la liberación*, 17; *Liberación latinoamericana y Emmanuel Levinas*, 21
dynamis, 155–57

Eagleton, Terry, 205
"Easter 1916" (Yeats), 209
Eastwood, Clint, 20
E-bay, 202
Eco, Umberto, 54
Ecuador, 107
egalitarianism, 53
ego, 30, 37. *See also* self
"Ego and Totality" (Levinas), 36
Elshtain, Jean Bethke, 51, 61, 197
emancipation, 20, 21, 190
Emancipations (Laclau), 191
emotions, 111, 118, 134–35, 205–207. *See also* affects; passion
English language, 48–49, 86, 184, 194, 209
Enlightenment era, 27, 52, 55

Entenado, El (Saer): *See The Witness*
equality, 33, 154, 168–69, 174
Equanil, 107
erfahrung, 213
erlebnis, 213
Esposito, Roberto, 164
Estridentismo, 67
Estridentistas, 64, 74, 87, 91, 101
Ethics of Deconstruction (Critchley), 14
Ethics: An Essay on the Understanding of Evil (Badiou), 14–15
Ethics-Politics-Subjectivity (Critchley), 14
"Ethics Without Others" (Hallward), 15
ethnocentrism, 12
"Ethnographer, The" (Borges), 13
ethnography, 64–66, 68, 73, 82–83, 94. *See also* folklore
Etica de la liberación (Dussel), 3, 17, 21, 22
Europa, rape of, 126, 129, 133
Europe, 52, 54, 106–107, 117, 161; modernism and, 64, 68, 79–80, 91; politics and, 4, 50, 66, 191; revolution and, 17, 21; theory and, 13
eventuality, 15–17, 121, 168; self and, 26, 30–32, 34–36, 38
exclusion, 16, 21, 38
existence, 22

family novel, 132
fantasy, 117, 124–26, 129–37, 140–41, 155, 158
Fate of the Senses (Stewart), 213
feminization, 64–65, 73, 80, 84–85, 87, 89–90; masks and, 91, 93–94, 96
Fernández, Roberto G., 184
fetish, 162, 204, 212
fidelity, 1, 15, 17, 25, 118, 168
finitude, 14, 21, 119

Fiord, El (Lamborghini), 112
Fish, Stanley, 205
Flaubert, Gustave, 51
folklore, 64–65, 69, 71, 73–74, 82. *See also* ethnography
Fon-Fon (magazine), 84
force, 149, 204, 209, 213
formal demand, 15
Foucault, Michel, 27, 39, 167
France, 47, 107, 197
Francisco Rojano Gutiérrez (*Morir en el golfo*), 153–54, 156–58
Franco, Jean, 63
Frankfurt School, 67
Freud, Sigmund, 27, 131–32, 140–41, 145, 188; *Wit and its Relation to the Unconscious*, 185
friendship, 129, 148, 151, 154, 159, 174–75
"From Saying to the Said, or the Wisdom of Desire" (Levinas), 32

Gabara, Esther, 4, 5, 101
Gaitán, Julieta Ortiz, 86
Galio Bermúdez (*La guerra de Galio*), 152–53, 159, 161–62, 164, 175–76
Gannon, Jeff, 48
García Canclini, Néstor, 63, 66
Garmendia, Salvador, 108
gaze, 75, 107, 205, 215; *See also* spectacle
gender, 65, 75, 90, 136, 191, 214
genealogy, 18
General Aguirre (*La sombra del caudillo*), 148
genres, 13, 118. *See also* detective genre
Gerbassi, Vicente, 108
Cueto, Germán, 91
Gillmor, Dan, 47
"Girl Drinking Coffee" (Ricardo), 80
Girondo, Oliviero, 64
Glaudes, Pierre, 130

global meaning, 19
globalization, 1, 12, 21, 80, 214
Godard, Jean-Luc, 106
González Marín, Silvia, 87
Gramsci, Antonio, 87, 188–90, 193, 196
Greece, 161
Greenberg, Clement, 94, 96
Guattari, Félix, 190
guerra de Galio, La (Aguilar Camín), 151, 153, 159, 163
Guha, Ranajit, 161
guilt, 25–29, 32–34, 36
Gutiérrez Alea, Tomás, 18

Habermas, Jurgen, 56–59, 191; "Chaos of the Public Sphere, The", 52; public sphere and, 51–55; *Structural Transformation of the Public Sphere*, The, 60
Hallucinated City (Andrade), 85
Hallward, Peter, 15, 166, 168; "Ethics Without Others", 15
Hardt and Negri, 201
Hegel, G. W. F., 27, 153, 161–62, 164, 176, 189
hegemony, 1, 176, 189–92
Heidegger, Martin, 14, 167
Helen of Troy, 129
Hell, 211
Henrich, Dieter, 15
Herder, Johann von, 193, 203
Herlinghaus, Hermann, 203
Hermann, Rosana, 60
heteronomy, 6, 26–29, 34–36, 165, 169–73; historical process and, 18
historieta, 89
Hitchcock, Alfred, 20
Höch, Hannah, 90
homelessness, 201, 202. See also *cartoneros*
homosexuality, 202
honesty, 12–14, 22

Honig, Bonnie, 192
Horkheimer, Max, 67, 71, 147
Howe, Irving, 52
"Hunger Artist, A" (Kafka), 204, 205
hyperlink, 46. See also links
hyperrealism, 128

iconography, 72, 73
identity, 68, 111, 134, 136, 162, 192; politics of, 3, 25, 37, 195, 198; Levinas and, 25–28, 36–37; otherness and, 107, 126–27, 203, 205, 208. See also self
Idiot of the Family, The (Sartre), 51
Igitur (Mallarmé), 164
Iliad (Homer), 149, 150, 177. See also Weil, Simone
immanence, 26, 166–68
In the Greek Tents (*En las tiendas griegas*) (Saer), 123, 126, 127, 129. See also *The Investigation*
incest, 130, 136
indeterminacy, 112
Indian reservation, 13
Indigo, 60
individuality, 19, 21, 82, 106, 195, 213; See also otherness; self
Infierno, Al, 211
Informe de la investigación del homicidio del licenciado Luis (Procuraduría General de la República), 149
Informed Comment (http://www.juancole.com), 47
infrapolitics, 6, 151, 158, 163–64, 174–75, 177; otherness and, 154, 166, 168, 170–73. See also politics
Inspector Morvan (*The Investigation*), 121, 122, 125–28, 130–31, 133–35
intellectuals, 7, 50–51, 53–56, 59–60, 117, 201; politics and,

19–20, 65, 108, 190. *See also* academics
Internet, 4, 5, 45–49, 56–59, 202; blogs and, 46–50; public sphere and, 52–56
Interpretation of Dreams, The (Freud), 185
interruption, 2, 158, 163, 192, 211; autonomy and, 25–26, 28, 34, 37; death and, 151; heteronomy and, 170; love and, 156
Investigation, The (*La pesquisa*) (Saer), 116, 123–24, 129, 136–37, 140; Inspector Morvan and, 121, 122, 125–28, 130–31, 133–35
Iran, 47, 48
Iraq War, 49
Irigaray, Luce, 15
Italy, 173, 188

Jacoby, Roberto, 202
Jitrik, Noé, 209
jokes, 185
journalism, 47–51, 73, 118, 162–63; Habermas and, 54, 57; Mexico and, 65, 87–88, 151–52
justice, 17, 19–21, 38, 110, 152–53, 186–87

Kafka, Franz: "A Hunger Artist", 204, 205
Kamuf, Peggy, 51
Kant, Immanuel, 150–51, 162, 164, 174–75; otherness and, 15, 18, 155, 167, 187, 207; self and, 25–26, 34–35, 37; *Metaphysic of Morals*, 174; *Perpetual Peace*, 147, 150
Kaz, Leonel, 84

l'Autre-dans-le-Même (the Other-within-the-Same), 31, 37, 38
Lázaro Pizarro (*Morid en el golfo*), 154–58

Lacan, Jacques, 1, 119, 121, 132, 141, 194; otherness and, 14–15, 18; self and, 25–26, 28–30, 35, 37–38; *Seminar VIII*, 28
Laclau, Ernesto, 33, 36, 190–91, 193, 196; *Emancipations*, 191
Laguna, Fernanda, 202
Lamborghini, Osvaldo, 5; *El fiord*, 112
language, 94, 111–12, 184–86, 192, 194–95, 196; modernism and, 96; novels and, 136–37, 169–70; otherness and, 31, 203, 206; poetry and, 209, 213–14; politics and, 2, 5, 13–14, 25, 32–33, 48; public sphere and, 53; Saer and, 115–17, 119–20, 122, 125, 131, 133
Lautremont, René, 133
Lautret (*The Investigation*), 127, 129, 133, 134
law, 26–30, 160, 176, 185, 194–95; Habermas and, 57, 59; infrapolitics and, 170, 174; otherness and, 154–55; politics and, 150, 158, 164; Saer and, 118, 124, 130, 134, 136; self and, 33–34, 39
Leite, Ivana Arruda, 60
Levinas, Emmanuel, 1, 3, 6, 21–22, 115–17, 207; otherness and, 13–16, 18, 167, 169, 186–87, 190; *Otherwise than Being*, 26, 32, 34, 36–37; self and, 25–29, 33, 35–38; *Totality and Infinity*, 30
Lévi-Strauss, Claude, 79
Lévy, Pierre, 55, 56, 60
Liberación latinoamericana y Emmanuel Levinas (Dussel), 21
liberalism, 69, 191–92, 194, 197
liberation, 3, 22
Lima la horrible (Salazar Bondy), 108
lingua franca, 185, 195, 196

links (hyperlinks), 4–5, 83, 203, 206, 212; blogs and, 46, 48–49; Habermas and, 55, 58–59; modernism and, 67, 80
Liscano, Juan, 108
List Arzubide, Germán, 91
lo popular, *See* popular culture
López Portillo, José, 153, 156
love, 152–56, 159–60, 193, 196, 211
Lyotard, Jean Francois, 191

Magazine of National Fashion, 83
magazines, 4, 65, 83–84, 96, 202
magical realism, 117
Malaise dans l'esthétique (Rancière), 20
Mallarmé, Stephen, 120, 133, 160–61; *Igitur*, 164
Managua, Nicaragua, 208
"Manifesto Pau Brasil" (Andrade), 74
Maples Arce, Manuel, 64, 74
Marchant, Patricio, 13
Marcos, Subcomandante, 164
markets, 29, 66, 89, 107–108, 209, 214; Saer and, 116, 118–20, 133. *See also* globalization; neoliberalism
Martín-Barbero, Jesús, 66, 69–73, 84–85, 194
Martini, Juan, 212
Marx, Karl, 189–90
Marxism, 17, 18, 188–90
Masiello, Francine, 6, 7
"Mask, The" (Villaurrutia), 91
masks, 91, 93–94, 96
mass culture, 94, 117, 121; *cultura de masas*, 4, 64, 66, 83, 86; Mexico and, 64–68, 84, 89, 91; modernism and, 63, 66–70, 72, 75, 80, 96
mass media, 70–73, 77, 89–90, 96, 117; Mexico and, 84, 86–87; modernism and, 65–69
mechanical reproduction, 72, 94

Media Matters (http://mediamatters.org), 58
mediation, 75, 80, 137, 170–71; mass media and, 66, 69–73; modernism and, 84, 96
Medios a las mediaciones, De los (Martín-Barbero), 69
Memorias del subdesarrollo (film), 18, 21
mestizaje, 70, 71, 98
metanarrative, 117, 125, 136
Metaphysics of Morals (Kant), 174
Mexican Revolution (1910–1920), 65, 86
Mexico, 91, 94, 101, 161–62, 177–78, 200; Aguilar Camín and, 151–54; crime and, 171–73; modernism and, 64–68, 73–74, 84–86; politics and, 4, 96, 149, 155–57, 164–65, state and, 87–89
Mexico City, 64
Mi vida revolucionaria (Palavicini), 88
Miller, Jacques-Alain, 130
minorities, 6, 183–85, 189, 194, 196
mise en abîme, 129
modernidad heterogénea, La (Herlinghaus), 203
modernism, 3–4, 71–75, 79–82, 89–91, 99; Andrade and, 98; Internet and, 46, 53; masks and, 94, 96; mass culture and, 63–67; mediation and, 69–70, 72–73; Mexico and, 64–68, 84–86; *modernismo* and, 84, 97
modernity, 77, 80, 82, 117, 195; otherness and, 17, 107, 203–204, 208–209; *modernistas* and, 209
modernization, 54, 79–80, 108, 152, 204, 208
Molloy, Sylvia, 11, 12
monoculturalism, 196

Moral burguesa y revolución (Rozitchner), 18, 20
moral insight, grammar of the concept of, 15
moral Law, 25
morality, 18–20, 147, 148, 155
Moreiras, Alberto, 6, 13
Morir en el golfo (Aguilar Camín), 153, 156, 158–59, 162–63, 175–76
Morrison, Toni, 183, 189
Moulitsas, Markos, 47
Muertos incómodos (Taibo and Marcos), 164
muralism, 65, 67
murder, 6, 126, 147–51, 157, 177; otherness and, 165, 169–71. See also crime; detective genre; infrapolitics
Murdock, ("El etnógrafo"), 214
Myers, PZ, 49
Mystic River (film), 20

Nadie, Nada, Nunca (Saer): See *Nobody, Nothing, Never*
Nafisi, Azar, 206
narración-objeto, La (Saer), 128
narration, 112, 120, 127–30, 133–34, 165; voice in, 139
Nation (magazine), 51
nationalism, 156, 176, 192, 214; heteronomy and, 172–73; modernism and, 64–65, 67, 74, 82, 86, 89
Native Americans, 203
Nature (journal), 49
neoliberalism, 118, 201–202, 214. See also globalization; markets
Neozapatista insurrection, 149. See also Zapatistas
New International, 57
New Orleans flood, 203, 205
New York, 50, 52, 79

Nietzsche and Philosophy (Deleuze), 160
Nietzsche, Friedrich, 27, 160, 161, 167–68, 196
nihilism, 16
Noblat, Ricardo, 47, 48
Nobody Nothing Never (*Nadie Nada Nunca*) (Saer), 127–28
Noriega Hope, Carlos, 89, 90
"Notas del presente" (Bellessi), 209
nouveau roman, 128
Novo, Salvador, 64, 68
Nussbaum, Martha, 12, 13, 206, 207

O Cruzeiro (magazine), 84
O Turista Aprendiz (Andrade), 82
object-narration, 128, 131, 134, 136–37
obligation, 26, 33, 36, 163–65, 170, 193–94
Octavio Sala (*La guerra de Galio*), 152, 159, 162
Œdipal theory, 124, 125, 130–36; detective genre and, 141
Öffentlichkeit (openness, public sphere), 51
Oil Maoism, 154, 158
online communities, 53, 55–56
ontology, 31, 186
Ortíz, Juan L., 120
otherness, 6–7, 13–17, 107–110, 165–67, 183, 207, 212–15; Bellessi and, 208–209; blogs and 45–46; democracy and, 193–95; Europe and, 21; Habermas and, 52, 54–57; *The Investigation* and, 123–28, 136–37; journalism and, 48–49; Levinas and, 25–31, 35–38; mass media and, 68–69, 71; modernism and, 75; otherwise concept and, 11, 18, 25, 49, 115–17, 195; politics and, 1–4, 151, 153–55, 163, 169–73,

otherness—*continued*
175, 186–90; popular culture and, 77; reading and, 203–206; realism and, 120; revolution and; 19–21
Otherwise than Being (Levinas), 26, 31–32, 34, 36–37, 115, 169
"Our Artists in Masks" (*El Universal*), 93
Oyarzún, Pablo, 13

Página 12 (newspaper), 202
Palavicini, Félix, 87; *Mi vida revolucionario*, 88
Pampillo, Gloria, 212
Paris (*Iliad*), 129
Partido Democrático, 80
Partido Revolucionario Institucional (PRI), 153, 176
passions, 188, 205–207. *See also* affect; emotions
Saint Paul, 15, 26, 29, 31, 32
Paulista Bandeirantes, 77, 79
Paulistas, 77, 78
Pavese, Cesar, 106
Pegamento (Pampillo), 212
"Pelo jornal somos omnipresentes" (Andrade), 70
PEMEX Corporation, 157
performance, 31, 36
performance studies, 1
permalink, 46, 58. *See also* links
Peronism, 137
Perpetual Peace (Kant), 147, 150
persona, 214
Peru, 107
pesquisa, La (Saer): *See The Investigation*
Pew Internet and American Life Research Project, 49
Pharyngula (http://scienceblogs.com/pharyngula), 49

photography, 64, 69, 72–75, 77, 80, 91, 94; politics and 4–5, 66–67, 82–84, 96, 156
Picasso, Pablo, 90
Picchia, Menotti del, 79
Pichón Garay (*The Investigation*), 121–24, 126–29, 132–36, 140
Piglia, Ricardo, 212
piqueteros (picketers), 7, 201, 214
Plato, 15
pluralism, 12, 26, 69, 195
Pobre gente de Paris (Salazar Bondy), 107
Poesía Buenos Aires, 137
poetry, 64, 74–75, 80, 90, 94, 117, 119–20, 210–11, *modernistas* and, 209; otherness and, 123, 208, 212–14; politics and, 84, 149; poverty and, 210–11
Poetry (Stewart), 213
poiesis, 213
political incorrectness, 17
politics, 1–3, 6, 20–22, 105–106, 111–13, 186–87; Brazil and; 188; civilization and, 162–64; crime and, 6, 169–73; democracy and, 191–94; Habermas and, 57–58; hegemony and, 189–90; Levinas and, 32–36, 38; mass media and, 69–70, 73; Mexico and, 65–67, 84, 86, 88–89, 151–52, 156–57; murder and, 147–51; novels and, 158–59, 165–66, 168, 174–75; otherness and, 16–20, 25, 27, 108–10, 153–55, 204–205; photography and 4–5, 82–84, 96, 156; poetry and 207; republican, 155; United States and, 47–50; utopia and, 191–93
Politics of Friendship, The (Derrida), 174
popular culture, 2, 84–87, 89, 91, 96; *cultura popular*, 4, 63, 66,

83; *lo popular* and 63, 71, 203–204, 207, 212–14; modernism and, 64–65, 68–70, 73–75, 80–82
porteño, 201, 208
Posner, Richard, 49
postcolonialism, 1, 15
postmodernism, 207
post-phenomenological theory, 12, 14
potentiality, 112, 155, 165, 167, 176
Poulet, Georges, 184
poverty, 107, 202, 209–12
pre-Columbian culture, 74
primitivism, 68, 91
Proceed with Caution, when engaged by minority writing in the Americas (Sommer), 183, 184
Procuradoría General de la República, 149
prose, 64, 117, 119–21, 123, 133, 137
psychoanalysis, 2, 117, 131–32, 135, 191
public intellectuals, 50, 51, 52
public sphere, 4, 50–56, 58, 60, 84
Puerto Apache (Martini), 212
Puerto Rico, 96, 188, 194

Rama, Angel, 1
Ramona (magazine), 202
Ramos, Samuel, 68
Rancière, Jacques, 3, 16, 20; *Malaise dans l'esthétique*, 20
Rather, Dan, 48
Rayuela (Cortázar), 109
reading, 1–2, 6–7, 11–12, 105, 183, 193; blogs and, 45–46, 54; law and 26; modernism and, 71–72, 89; narration and 128–29; novels and, 115–16, 118, 152; otherness and, 13–14, 108–109, 187, 203–206, 209, 215; poetry and, 211–14
Readings, Bill, 51

realism, 51, 109–10, 118–21, 123, 125, 133
real, 71, 90, 94, 116–19, 157–59, 202; *The Investigation* and, 121–22, 130, 132, 135; otherness and, 14, 28, 30, 54, 123–25, 189; poetry and, 213–14; politics and, 2, 5
rebelión del instante, La (Bellessi), 209
rebellion, 106, 109, 209
reciprocity, 38, 183, 184
regulative Idea, 118
Relación de abandonado, 136
religion, 49, 91, 111, 190, 193–94; Enlightenment era and, 27
religious Right, 49
representation, 2–7, 94, 105, 112, 149; *The Investigation* and, 124, 130, 137; Levinas and, 27, 29–33, 35–36, 38; modernism and, 64, 96; otherness and, 108, 155, 203, 207, 214
república, La (newspaper), 151, 152, 162
Republican Party, 47, 49
republicanism, 150, 163, 166, 168, 173–75
responsibility, 1, 3, 34, 169, 215; otherness and 16, 19–20, 126, 186, 188; self and, 26–29
Revista (magazine), 84
revolution, 164, 190–91, 204, 208; Mexico and, 85–86, 88, 152, 154; otherness and, 17–21
Revolution of 1930, 65, 80
Revueltas, José, 5, 110–12; *El apando*, 111–12
Reyes Palma, Francisco, 74
Ricardo, Cassiano, 65, 79; "Canto da Raça", 81; "Girl Drinking Coffee", 80
Riera, Gabriel, 5, 6, 115, 140, 142, 145
Rimbaud, Arthur, 120, 133

Rio de Janeiro, 77
Río sin orillas, El (Saer), 123
Rodríguez, Renato, 5, 107, 110; *Al sur del Equanil;* 107–10
Rome, 161
Ronda nocturna (film), 202, 215
Rowe, William, 63, 69
Rozitchner, León, 18–20
Rubenstein, Anne, 87
The Rude Pundit (http://rudepundit.blogspot.com), 47
ruralism, 69, 71, 74, 80, 86–87, 204
Russian formalism, 215

Saer, Juan José, 5, 106, 115–19, 130–33, 144; "La cuestión de la prosa", 133; Inspector Morvan and, 121, 122, 125–28, 130–31, 133–35; *In the Greek Tents* (*The Investigation*), 123; *The Investigation*, 116, 121, 123–24, 129, 136–37, 140; *La narración-objeto*, 128; *Nobody, Nothing, Never*, 127–28, 137; *El río sin orillas*, 123; *The Witness*, 120–21, 124, 136
Salazar Bondy, Sebastián, 5, 107–108
Salinas, Raul, 149
sameness, 1, 2, 7, 40, 91, 184; Bellessi and, 211; Levinas and, 25–26, 28, 36–38; love and, 156; mass media and, 68, 71; otherness and, 14–16, 19, 56, 108–10; utopia and, 192; Saer and, 115–17, 123, 131, 136
São Paulo, Brazil, 64, 75, 77–80; modernism and, 79–82, 84–85, 99
Sarlo, Beatriz, 63
Sartre, Jean-Paul, 51
Schelling, Vivian, 63, 69
Schiller, Friedrich, 188
science, 38, 48, 49, 189–90

scienceblogs.com (http://scienceblogs.com), 48–49
secrecy, 6, 141, 212; heteronomy and, 169–72; politics and, 6, 111, 163, 165–66, 175
secret police, 88
self, 6, 30–34, 75, 175, 184, 195; centrality of, 28; detective genre and, 130, 133; Levinas and, 25–29, 35–38; otherness and, 16, 18, 166, 186–87, 207, 214; self-awareness and, 12–14. *See also* subjectivity
Seminar VIII (Lacan), 28
semiosis, 212, 214
sequencing, 16
Sergio (*Memorias del subdesarrollo*), 18
Serviço do Patrimônio Histórico e Artístico Nacional (SPAHN), 83
sexuality, 131, 134, 140–41
Shklovsky, Victor, 185, 188, 215
signifying order, 30
Signs of Borges (Molloy), 11, 12
Simenon, Georges, 139
sin, 29
Slave Who Is Not Isaura, The (de Andrade), 70
Social Democratic Party (PSDB), 47
social movements, 17, 85
Soldi (*The Investigation*), 122, 126, 129
sombra del caudillo, La (Guzmán), 148, 149, 164
Sommer, Doris, 6; *Proceed with Caution*, 183
Sontag, Susan, 51, 52
sound, 21, 34, 53, 75, 195, 206; poetry and, 208–209, 212–14. *See also* poetry
spectacle, 56–57, 94, 122–23, 132–33; reading and, 203–204. *See also* gaze
Spectres de Marx (Derrida), 57
speech, 119, 208–209

Spinoza, Benedict, 167
Spivak, Gayatri, 15, 20, 171; "Can the Subaltern Speak?", 20
state, 14, 71, 77, 178, 185–86, 194–96; civilization and; 161–63; hegemony and, 190–92; *The Investigation* and, 123, 126, 133, 137; Mexico and, 86–89; modernism and, 73, 79–80, 82, 90; novels and, 116, 118–20, 149, 153, 155, 157; otherness and, 20, 27, 29, 107–108, 207–208, 212; politics and, 3, 49, 65, 69, 112, 175. *See also* politics
status quo, 2
Stewart, Susan, 213
strangeness, 134, 185, 187
stress, 89, 209, 212
Structural Transformation of the Public Sphere, The (Habermas), 60
subaltern, 1–2, 171–72, 188, 203, 215
Subcomandante Marcos, 164
subjectivity, 37, 107, 132, 198; definition of, 17, 25; desubjectification, 167–68; intersubjectivity and, 27, 196, 213; performance of, 32; politics and, 1, 3–4, 21, 158; postmodernism and, 207; self and, 26–30, 32–36, 38–39; tragic and, 3–4, 25–29, 33–35, 158, 161, 163. *See also* self
superego, 27, 33–34, 36
superstition, 3, 11
"Superstitious Ethics of the Reader, The" (Borges), 11
Sur del Equanil, Al (Rodríguez), 107–10
Surfistinha, Bruna, 60
symbolism, 107, 110, 120, 148; *The Investigation* and, 130–32, 134, 136; real and, 117, 124–25; self and, 28–29

Taibo, Paco Ignacio, 164
technology, 52, 55–59
Technorati (http://www.technorati.com), 48, 49, 60
temporality, 16, 35, 128, 171; diachronic, 32
Terada, Rei, 207
terrorism, 195
textuality, 12–13, 18, 22, 113, 207
thrillers, 6, 138, 147–48, 150, 155–56, 169–72; infrapolitics and, 6, 151, 154, 158, 164, 175. *See also* crime; detective genre; infrapolitics; murder
"Toada" (Andrade), 75
Tocqueville, Alexis de, 193, 197
Tomatis (*The Investigation*), 122, 126, 129, 133, 134
Totality and Infinity (Levinas), 30, 31
tourists, 214
Toussaint, Manuel, 68
traces, 3, 30–32, 35, 37, 203, 213
tragedia de Colosio, La (Aguilar Camín), 149
tragic subjectivity, 3–4, 26–30, 33–35, 158, 161, 163; definition of; 25; intersubjectivity and, 27. *See also* subjectivity
Trejo, Oswaldo, 108
truth, 17, 20, 71, 109, 112, 204; ethics of, 14; Habermas and, 50, 56; Levinas and, 26, 31; novels and, 123, 148, 155–56, 158, 162, 168–69; "truth effect" and, 47
2666 (Bolaño), 165–66
Twenty Poems to be Read on the Tram (Girondo), 64

United States, 47–51, 58, 195, 198
Universal Ilustrado, El (newspaper), 67, 74, 85, 87–96

Universal Ilustrado and Revista de Revistas, El (Reyes), 74
universality, 33, 54, 164, 168, 173, 208; democracy and, 191, 193, 195, 197
University in Ruins, The (Readings), 51
unsayable, 2, 5–6; Saer and, 116, 119–20, 133–34, 137
urbanism, 64, 83, 85–87, 108, 204, 207; mass media and, 69–71; Sao Paolo and, 77, 80, 82;
urszene (primal scene), 132, 135, 141
Uslar Pietri, Arturo, 108
utopia, 109, 156, 161, 190–93

Vallejo, César, 123, 124, 133
Vampré, Leven, 79
Vanitas (magazine), 83
Vargas, Getúlio, 80, 82–83
Vasconcelos, José, 65, 90, 98
Vela, Arqueles, 64, 91
Venezuela, 108
victimization, 3, 16–17, 33–34, 69, 167; guilt and, 25–26, 28; revolution and, 17, 19–21;
Villa (Aira), 212
Villacañas, José Luis, 175
Villaurrutia, Xavier, 64, 68, 94–96; "The Mask", 91
villismo, 152

Viñas, David, 19
"Violence and Metaphysics" (Derrida), 30
Vlaminck, Maurice de, 97
von Trier, Lars, 20

Week of Modern Art, 64, 79, 84
Weil, Simone, 149, 150, 163, 177
weltgeschichte (world history), 161, 162, 176
Williams, Daryle, 83
Wilson, Edmund, 52
Wit and its Relation to the Unconscious (Freud), 185
witness, 31–34, 36, 212; law and, 26, 28, 30; revolution and, 18, 21
Witness, The (*El entenado*) (Saer), 120–21, 124, 136
Wittgenstein, Ludwig, 186
Workers' Party (Brazil), 47

Yeats, W. B., 208, 209; "Easter 1916", 209
"Yo persigo una forma" (Darío), 208

Zambrano, María, 173
Zapatismo, 152
Zapatistas, 149, 202
Zeus, 126, 129, 133
Zupančič, Alenka, 30, 38, 176